The Texture of Treatment

The Texture of Treatment
On the Matter of Psychoanalytic Technique

Herbert J. Schlesinger

Routledge
Taylor & Francis Group
www.routledgementalhealth.com

Routledge
Taylor and Francis Group
270 Madison Avenue
New York, NY 10016

Routledge
Taylor and Francis Group
2 Park Square
Milton Park, Abingdon
Oxon OX14 4RN

Published by The Analytic Press, Inc.
101 West Street, Hillsdale, NJ 07642
www.analyticpress.com

Library of Congress Cataloging-in-Publication Data

Schlesinger, Herbert J
The texture of treatment : on the matter of psychoanalytic technique / Herbert J. Schlesinger
p. cm.
Includes bibliographical references and index.
ISBN 0-88163-382-8
1. Psychoanalysis—Methodology. I. Title

RC506.S2965 2003
616.89'17—dc22

Reprinted 2009 by Routledge 2003057875

CIP

10 9 8 7 6 5 4 3 2

I dedicate this book to my wife, Ann H. Appelbaum, M.D., whose gentle, persistent encouragement finally paid off. If only she had allowed herself to be the nagging shrew my procrastinating seemed designed to evoke, this might have been a second or even third edition.

Acknowledgments

I want to acknowledge first the contribution of my wife, Ann H. Appelbaum, M.D. Her steadfast encouragement for me to get on with finishing this book and willingness to overlook the many undone household chores were instrumental, especially when I would much rather have shoveled and lifted than write. It does not detract from her contribution to note that writing does not deprive us of each other's company, for we write at adjacent desks, each trying to set a good example for the other.

Stanley Goodman, M.D., old friend and colleague, is the sounding board every writer hopes for. He read and commented forcefully, if generally approvingly, on every early version of these chapters, and I adopted his suggestions gratefully. I offered to include his address here so that any reader with a complaint could take it to the proper source, but, with modesty exceeded only by good judgment, he declined.

Phil Holzman read several of the chapters, and I profited from his critical observations. Bob Schlesinger caught some obscure allusions and infelicitous expressions that I had missed. If any remain—finders keepers.

Over the years, several colleagues, notably Dick Simons, Cal Narcisi, and Diana Diamond, and many students have urged me to clean out my desk drawers of unpublished lectures and put them together as a book. This book draws on the ideas, mostly freshly written, in those lectures and should quiet their urging.

John Kerr has been after me to write this book for more years than I care to acknowledge. When finally we arrived at a serious commitment to it, he stayed with the project as editor and matched encouragement with a keen eye and sense of form as well as content. The book owes much to his good taste and clinical as well as literary judgment.

Once I had submitted the manuscript, Eleanor Starke Kobrin picked up where John had left off. She caught the slips we had missed and asked the penetrating questions that familiarity with the text had led us to overlook. As a former editor, I appreciate how important is careful editing to converting a good manuscript into an even better book. In both John and

Lenni I found the indispensable passion for quality that marks the best among editors.

Finally, I must acknowledge the indispensable contribution of Rudy Ekstein, who surely will recognize that the point of view of this book was inspired by his ancient tutelage and will recall that in our extended conversations was the Ur-source of many of the ideas in it.

Contents

Introduction

I expect that some readers do much of their reading of new professional books as I do, while standing at publishers' displays at meetings. By skimming the introduction, one can generally find everything an author has to say, put concisely, and spare an actual reading, let alone purchase, of the book. You would have had that opportunity to discover what I have to say at low risk if an editor had not urged that I collapse the first introduction I wrote into the first chapter.

Fellow browser, the material you may be looking for is in the first two chapters. You can get from them my point of view and primary assumptions, and they are an easy read. If you have not satisfied your curiosity by then, you may have no choice but to continue until feet or back give out or you put the book down. I hope you will choose the former, more righteous path, but I will understand if you don't. I too have resisted temptation only later to wallow in regret.

There is, of course, a third possible choice. You could buy the book and resolve to read it later. I have often done so when I could not bear to put the book down, but neither could I bear to stand a minute longer. And my bookshelves give mute but dusty testimony to how often my resolve proved no stronger than my back. I hope, if you are intrigued, you will keep standing and read on rather than put the book down. But, if you do buy the book, I hope you also will read it, for a book unread is like a bride unkissed, or so I have been told by the brides I have skimmed on tables of publishers' overstocks.

Since you have read this far, let me warn about what you will not find in this book. It is a personal statement. I have not attempted a comprehensive review of the literature on psychoanalytic technique and have referred only to the few authors whose similar or usefully contrasting views called for acknowledgment. I have drawn mainly on my own clinical experience as it has been deepened and expanded by the necessity to explain matters in teaching and supervision, and on some of the findings of research. I have put my ideas in the same simple, everyday language we use when talking with patients. You will find only a few higher level concepts and terms that I could not avoid using.

Although I was raised, analytically speaking, in the tradition of ego psychology, I have tried to stay free of its doctrinal implications, including much of metapsychology, as well as those of the other schools of analytic thought that have emerged during my professional lifetime. I do not find scholastic disputes interesting. I have tried to indicate when I was aware that I was making use of an idea from a source other than a patient.

To keep the length of the book within bounds, I have reserved the sections on ending and termination and impasses and stalemates for separate publication.

1

In the Beginning . . . Was Technique

In Defense of Technique

Perhaps most analysts were introduced to the mysteries of psychoanalytic technique as I was: that it was not so much a cohesive body of structured knowledge and practice as a loose collection of do's and don'ts. A chill in the heart warned me that to violate any one of them would ruin the analysis. Cowering before gray eminences, I and my fellow candidates had a bad case of transference to the Institute, for none of our teachers had literally laid down any such doctrine. It was more that no one troubled to disabuse us of the idea that, if somehow we were lucky enough to avoid all the pitfalls set by our natural enemy, the patients, the residue of our avoidance would be pure essence of psychoanalysis. We feared analysis was a fragile flower, one easily crushed in the hands of clumsy beginners. And the patients, we feared, were secretly out to do us in, to abort our nascent careers. Simply through recalcitrance, they could keep us from graduating. It took a while to discover that our patients were even more frightened than we were. It took more time to discover that analysis is not a fragile flower, but a sturdy affair. What we once regarded as fatal mistakes turned out mostly not to matter that much; sins of omission—what we failed to do—proved much more harmful.

It also seems to me, after later reflection, that we were working with more than a collection of rules of thumb, that there was a structure to the knowledge we use when analyzing patients and that it would be useful to spell out this structure. Karl Menninger and Philip Holzman (1973) have offered us a systematic theory of technique, one that makes great sense to me. The reader will find resonance of this approach in what follows. But their overall approach seems to me too heavily committed to the model of a rational "compact" between analyst and patient, an idea that does not fit with my experiences in the analytic situation.

I am not offering here an altogether new view of psychoanalytic technique. Rather I am attempting to make explicit that there is a logic to the way we go about analyzing as we listen to our patients and follow their associations. We generally do not pay attention to that logic while analyzing any more than we think about the physics of keeping the bicycle upright while riding (Schlesinger, 1994). But one needs to pay attention to the science when designing a bicycle or when designing a treatment for a particular patient, which after all is what one does when one analyzes. In this book I will present the technique of psychoanalysis and psychotherapy in a way that is both more systematic and simpler than I recall it being taught to me.

The very term technique strikes some clinicians as repellant when applied to psychotherapy or psychoanalysis; it seems to signify a manipulative intent rather than a collaboration and tends to substitute a mechanistic approach for intuitive and empathic understanding. But the term has other implications that are inescapable for a clinician. Psychoanalysis certainly ought to be collaborative: to rest on the analyst's intuitive and empathic understanding of the experience of the patient and to encourage the patient in intuitive self-understanding. But the analyst or therapist is more responsible for the conduct of the treatment than the patient is, and the analyst is expected to know what she is doing and why and what to expect when she intervenes. "Technique" refers to this responsibility of the clinician to conduct a rational treatment.

"Technique" has a politicized history. Almost from the beginning of the psychoanalytic era, the field has been marked by fervent arguments about preserving the integrity of the method. Self-appointed custodians of the field have worried that any deviation from received wisdom would spoil what was truly psychoanalytic, would dilute the purity of its technique and lead inevitably to seduction of the innocents. The debate has taken different forms and has used different terms across the generations but always within the general concern that, on one hand, ill-considered modifications would impair the integrity of Freud's legacy and, on the other, hide-bound adherence to outmoded doctrine would make the field irrelevant.

The struggle has often had the character of a religious war with clinching arguments based on quotation from authoritative texts rather than experiment and data. The crowning denunciation from the right has been "But that's not analysis," and, on the left, "But it works." Neither charge is apposite. Both are flawed, logically and psychologically—and also analytically.

To pursue this discussion of technique with less heat it is necessary to clarify the operative terms and to set down some ground rules: I do not use the word analysis to describe the process under consideration.

Processes must be described with verbs, and, as I consider "analysis" to be a noun, a process, the appropriate verb is "to analyze."[1] Rather than permitting the wholesale derogation of a clinician's work with the denunciation, "That's not analysis," or, in its ultimate form, "We all know he doesn't do analysis, and between us, neither did his analyst," we require that objectors specify at what point(s) they believe the clinician under observation failed to analyze, either by not attending to something at all or by attending to it in some way the objector considers "unanalytic."

Not everything an analyst does, or a clinician of any stripe does, has "technical" intent. After all, the analytic situation is a subset of the larger social situation and is, to a considerable degree, governed by the customs, manners, and expectations prevalent in the culture at large as well as the social subcontext of the doctor–patient relationship. The expectations of these larger contexts may, but do not inevitably, conflict with those of the analytic situation. It becomes a matter to be determined, at the moment under review, if these expectations conflict, and if they do, which context should govern.

I reserve the term technique for those actions (including withholding intervention, or silence) the analyst undertakes with specific analytic intent. For these actions, the analyst should be able to state what he believes the effect ought to be, how he would know if his action had had the intended effect, and what ought to happen next. Much of what the analyst does is not technical in this sense but is either nonspecifically facilitative or, more generally, in the service of preserving the analytic situation or not offending the expectations of the larger social context (Schlesinger, 1995a).

I avoid professional jargon unless the descriptive powers of ordinary English prove insufficient. It has been my experience that jargon often is used to conceal a lack of clarity, and it is my purpose to expose that lack rather than conceal it. I have tried to write in such a way as to demystify the topic of technique. Though my topic is serious, I see no reason to be solemn about it or to affect the dense style that announces itself as scholarly and pretends to profundity. My goal has been to write so that an intelligent layman interested in this topic could understand all of it.

I mean to show that both psychoanalysis and the dynamic psychotherapies derived from it are governed by the same technical

[1] A warning to the reader: I will object later to this use of "to analyze" in a transitive sense to emphasize my view that it is the patient who analyzes himself, with the help of the analyst. I distinguish this view from the more common usage that implies, I believe incorrectly, that the analyst is the agent who analyzes the passive patient. I recommend that we consider "to analyze" to be a reflexive verb.

principles. I deal with the differences and similarities between them in a chapter that, logically, ought to appear early. But in that position it would interrupt the general argument and so it appears closer to the end.

I discuss psychoanalysis as a process. In common usage within the profession, the term process is often employed as an intensifier, when the user means to invoke the ineffable essence of psychoanalysis, as in, "I guess he does all right clinically, but he doesn't grasp the psychoanalytic process." I intend to show that the term process has much more specific meaning, and that viewing such standard topics as resistance, regression, transference, and interpretation as processes promotes clarity and adds power to our understanding of technique.

Since my view of psychoanalytic technique is based on "system" and "process," the organization of this book is necessarily recursive; these key ideas reappear in different contexts. While I may seem to be offering a textbook of psychoanalysis (and secretly I hope to have filled the need for one), I have adapted my ambition to the less formal and less demanding and perhaps less off-putting style of simply thinking aloud.

What Do We Mean by "Technique?"

Technique is a term used in many fields of practice. Freud (1912a) liked to draw an analogy between the position of the analyst at work to that of the surgeon (Stepansky, 1999). But, for a surgeon, technique has several important implications that analysts tend to ignore. For instance, a surgeon will choose the point of incision depending on his purpose in undertaking the operation. When he opens the abdomen he will have a clear expectation of what he ought to find. He will also have a clear idea about what should not be present, and how and with what instruments he will undertake to correct matters.

The general term I use for the "instrument" of the psychoanalyst is technical intervention. The term analyzing instrument was used by Isakower (1957) for processes in the mind of the analyst that lead to interpretation. I have no quarrel with his usage, but prefer to focus on the outcome of that process, that is, what the analyst does or refrains from doing. Among the various technical interventions, analysts favor particularly interpretation. Compared with the surgeon's scalpel, interpretation must seem a blunt instrument. But an analyst can aspire to something like surgical precision if he holds the same attitudes of purposefulness and expectancy as the surgeon. Like Fenichel (1941, p. 52) I believe the analyst should accept analogous responsibilities to direct an interpretation toward an issue of immediate analytic significance and to have an idea of what the patient's response might be if the interpretation is correct. The analyst should also have an idea of what ought not to happen in response to an intervention.

It might be objected that even in ordinary conversation, one making any comment will have an expectation of what the response is likely to be inasmuch as the context in which the parties are conversing sets the bounds of appropriateness of response. But interpretation is the kind of intervention that seldom occurs in ordinary conversation, a context in which we, of course, are not privileged to offer interpretations. By interpreting we intend to disturb the expectation of the other; by changing the meaning of an idea in play, we violate the apparent context in which it was offered originally. It is, therefore, incumbent on the analyst to anticipate how the patient will respond to a disturbing, if enlightening, message.

Although the analogy to the surgeon has much to teach analysts with regard to intentionality, it is too limited in other important respects to serve as a general guide. It could be taken to imply that an analyst must always know precisely what is going on and make no utterance without both a specific purpose and a clear idea about what ought to ensue. To the contrary, one of the main lessons an analyst must learn is to be comfortable with ambiguity, with not knowing instantly where he is. And much of what the analyst does is in the interest of expectancy, of allowing matters to develop.

Classifying Interventions

The activities of the analyst in the analytic situation can be arrayed in a simple table (see Table 1). The headings "Technical" and "Nontechnical" imply that some interventions may not have technical intent; the labels "Specific" and "Nonspecific" refer to the extent to which the analyst's activity is planned and deliberate, rather than casual. Table 1 represents systematically our general awareness that the analytic situation includes more than the purely technical activity of the analyst. While it oversimplifies matters, this matrix does permit organizing some of the familiar terms with which the analytic situation has been described (Schlesinger, 1995a).

For instance, "Technical and Specific" includes the named, planned interventions that particularly characterize analysis. They have been categorized by Bibring (1954) and others. While these activities may define

Table 1. The Activities of the Analyst

	Technical	Nontechnical
Specific	Interpretation, clarification, etc.	Suggestions, prohibitions, ultimatums, etc.
Nonspecific	Facilitating comments intended to build toward interpretation.	Socially appropriate comments intended to promote relationship

psychoanalysis, I do not believe anyone would claim today that, if only these activities were carried out, an analysis would occur. Obviously, more than strictly technical activities are necessary.

"Nontechnical and Specific" is also easy to characterize. It includes all those things that analysts do, with plan in mind or not, that are not engraved in the canon of technique but generally have a considerable influence on the analytic situation. Over the years, these interventions have been given various names—blunders by some, parameters by others; they may include orders, ultimatums, advice, and other therapeutically intended interventions that are not, strictly speaking, analytic.

"Nonspecific and Nontechnical" encompasses all those aspects of the human relationship between analyst and patient that promote its continuance, whether that continuance has the form of a therapeutic or working alliance, or a stalemate, or a transference–countertransference bind sustained by mutual acting out. Friendliness, attentiveness, and more could be included.

"Technical and Nonspecific" might seem at first glance to be a puzzling, even confusing designation. But, if one thinks of interpretation as a process, one could define its vector with increasing specificity—in its earliest phase as largely nonspecific and facilitative (perhaps merely encouraging grunts) as the analyst attempts to determine the readiness of the patient to explore, analyze, absorb, or otherwise get into the conflict that is at the root of the disturbance of the moment. Later, the interpretive process becomes more specific and focal. At all times, however specific or nonspecific, the intent of the analyst is to build toward interpretation and hence is technical.

My purpose in organizing interventions in this way is to support the idea that the effectiveness of an interpretation depends not only on its correctness, its "truth value," but also on a number of other variables.

This idea is of course not new. Supervisors constantly stress in their teaching the importance of timing, tact, and dosage, along with the empathic quality and the accuracy of the interpretation. Notice that I did not include tact, dosage, timing, or empathy in this matrix of technique, even though we talk about them repeatedly in seminars on technique. But, if I may anticipate the end of this argument, tact, dosage, and the rest are desirable attributes of all the interactions in the analytic situation and elsewhere (Loewenstein, 1958; Poland, 1975). They are, after all, basic to our code of social manners. If we were to include them in the matrix, perhaps they would fit best among the nonspecific aspects of technique rather than among such specific aspects as interpretation, clarification and confrontation (Schlesinger, 1995a).

Intervention versus Interpretation?

I have used the term intervention to cover the analyst's deliberate activity without distinguishing the various forms that intervention can take. A comprehensive discussion of analytic technique certainly seems to need to address these distinctions inasmuch as so much has been made of them in the literature. In particular, I must deal with the defining act of psychoanalysis, the interpretation. I have left unchallenged the implicit notion that it is sensible to label an intervention as an interpretation or as something else on the basis of formal definitions. But I believe much too much importance has been given to categorizing interventions and to rating their presumed analytic value. According to convention, one decides if an intervention was an interpretation from the way it was phrased and from the intention of the analyst. I do not believe this approach is useful. An old story may make my point clear:

> Three aging baseball umpires were bragging about their exploits at judging on the field and compared their sense of conviction about calling balls and strikes. One declared, "I call them the way I see them." The second umpire averred, "I see them the way I call them." The third, most senior, umpire quietly ended the discussion by saying, "They ain't nothing until I call them."

In analysis the patient, not the analyst, is the umpire. Whether an intervention is an interpretation, a suggestion, a confrontation, or a dud depends on how the patient takes it. And how the patient takes it is what the analyst should be listening for so he can include the patient's judgment in his next intervention (Schlesinger, 1995a). If the analyst listens carefully, he will notice that, whatever the analyst might have intended, the patient always takes an interpretation as a suggestion; at the very least he assumes that the analyst wants him to think in a new way about the matter. If the analyst fails to notice it, that nidus of suggestion can build to a formidable resistance.

The term technical intervention implies a planned, deliberate action offered with the expectation that certain desired outcomes are likely to occur. For instance, if the analyst considers a comment to be an interpretation, he should be prepared to describe the intended immediate consequences and how he would know if they had occurred (Schlesinger, 1995a). (How to know whether or not an interpretation has had an effect and what to do about it is discussed in several of the following chapters.) In brief, the analyst should expect to see some signs of disturbance and the patient's efforts to take account of the disturbance or, more likely, efforts to restore the status quo ante. Of course, one should have similar, if less specific, expectations of technical interventions that are less ambitious than interpretation.

"Intervention," narrowly defined, seems necessarily to imply an action, that is, an activity in the everyday sense, something the analyst does. At times, however, the analyst's silence, that is, seeming inaction, also may have the power of an intervention, especially when the analytic (or social) situation would call on the analyst to make some utterance, whether intended technically or not. It would be accurate to say that the analyst is always an "active ingredient" in the analytic situation whether he is noisy or silent. (The implications of this position are spelled out later.)

Let us return to the limited applicability of the analogy to the surgeon. Consider: a surgeon typically operates on a patient who deliberately is unaware of what is going on and who therefore has no responsibility for the operation other than to give consent. But the analyst, that is to say, psychoanalysis, requires a conscious patient able to give and withhold cooperation from moment to moment. Indeed, the quality of cooperation, which is to say the issue of "resistance," may be the main issue much of the time.

A better analogy than the technique of a surgeon is the technique of a musician. Like the analyst, the musician intends to influence the emotional state of the listener, who, like the patient, has offered himself to be influenced. Like the analyst, the musician has to know how to play the notes so as to have the intended influence, so that the performance is musical rather than merely literal.

Let me extend the analogy of the musician to the teacher. If one listens in on a master class in which a talented teacher tries to help a pupil to achieve musicianship, one will witness a process quite like a psychoanalytic supervision when the supervisor tries to get across to the candidate how and when he might phrase an intervention so as to have the intended emotional effect. A common, but incorrect, criticism of an unsatisfying musical performance is that it was "technically perfect" but emotionally cold. "Technically perfect" in that usage means that the performance merely was "note perfect." For the analyst as well as the musician, technique is more than a matter of getting the words or notes right. Actually, a musical performance cannot be both technically perfect and emotionally cold; that is unmusical. Technique for the musician, as for the analyst, is about how to make emotional contact with the listener for a professional purpose.

The Logic of the Case Example

Like all analytic writers, I use case examples to illustrate the concepts I discuss and the technical procedures that follow from them. Psychoanalysis has been criticized for holding itself out as a science while behaving unscientifically in demonstrating and testing what it holds as its truths; that is, an analyst typically offers case examples to make his point. Some philosophers of science (such as Adolf Grünbaum, 1990) dismiss such evidence as anecdotal, flimsy stuff from which one cannot generalize or use to test the truth of a proposition in any "normal" science. The preferred method of testing propositions in a normal science, in which one can manipulate variables, is the experiment. In the rare instance of the failure of a crucial experiment, the entire theoretical edifice that gave rise to the proposition may fall. Most experiments are not that determinative and, at best offer or withhold support from the hypothesis under test.

The logic of the experiment is clear, but what might be the logic of the case illustration? Indeed, does it have a logic? If manipulation is practically impossible, as in astronomy, meteorology, and macroeconomics, or ethically impossible, as in psychoanalysis, can predictions derived from theory be tested and falsified? Is the case example perhaps the equivalent for the psychoanalytic narrative that the drawings of Phiz are for the characters of Dickens? We all "know" what Mr. Pickwick looks like, even though he never existed other than in the imagination of Dickens's illustrator. But our "knowledge" of these characters is purely imaginary; is our knowledge of the characters in a case example of any higher order?

The case example does have a logic even though the chain of reasoning may not be as tight as for the *experimentum crucis*. A well-written case example based on an accurately observed patient is more than a mere illustration, though it is at least that. It has something of the nature of a prediction. It says to the (analyst) reader, "This is the sort of experience that led me to arrive at my theoretical position." The reader is invited to test the position by asking himself, "Have I ever seen anything like that under those circumstances?" The reader is invited to test the idea further by waiting until those circumstances arise in his own practice and then checking to see whether the critical observation can be made or whether the suggested intervention produces the predicted results. In this sense, the well-written case example has a scientific status that is more "scientific" than the economist's prediction of the next movement of the business cycle, even if it is not quite up to the astronomer's prediction of the next solar eclipse.

This is not to make the weary claim that what the clinical psychoanalyst does is science, in any sense. The psychoanalytic enterprise is not engaged in primarily to discover truth but to relieve pain by altering the circumstances that led to the pain, particularly the politically correct untruths that have persisted untested in the patient's personal ideology. It does not follow the logic of science but rather something closer to that of the voyager; it is a self-correcting process much like that of the seafarer who uses a variety of guides ranging from landmarks to celestial navigation to stay on course. But where the mariner seeks to end up at a particular port, the analyst seeks navigational aids that will help him help the patient to cease sailing in circles. And, when the patient discovers how to steer his own course toward whatever goal, the analyst may recuse himself (Schlesinger, 1995b).

The operative term for the useful case illustration is "well-written." Unless the phenomenon at issue is carefully and fully described and the circumstances under which it appeared are equally well documented, the element of prediction in the example would fail because of vagueness. The reader would not know whether the analyst is fulfilling the necessary conditions of observation or filling in the missing elements from his own imagination. A vague proposition cannot be tested. A vague prescription cannot be followed. Psychological propositions have been charged in general as being incurably vague.

But a case example that refers to the behavior of the patient in the analytic session need not fall under that criticism. The analytic situation is conceptually much simpler than are most situations in life, and an analyst of any experience is familiar with its dimensions and possibilities. Most of the forces of everyday life are present, but the fixed elements of the situation that permit transference to become obvious and salient make easier the task of predicting to another psychoanalytic situation. In essence, one predicts from one narrative to another, that is, if my inference is true that the process in which the patient is now engaged is of type "A" and the patient said "X" in this session, he is likely to say some variant of "X" in another session if he again is in state "A."

Predicting to another session is a common event in psychoanalytic supervision, and supervisors are awarded unearned status by remarking, off handedly, to candidates, "I guess the patient will soon tell you XXX." The dazzled candidate confirms that the patient indeed said just that in the session after next. But, in my experience, he is not likely to ask the supervisor what his theory of the interaction was and on which of the circumstances of the reported session he relied to permit this wizardry. Most students seem to prefer not to delve into such mysteries. But, if he were to ask and if the supervisor were articulate, the predicting would likely seem transparent. Then, the supervisor would turn out to be just a good clinician and not a wizard. I am afraid that most candidates and some supervisors would prefer that supervisors retain the unearned status of wizard, and hence they collude in preserving the mystery.

Predicting what a patient will say or do next in the analytic situation is not a trivial matter. We assume correctly that what the patient reports can be different from what actually takes place outside the session. Transference, self-deception, and wishful thinking powerfully color patients' reports, but in time, the competently conducted analysis is self-correcting, and truth, that is, a greater correspondence between external actuality and the internal processes of memory and perception, will emerge (Schlesinger, 1995b). It would be feasible to set up a research project in which an analyst reported sessions to a group of analysts charged with making such predictions and making clear the grounds on which they felt comfortable in making a prediction or, equally important, when they did not feel comfortable enough to make one.

To make such predictions, the analyst must have a grasp of the process of psychoanalysis, a matter I deal with later. In anticipation of that discussion, note that the concept of psychoanalytic process implies that the analyst focuses primarily on what the patient *does* during the session (and on what the analyst does), not just on the content of what the patient *says*. While I dare say most analysts would agree with this definition of psychoanalytic process, in practice it is not easy for analysts, particularly beginners, to maintain this focus consistently.

2

The Systems Approach

The Centrality of Consciousness

Much of this book deals with how analysts acquire and maintain a focus on process. Before discussing the systems approach to personality as it relates to clinical psychoanalysis, I must open for consideration a basic assumption: the nature of consciousness as a process and its relationship to the idea of unconscious mental functioning.

I have long entertained the idea that the important concepts of psychoanalysis, at least those that refer to the working of the mind in psychoanalytic treatment, could be derived from a single assumption or axiom. My favorite, if seemingly quixotic, choice for this fundamental idea is that the mind is always "on"; or, in more familiar terms, consciousness, that is, mental activity that could be open to awareness, goes on continuously. It may seem odd for an analyst to suggest that a proposition about consciousness is fundamental to the clinical application of psychoanalysis. The mainstream idea seems to be closer to the proposal of Solms (1997), who, drawing on Freud's writings after 1915, proposed that "mental processes are in themselves unconscious" (p. 681). But this statement seems to me close to a tautology. By "unconscious," in formulations such as this, Freud did not mean dynamically unconscious, not as in "the repressed." He meant that, while one can become aware that one is engaged in a mental process, the process itself is not conscious. Only its object appears in consciousness. Such mental processes as perceiving and memorizing cannot be the content of consciousness, though one can be aware that one is seeing or memorizing. Thus, the idea that mental processes are unconscious hardly seems particularly psychoanalytic, let alone fundamental.

Consciousness was central to the thinking of William James (1892). At about the same time he was writing, consciousness was also important to Freud. Apparently without knowledge of James's views, Freud (1894) built his first theory of neurosis around the problem it makes for one to have incompatible ideas in mind, that is, in consciousness, at the same time. He did not arrive at the idea of a dynamic unconscious until somewhat later, when he considered anew how consciousness seemingly comes to have gaps in it, and the real action, so to speak, takes place in those gaps. When Freud (1900) began to develop psychoanalysis as a psychology, he proposed that, "The unconscious is the true psychical reality . . . and it is as incompletely presented by the data of consciousness as is the external world by our sense organs" (p. 613; see also Herzog, 1991). Note that the case Freud made for "the unconscious" being the true psychical reality derived from the evidence of consciousness, specifically from the incompleteness of the conscious record.

The Derivation of Unconscious Mental Functioning

I must emphasize that, by reverting to Freud's early theorizing, I am restricting my argument to the working of the mind in the psychoanalytic situation in order to develop a consistent approach to the technique of analyzing. Since in his analytic endeavor, the analyst has access only to what the patient presents, mainly his words, it is heuristic to assume that those words present a complete picture of what is going on in the patient's mind. It then becomes an empirical matter to discover the many interesting ways in which that proposition turns out to be only partly true. The situation is analogous to the position of a witness in a court of law. He swears to tell the truth, the whole truth, and nothing but the truth, but the trial then consists largely of testing this idealistic assumption.

If you agree, for sake of argument, to follow me in retracing Freud's early footsteps from 1894 on, and if you accept my working assumption that consciousness is continuous, you immediately will have to protest that it does not always seem so. I agree. We might then infer, as Freud (1900) did, that the seeming discontinuity or interruption of consciousness or mental activity is only apparent; perhaps the missing thought or feeling is not really gone. Rather, something may be preventing it from appearing. Notice that I have sneaked in an idea vital to psychoanalysis: the possibility that some mental contents and processes may not be conscious in the sense that they are not readily available to focal awareness.

It follows, then, that this idea, so vital to psychoanalysis, is a derivative, a finding, rather than a primary assumption, as many analysts seem to take it. Corollaries to this idea include that consciousness must be layered in terms of degrees of awareness, that is, that consciousness must be a "more or less" matter, not an "all or none" matter. Similarly, armed with the assumption of continuity, we would soon observe that there seem to be many ways to interfere with the appearance of an idea in consciousness. And with closer observation we likely would be able to discern the various ways in which we deceive ourselves, including the so-called mechanisms of defense (so called in that there are no "mechanisms" that are exclusively defensive in purpose, no special ways of defending that are not also ways of adapting or coping).

And we would also discover that certain matters, rather than others, tend to be kept out of consciousness. We would notice, too, that the omissions seem to be motivated; they are intentional, purposeful. We would also notice that the omitted items seem to be connected; in other words, that there seems to be an organization to what is omitted from, or better, denied access to, consciousness. We are now well on our way to deriving the ideas of conflict, unconscious fantasy, and neurosis. Notice that, with only the one embattled assumption that consciousness is continuous, we would have been able to repeat Freud's early journey and, like him, derive the key ideas of clinical psychoanalysis by using analytic observation.

I have another purpose in thus enshrining consciousness (only then to point out that in practice it is more tattered than continuous). If one attends clinically to the continuity of consciousness, one is in an ideal position to observe the patient as a self-aware organism, continually involved in interchange with its surroundings (including, of course, the analyst). From a formal point of view, the patient may be considered a system. This system approach to the analytic situation informs my view of technique.

A Systems View of Analyzing

Just as the major clinical concepts of psychoanalysis can be contained in a single axiom, that consciousness is, or ought to be, continuous, so I believe the major principles of technique can be derived from systems theory. It is a point of view that now informs all thinking in the social and biological sciences but has made only a little inroad on psychoanalysis.[1] In brief, it assumes that the society, the organism, or the personality can be viewed as a system, that is, as a self-regulating organization that is purposive and adaptive and also is "open" and able to make use of the information it trades with its environment. For my limited purpose, a fairly low-level application of systems thinking will do.

[1] There have been many attempts in the last 30 years to use general systems theory and information-processing theory to make psychoanalytic theory look like the other "normal sciences." For a representative effort, see Peterfreund, 1971.

The notion of the centrality of consciousness could itself be derived from the systems point of view, from the principle that the organism is always in contact with its environment. Consciousness is the "sense organ" of the personality that guarantees continuous contact. Consciousness, in the sense of awareness, is never interrupted except by organic insult, anesthesia, or intoxication. It may, however, be diverted, for instance, defensively to another topic or object of attention or to internal affairs, as in dreaming. Note that when a patient says that his mind "goes blank," he is still aware of the room, the analyst, and his own breathing.

In addition to providing a platform on which to build a consistent approach to technique, the systems point of view suggests an overall attitude toward analyzing that I commend to you. Consider: explanation in the physical sciences is properly reductionistic. But in psychology and psychoanalysis, explanation, that is, interpretation, expands meaning. It does not reduce complexity to simplicity. As philosophers Herbert Feigl and Maude Brodbeck (1953) put it, psychoanalysis is not a "nothing but" science; it is a "something more" science. As a teaser, a foretaste of what will occupy us in great detail later, consider that an implication of this point of view is that the proper general form of an interpretation, is not, "What you *really* mean is . . . ," but rather, "You may *also* mean. . . ."

Vis Medicatrix Naturae *(The Healing Power of Nature)*

You may already have anticipated that my argument is ultimately going to sound curiously old-fashioned. Are the implications of a plea to view personality as a system all that different from the medieval doctrine of *vis medicatrix naturae*? That ancient caution and reassurance that we should rely on nature once comforted clinicians who had little specific to offer the afflicted who fell into their care. But there was also clinical wisdom reflected in that doctrine, the awareness that the body and soul have inherent power to heal themselves, to go back, more or less, to their previous states once the illness runs its course.

This is the key idea. Systems are conservative. Whatever disturbs a system, once it is removed, the forces operating within the system will restore the system to its previous state of semistability. If given the chance, body and soul return to their previous states. For the personalities we see in our consulting rooms, that "previous state" is the neurosis, and the "whatever" is usually an intervention, in its best guise, an interpretation. The interpretation will have rattled the system, sending it into a self-protective spasm. But, if the analyst relaxes at that point and allows time for the system to recover, it will revert as closely as possible to its previous state. The analyst must understand the effect his interpretation has had and be prepared to follow up, guided, of course, by the principles of tact, dosage, and timing. In that way he can capitalize on the vulnerability of the system in its shaken, postinterpretation state. If he fails to observe the effect of his intervention and does not grasp the need to follow up, he is likely to withdraw, discouraged, under the mistaken belief that he gave it his best shot and "nothing happened."

A Systems View of Neurosis

The term neurosis is admittedly an old-fashioned one, no longer recognized in the *Diagnostic and Statistical Manual* (American Psychiatric Association, 2000). It once distinguished milder forms of disturbance from psychosis, the more severe form. For the psychoanalyst, the term still is useful, and I use it to describe a pattern of behavior driven by an unconscious fantasy. A neurosis tends to follow a script rigidly and repeatedly and does not easily adapt to changes in reality. A neurosis generally comes to clinical attention when the life circumstances of the sufferer have changed sufficiently so that it becomes obvious that the person who is now a patient has been long been marching to a different drummer. What could it mean to describe this state of affairs from the point of view of a system?

As a system, both the body and the personality are able to function under a wide range of conditions, but they function best when conditions are optimal. Optimal, of course, is a matter for individual definition. Some (bodies) like it hot, others cool; some personalities prefer clear structure, others prefer to "hang loose." It is characteristic of systems that their parts are interdependent, so that an action (for example, an intervention) at one point can have (perhaps unanticipated) effects elsewhere in the system. Freud (1913) anticipated the systems point of view when he remarked, "A neurosis as well has the character of an organism. Its component manifestations are not independent of one another: they condition one another and give one another mutual support" (p. 130). This quality of interdependency is what permits analysts generally to refer to neurosis as having a "structure." The term structure may evoke architectural implications of solidity and stability and permanence. But the structure of a neurosis, like that of personality in general, is of a different sort.

In energic terms, psychological structures can be thought of as systems capable of maintaining internal tension or as processes having a slow rate of change (Rapaport, 1957). Viewed phenomenally, a neurosis is a pattern of repetitive behavior; it is a "structure" only in the sense of being a quasi-stable set of functional arrangements that are not completely fixed but, within limits expressed as the "severity" of the neurosis, are responsive both to outside influence and to changes in internal conditions.

I should emphasize that neurotic styles (Shapiro, 1965) have the same characteristics but with wider limits. When clinicians use the epithet "neurotic," it should be understood as a kind of shorthand judgment about the degree of limitation or maladaptiveness in the functioning of the personality, considered as a system. A neurosis can even be adaptive within a limited range of circumstances. An obsessive person may earn a good living as a bookkeeper. While we commonly speak of one as "having" a neurosis, it would be more correct to think of a neurosis as something one *does*, something one lives out. It is emergent rather than existent, and it must continuously be re-created as circumstances change.

Psychoanalysts are familiar with the point of view of process and are accustomed to contrasting it with a point of view called "structural." But the relationship of "structure" to "system" may not be so familiar. Both system and structure refer to the internal organization of and relationships among subsystems or substructures, or among external systems or structures, at a moment in time. But the two terms, system and structure, have quite different implications. The image of a structure carries with it a sense of solidity. In a structure, the parts have relatively fixed positions in unchanging relationship with each other. "System," on the other hand, evokes images of looser arrangements, of functional stability achieved over time, not necessarily in the moment. And there are more important differences to be discussed, differences less based on the power to evoke images.

The general concept of process refers to changes in or between systems or structures that take place over time. In clinical psychoanalysis, "process" has other, special meanings. For one, it refers to the analyst's consistent focus on the effort of the patient to communicate his current experience, which is a conflation of his current reality and unconscious scripts or fantasies laid down in early life. The psychoanalytic situation allows the patient to tell his story through every means possible—and especially through reenacting, through the medium of transference—aspects of the story that are not available to declarative memory; that is, some aspects cannot be told as a narrative because they either have never been put into words or have been repressed.[2] But in the safe and permissive ambiance of the psychoanalytic situation, an unconscious

[2] Metaphors, dreams, and other ways of reliving unconscious fantasies are taken up in later chapters.

fantasy may be dramatized, reenacted, using as raw material the details and props of everyday life, events of the remembered past and the "stuff" of the current analytic relationship.

How Systems Respond to Disturbance

Some further musings about the nature of systems in general may be in order. Any nonbiologic system, for example, an organization such as a hospital, if undisturbed tends to settle into a state in which the energy expended is sufficient only to maintain the system at that level; it looks like inertia. The longer a person is in such a system, the more he potentially contributes to the inertia. In such a system, the least important person can gain power, depending on his tenure; but it is a limited kind of power, the power to obstruct, not the power to create. The power to impede is much easier to acquire than the power to initiate, and it is much easier to impede change than to exert the sustained effort required to change the system. Without such sustained effort, all systems tend to slip back into a routine that serves only to maintain the system. Inertia is a steady state that may serve the survival of the system but may also thwart the accomplishment of the aims for which the system was devised in the first place.

These considerations also apply to personality as a system. Personality systems, like hospitals, are rarely changed by a single act, no matter how disturbing. An intrusion, whether the firing of an administrator or a brilliant interpretation, may cause temporary chaos, but damage control soon takes over. If effort is not sustained, the system will slump back into a condition much like its original state. It takes sustained effort to change a bureaucratic system and sustained follow up to change a personality system. In a personality, as in a hospital, a relatively small force exerted at the right point but sustained for enough time will permit change to become incorporated into the system. Thereafter, people in the system will not even remember how it used to be. Similarly, persons whose personality has changed often will hardly remember how they used to be. The therapist will have to point out that three months ago the patient could not have done "this," and a year ago he wouldn't even have thought about it.

The neurotic system has limited flexibility because it embodies assumptions that are unrealistic, assumptions that might have been realistic in the infantile years, but even then might have been fantastic. With only a mild degree of neurosis, one can often find life settings in which one can fit, survive, and even prosper as long as the assumptions built into the neurosis conflict only minimally with a tolerant "reality." Persons with mild neuroses do not generally come to the attention of analysts until the "fit" with the current "reality" breaks down, as when the changing demands of the situation exceed the neurotic person's ability to adapt.

This formulation of the idea of neurosis as a system permits recasting the idea of analyzing. Rather than viewing analysis as an attempt to dismantle or destroy an architectural structure (for instance, to "undermine" or "break down" resistance), one could view it as repeatedly interfering with the patient's efforts to re-create the neurosis in the analytic situation. The analyst interferes with the reassembling of erroneous constructions, emotion-laden perceptions, and idiosyncratic ways of thinking that draw inspiration from, and are intended to support, neurotic assumptions and to avoid awareness of alternatives. To the extent that one has relatively fixed internal commitments, such as to the unconscious fantasy underlying a neurosis, one's personality is a semiopen system. From a cognitive point of view, one could say that it avoids recognizing disconfirming evidence; a neurosis is relatively "data proof."

A neurosis can be viewed as a set of internal operating conditions that were imposed on the personality, or better yet, created by the personality during early development. These conditions are in the nature of fixed, erroneous, and conflicting assumptions about the nature of the self, the nature of the object world, and the contingencies that relate them to each other. In analytic terms, these fixed assumptions are not independent but are embedded in unconscious fantasies that originated in efforts to solve an unconscious conflict. Being programmed by certain unconscious fantasies might have made it easier at one time to adapt to a particular pathological family constellation or to a fantasy about one, but more than likely it will later make adapting to the world at large more difficult. In general, fixed assumptions of any kind are likely to limit the ability of the organism or the personality to adapt to the vicissitudes of life. Our patients generally come to us when their fixed assumptions, that is to say, their beliefs about themselves and the world, do not square with the expectations of a new job, a new relationship, or other changed circumstance. For example:

> A business executive came with a depression and an acute marital problem for which the immediate precipitant was that he had learned that his firm would be downsizing. It had been hinted that not only would he not be getting the promotion he thought he deserved, but also the firm was planning to let him go and that it would be best for him if he would leave the firm voluntarily.

At graduate school, he earned a stellar record and had his pick of several prominent companies that were recruiting him. He thought he had been doing marvelously at work: he was well liked; he had been credited for some good ideas; and he had put out a great deal of effort, if sporadically. He said he could not understand why he was being passed over and resented that the "rules" had been changed without anyone telling him. But later it turned out that he had been told repeatedly about the disorder in which he kept his affairs, including his messy office. He had always taken these comments as a kind of friendly joshing. More seriously, it turned out that a significant proportion of the work he had begun with great promise was never finished, or was not finished in time for it to pay off.

In analysis, these patterns of dilatory behavior at work could be seen as current versions of childhood patterns in which he would frustrate his mother, a persnickety housekeeper, by not cleaning his room and, later, his teachers, by failing to turn his homework in on time. The tension between him and them was erotized, of course, and his sloppiness kept mother's attention focused on him, rather than on his well-behaving younger sister. His grudging compliance with requirements at home and at school was generally forgiven since the work he would finally turn in, nearly always late, was of high quality. He had imported these character attitudes into his work situation and expected the same response: that he would be noticed, perhaps with loving annoyance, but ultimately with indulgence because his work, when he finally got around to producing it, was excellent. These traits, while endearing though annoying at home and at school, on his job were correctly seen as signs of immaturity and lack of seriousness and were not forgivable. With analysis, the patient was able to approach his next job in a more mature way.

Systems are characteristically conservative and resistant to change. If you have ever tried to challenge a bureaucracy, you have discovered this for yourself. It is also characteristic of systems in distress that the locus of complaint is not necessarily, or even usually, where the underlying problem is located or where it can be most easily addressed. Although a conflict usually will sound loudest in the transference, as in civil disorder, the root of the problem is not in the street where the crowd is shouting. Multiple complaints may reflect a common systemic issue.

3

Working Principles Of Technique

We need some guidelines to tell us how to use the concepts we have derived from the axiom that consciousness is continuous. A small set of principles has wide application. I am dealing here largely with the formal aspects of technique, *how* and *when* the analyst interacts with the patient, and only secondarily with the content of the patient's associations. When the analyst attends to the content of the patient's thoughts and feelings, he may frame his understanding from any of several points of view, including, for instance, development, adaptation, genetics, dynamics, and structure. The approach I am suggesting is entirely consistent with this customary view but considers primarily the process of analyzing, why the analyst intervenes when he does and his purpose in doing so. I have come up with a brief list of major principles. I am not sure my list is yet complete or that the principles I list are independent of each other, but the first three of these I can offer are:

1) The patient is always right.
2) Analysts don't analyze, patients do.
3) The patient is doing the best he can.

These statements may seem to be put too frivolously to be taken seriously as principles of technique. Are they principles of any kind, let alone psychoanalytic principles? Nevertheless, although I have put them colloquially, I mean them to be taken literally and hope that you too will find them indispensable.

The Patient Is Always Right

If you have been to Chicago you may recognize that I have paraphrased Marshall Field's marketing dictum, "The customer is always right." This dictum might be taken cynically as an injunction to salespersons to yield to the customers, to placate them; since we want their money, it doesn't pay to offend them. That understanding would be sufficient for a wide range of commercial transactions, except perhaps the most trivial ones and those involving commodities, that is, those in which the customer knows precisely what he wants and where to get it and is free to purchase by price.

But many retail transactions are more complex. They have to do with satisfying customer demands that range in urgency between needs and desires but largely are elective; they can be postponed, so that the customer may shop elsewhere (thus excluding emergency medicine, for instance). Facing such a shopper, the salesperson must also be a diagnostician. Frequently, the customer knows he wants "something" and goes to the place he believes might have the something that would fill that need. But he is not certain what "goods" would be right for him, or if any would suffice. Which computer of the 50 on display is best for him? Does he need a new computer at all?

This customer will enter a functional relationship in which the first issue is whether he feels comfortable with the salesperson. Even though this relationship is likely to be brief, perhaps limited to this simple purchase, the issue remains, "I must depend on his expertise, but can I trust him?" The wise salesman will not yield to narrow self-interest and try to push an item of which he has an overstock or one that clearly is out of the customer's price range. Even if he does make a sale, the item is likely to be returned. A consequence will be the probable loss of the customer's "good will," that vague but legally recognized value represented by the customer's inclination to return to a store where he has felt well treated, and to refer his friends. Instead, the wise salesman will interview the potential customer to determine if his needs can be met by what the salesman is authorized to sell and is within the range of what the customer is ready to spend; perhaps his needs might be met better by another department of the store. It may be that the customer's need is unlikely to be satisfied by goods of any kind. The folklore of architecture and plastic surgery is replete with tales of unfinished houses and lawsuits for unsuccessful nose jobs that ensued when this essential diagnostic step was insufficient.

The parallel to psychoanalysis and psychotherapy is clear: as a potential customer for the analyst's services, "the patient is always right." The first task of the analyst (or any clinician) on meeting a new patient is to determine what the patient thinks is causing pain, whether or not the conditions that produced it are remediable by the skills available to the analyst, if the life circumstances of the would-be patient permit treatment now, and if the patient is willing. During the initial meetings the patient may resolve whether he "trusts" the analyst sufficiently to follow his advice to enter one or another form of treatment with him, to accept a referral, or to consider other possibilities.

It is important to recognize that neither the good salesman nor the analyst initially challenges the patient's belief that he needs "something." At least in that sense the customer/patient implicitly is deemed to be "right." The analyst, for instance, is not likely to tell the patient, "There's nothing wrong with you; it's all in your head. You're just one of the worried-well. Pull up your socks and get on with life." True, the analyst might conclude that the patient does not need extensive treatment now, but he will not hold that one can be significantly worried and yet altogether well. But consider this example. Is it a contradiction?

> A woman came for a consultation to seek immediate therapy. Her husband, who had recently disrupted her career by moving the family to this distant state so that he could accept a better position for himself, had just asked her for a divorce. She had been in therapy before and had found it helpful. After listening to her story, the analyst told her that he thought that right now she needed a lawyer to help her with her practical problems. He feared that if she would involve herself in therapy to discover how she might have contributed to the breakdown of the marriage, she might well fail to look after her own immediate interests. He suggests that, after she had engaged a lawyer to protect her interests, if she still thought she needed treatment, she might return to discuss additional therapy.

Unlike the brief retail transaction I used as an introductory model, the delivery of psychoanalytic services takes place over a long stretch of time, and thus other considerations come into play. The analyst must continue to be a diagnostician as he keeps open the question whether or not the patient still needs his services. Does the patient need more treatment now, or can she continue alone? It may seem jarring to raise the issues of ending and termination at this point, but I do so to emphasize that ending ought to be a concern of the analyst from the very outset of treatment. By analogy to the surgeon's maxim, "Getting in is easy; getting out can be problem."

The Centrality of Unconscious Fantasy

There is a much more profound sense in which the analyst must hold as a tenet that "the patient is always right." It is the analyst's working assumption that a patient's sense of unsatisfied need is rooted in conflictual unconscious fantasies that drive her to seek, repeatedly and unsuccessfully, solutions to the conflict. The patient repeatedly finds and adopts the same inadequate solution, which leads once again to the sense of dissatisfaction that opened the cycle. Though she may feel uneasy about what she is doing, may even admit when challenged that it makes no sense, she generally lacks full awareness that what keeps her stuck are the "choices" she has made that unconsciously were compelled.

I must clarify the term unconscious fantasy as it recurs throughout this book. The term fantasy implies a formulated text and hence that there must have been a time when the text was formulated. The question may then be asked if the fantasy was in consciousness when formulated and if it only later became unconscious—an iffy question about which much speculation exists. It would not do, for instance, to insist that all stable, repetitive, perhaps maladaptive patterns of behavior are driven by a current conflict that is not in consciousness. Some such patterns seem as if they are governed by such an unconscious script but developed as a kind of unclearly formulated rule or habit. Perhaps these patterns emerged in imitation of elders as an effort to find a way to get along in the family; they might represent an effort to avoid conflict rather than to solve a conflict of which one is unaware.

Examples of the latter range from behaviors that, indeed, appear to be conflict driven and that lead one to question their status only when one notices that several members of the family, different in other respects, manifest the same odd behavior. More common examples that only infrequently are confused with unconscious fantasy include mannerisms and accents that are difficult to change. It is entirely possible that such a pattern of behavior was once laid down for dynamic reasons and, although those dynamic reasons are no longer compelling, the pattern of behavior remains as a habit. As long as the pattern is not grossly maladaptive, it may persist as an idiosyncrasy, crotchet, or style. It may even acquire new functions that reinforce it so that it may persist long after it has lost connection with its dynamic roots.

Some analysts may insist that this softening of the idea of the unconscious fantasy is unwarranted, that all such patterns must have current dynamic support. Those analysts may be right. My position is that one can treat such patterns as if they do have such support without insisting on the factuality of one's plausible reconstruction. The usefulness of this observation may be in discouraging young analysts from hunting for the presumed specific causative conflict when there may not have been one. Old theory may have required the hunt, but current therapeutics does not. The clinical approach to both varieties is the same; it is based on first understanding the function of the behavior and only secondarily, and when indicated, connecting it with its presumed origins. In what follows, unless I specify otherwise, unconscious fantasy is presumed to be conflict based. But you should understand that the broader sense is intended.

It is highly useful, even essential, as one gets to know one's patient, to construct a script or formulation of the patient's repeated life-course deviations that would appear sensible, rather than, "nonsensical," as the patient and family may label them. This is, of course, an important application of the principle that the patient is always right and that the analyst's task is to discover or invent the premises that, if followed logically, would lead to the adoption of just that odd pattern of behavior. I believe this position is close to that of Spence (1982) regarding the distinction between historical and narrative truth. Such constructions or formulations help both patient and analyst talk about the troublesome behavior and recognize that what looks like foolish error is better understood as part of an elaborate but not yet clearly seen plan. Holding, even tentatively, to such a construction also may help to facilitate change in that it permits one to highlight the decision points in what formerly seemed to be a seamless and automatic process.

The analyst views the patient's unsuccessful and frequently expensive and hurtful efforts as attempts to solve the archaic problem embedded in the presumed unconscious fantasy. In that sense also, the patient's problem-solving activities are "right." As experienced by the patient, they are painful and frustrating. As seen by an "outsider," and occasionally by the patient too, the efforts are misdirected and doomed to failure. But at one time, they probably were successful in reaching the best possible compromise among the various forces represented in unconscious fantasy. The analyst helps the patient to understand that his efforts, which seem to reflect only failure from the "outside" point of view, ironically also are at least partial "successes" from the point of view of others among the internal contending forces. By failing, (in the "external" sense), the patient's behavior will have fulfilled successfully at least one of the conditions of the unconscious fantasy, generally the condition that required punishment.

I could have taken inspiration from a source closer to home than a master retailer; for I have only restated for neurosis the major application of systems thinking that Virchow (1866) proposed for somatic disease: that disease is the body's response to altered conditions. In our usage, the principle implies that the analyst ought to take the position that, however miserable and mixed up the patient seems to be, he is doing the best he can under the circumstances. The disturbed and disturbing behavior represents the best solution the patient can come up with inasmuch as he keeps himself unaware of the true nature of the problem. He is unaware, as well, of the full resources he might bring to bear to achieve a less costly solution were he not burdened by some anachronistic assumptions. It is the business of the analysis to discover the dimensions of the problem, to help the patient appreciate in full consciousness why the solution he arrived at was indeed the best available to him at the time, and to help him to consider whether or not the "problem" is a currently valid one and thus if it needs solving at all.

In the most general terms, the kind of psychopathology that psychoanalysis is most suited for is an inhibition of function that results from compromises designed to satisfy the paradoxical conditions of unconscious fantasy. In regard to paradox, unconscious fantasy is like the dilemma the Mikado presented to Koko. Recall that, to fulfill his credo to "make the punishment fit the crime," the Mikado sentenced Koko who had been found guilty merely of a misdemeanor, first to be elevated to the post of Lord High Executioner and then, before beheading the next condemned man, to cut off his own head (Gilbert and Sullivan, 1885).

We can appreciate fully the absurdity of the Mikado's paradoxical sentencing while enjoying the operetta, but Freud's (1894) original idea of neurosis pivoted on the difficulty of keeping incompatible ideas in consciousness at the same time. Unconscious fantasy, since it must satisfy contradictory premises, permits no constructive solution. And since it contains and must reconcile forbidden wishes, neither can it be allowed full access to consciousness. Again, the task of analysis is to make it possible for the patient to appreciate the absurdity of the conditions to which he has subjected himself.

Briefly, then, the issues analysis attempts to clarify are the nature and source of the unconscious conflicts embedded in the unconscious fantasy, why the compromise-solution seemed inevitable at the time, and why it has persisted anachronistically. This kind of psychopathology, based on unconscious conflict, may occur in a wide range of personality types and personality disorders. Of course, whether or not psychoanalysis is the appropriate treatment for a patient is a question that entails consideration of other factors in addition to the inhibiting, unresolved unconscious fantasy that is present.

Analysts Don't Analyze, Patients Do

The ultimate aim of psychoanalysis is to promote the patient's activity, to promote the patient's living in the world rather than in fantasy. The immediate (that is, tactical) purpose for the analyst to intervene technically also is to promote in various ways the patient's activity within the analytic situation. First, the analyst will want to facilitate the patient's giving voice to the stream of consciousness, that is, to associate freely. The analyst also will want him to recognize the obstacles he puts up both to associating freely and to recognizing the import of what he has said or failed to say. And the analyst will want him to take responsibility for his reluctance in both matters, that is, to acknowledge that it is something he is doing, not something that is happening to him.

Another important function of intervening technically is to keep the processes of discovery and recognition open, to keep the patient's personality system from slipping back into the previous neurotic state (Schlesinger, 1995a). Left to itself for only a little while, a personality system that has been shaken up by an accurate interpretation will slip back into its customary ways unless the analyst "follows up" by immediately addressing the "pull" to restore the status quo ante (that is, "the resistance"). For example:

> The patient had been struggling against recognizing how attached she was to her husband who, after years of acrimony had decided he had had enough and asked for a separation. "Good riddance," she tried to maintain, "who needs such a wimp." But her dreams told a different story as did her associations that regularly expressed metaphorically the despair of one left behind. The analyst pointed to the confluence of themes from these two sources and, after a moment the patient began to cry, a highly unusual event. After several minutes of sobbing, she pulled herself together, wiped her eyes and, in her usual brittle way, said, "Thanks for letting me have my little cry. I'm all right now. Let's get back to work."
>
> The analyst was tempted to go along with her plea to let her regain her composure, but he realized that she clearly wanted to deal with the episode as she always had, by disowning any depth of feeling. He suggested that she wanted to put behind her the sad acknowledgment of how lonely she felt and how she missed her husband.
>
> "You're cruel," she almost shouted. "Why won't you let me forget about him. He'll never come back."
>
> Again, the analyst addressed her defensiveness. He pointed out how embarrassed she had become when she could not prevent the outburst of normal emotion and instead reached for her characteristic readiness to accept punishment and get on with "the work." It would be too painful to entertain the possibility that the situation might be retrievable.

She was silent but the analyst observed that her posture was not tense. He then added that he thought she was also scolding herself for allowing herself to cry: "I think it felt good to let yourself go, as you so rarely do, and when you noticed that it felt OK, you had to reject it as if it represented an unpardonable indulgence."

The patient remained silent for a while and then wiped her eyes and shook her head. She said softly, "I never do that." The analyst added, "Perhaps you never did that before, but you were able to do it just now."

By helping the patient to stay with her emotional reaction and to accept that she was hurt, whatever the cause of the breach with her husband, the analyst has helped the patient enter, however gingerly, a new area of experience.

That episode occurred early in the analysis. At a later time, the same issue arose again.

After many months of separation, the couple reconciled sufficiently to try to live together again. But, once again, the longer the patient remained in a situation that permitted intimacy and dependency, the more she felt driven to criticize, to expect the worst, and to feel that she had to protect herself against being vulnerable to someone who inevitably would let her down. While the character pattern had been apparent for some time, the patient's associations to her childhood made it possible for the analyst to attempt a tentative construction of the unconscious fantasy that she might be reenacting. The analysis reached a point homologous to the one described earlier.

The patient had been anticipating with defiance, but also with a more easily recognizable note of dread, that her husband again might become fed up and leave. Again she was readying herself to take the blame and carry on alone, bravely. Once again, the analyst interrupted this repetitive pattern by noting her readiness to write off the relationship. This time her protest was more muted and eventuated in her wondering, puzzled, why it always seemed to turn out this way. The analyst heard this new expression as something between active curiosity and shrugging it off because there was "no good reason for it," hence, by definition, a matter of no interest to a logical mind.

The analyst took a chance that the patient might be more ready now to engage the issue. He suggested that, far from being an inevitable outcome, it was a development the patient had to work very hard to achieve for her husband was not easily discouraged. Half recognizing some truth in this comment, the patient nevertheless spluttered her disagreement and after a while again tried to shrug it off by wondering, "Why would I do such a thing?" Her tone of voice implied that, since she could not think of a good reason, she could not have done it.

The analyst adds that getting her husband to leave was the whole point of her behavior. Unless he left her, she would not be able to return to the familiar, uncomfortable, but safe, position of the lonely, abandoned child, a victim who will both suffer punishment for and be forgiven for her sins. The patient was silent for a few moments and then said that she had just thought of one of her favorite "jokes," a cynical one-liner about the man who killed his parents and then threw himself on the mercy of the court because he was an orphan.

The patient, now hearing this "joke" in a different way, saw, that its appeal to her was that she too had to be rid of someone in order to enjoy the status of victim. It began to make sense to her that she has been avoiding recognizing that she was active in creating and maintaining her "neurosis" and equally avoidant of actively engaging in her analysis.

The point of these examples is to emphasize the importance of attending to the defensive position of patients who prefer being analyzed (passive) to analyzing (active). The usual way patients and analysts refer to what we do favors this misleading passive usage and promotes wrong expectations, for example, from patients, "I am *in* analysis," and from analysts, "*I* am analyzing *her*."

The principle that we aim to promote the patient's activity has several corollaries and many applications. It follows that the analyst should avoid doing for the patient what the patient can do for himself. In particular, the analyst should avoid spelling out what she means in great detail as if the patient were a dull student. The analyst should be laconic and emotionally evocative when intervening. As I discuss in more detail later, she should fractionate complex ideas or constructions and offer a partial rather than a complete idea; she should expect that, if the patient is ready to "get it," his subsequent associations will fill out the idea with examples. If the patient is not ready, it is preferable that the analyst help him to recognize that he is not ready and why, rather than attempting to do the work for the patient by continuing to elaborate and explain her idea, as if in this way she could overcome the patient's unreadiness.

I am describing intervening or interpreting as a process that is at once analytically therapeutic and also analytically diagnostic. The analyst can learn from the patient's response to a partially expressed idea how ready he is to get further into an issue. The analyst aims to open issues rather than to close them. Of course, the analyst will not be relentless in the service of "openness" and promoting the patient's activity. As a good clinician, the analyst will sense when the patient has seen as much and done as much as he can stand for the moment. Which is to say that the analyst will bear in mind my third principle, "The patient is doing the best he can."

While the analyst will be guided by the principles of neutrality, anonymity, and abstinence left to us by Freud (1912a–1915b), the systems approach may make it clearer how they should be applied. A corollary of the principle that the analyst should promote the patient's activity is that the "analytic material" is what the patient *does*—his actions—which, of course, include his vocalizations, but other behavior as well (Hellmuth Kaiser, cited in Fierman, 1965; see also Shapiro, 1999).

We may say, then, that all analysis is self-analysis; "to analyze" is, so to speak, a reflexive verb. The patient analyzes himself, with the occasional assistance of the analyst. Keeping this distinction in mind will make a large difference in how we analyze, that is, how we engage the patient. We can act toward the patient in a way that encourages him to be active rather than conveying that analyzing is the analyst's business.

Activity in Analysis

The analyst does not analyze the patient as a biochemist might analyze a urine specimen, by reducing it to its constituents, or as a surgeon might operate on an anesthetized patient. The analyst's position is analogous to that of the midwife who assists the mother-to-be by attending her expectantly and encouragingly, while mostly staying out of the way of the natural process of childbirth.[1] She facilitates matters when necessary, removing obstacles the mother cannot handle alone. Moral: neither obstetricians nor midwives deliver babies; mothers do it. This point of view has many implications for analyzing.

For one, analyzing can be construed as a natural process, like childbirth. Free association is the way the mind works when it is not constrained or focused by a task, whether the task is assumed voluntarily, assigned by another, or imposed by the constraints of an unconscious fantasy

[1] Stepansky (1999) has pointed out that Ferenczi (1919) proposed that an obstetrical metaphor be substituted for the surgical one.

(Schlesinger, 1993b). Thus, the analyst does not have to force the patient to associate [as Freud (1895b, p. 110; 1924) thought he had to in his early efforts with the pressure technique]; neither does she have to teach the patient to associate. Rather, she must diagnose what keeps the patient either from allowing this natural process to occur or from lending it his voice, and to help the patient recognize when he is slowing things down and why.

As anyone who has tried can tell you, following the "basic rule" literally is very difficult. Conscious intentions tend to divert and redirect the train of associations, and, after a while, you cannot be sure whether you are associating, or are deliberately talking nonsense. We do not usually hear about the seemingly opposite problem: that it is also difficult not to associate freely. We all know of persons, not necessarily patients, who cannot keep to a point when speaking, whose ideas seem to wander unpredictably and who seem oblivious when the end of a thought is unrelated to its beginning. These people may demonstrate a high degree of looseness of associations, to use the clinical term, but they differ from the rest of us only in degree of obliviousness.

We all listen to ourselves more or less closely when speaking. We monitor our speech for sense and continuity—one might say, to keep from free associating. Slips of the tongue tell us that, when unguarded, when our self-monitoring relaxes, we are likely to say more and differently from what we intended to say. The art of clinical listening takes advantage of the fact that, whether or not a patient has been given the basic rule, if given enough time and lack of external stimulation, the several parties in a patient's intrapsychic conflict will either make themselves heard or make their wish to be heard obvious. The struggle to gain the floor is revealed in the way a patient shuts down or pauses when his story does not require it, or when his story diverges from the line it has been following, or when the story is replaced by another line of thought altogether. The patient may not be aware of the dysfluency and, even if he is aware, may not comment on it, but to the analyst, at least, the way the patient speaks will betray that he has several incompatible agendas.

It is not often mentioned that an additional reason for the patient to voice his associations is so that he himself can hear them. It is quite a different matter to listen silently to one's thoughts than to hear them through one's external ear, all the while knowing that the analyst, too, is listening. It is much easier to fool oneself when the story-telling is totally within one's head. The general reason for not voicing associations is that it would not feel safe for the patient to recognize and express what has come, or might come, to mind. It is the analyst's job to help the patient discover why he feels unsafe and whether and when to take the risk of allowing his mind to "play" (Schlesinger, 1993b).

You will have noticed that here the analogy between analyst and midwife tends to break down. If a delivery is impeded for long, it will be dangerous for both mother and child, and more drastic intervention might be called for. But reluctance to associate freely seldom constitutes an emergency in analysis, although the analyst may feel frustrated and mistakenly view it as such (Schlesinger, 1989). I am not offering a recommendation just to "sit it out," for time is not necessarily on the side of the analysis, and turning a deaf ear to the patient would only express the analyst's annoyance for being frustrated. On the other hand, it is a common transference position for the patient to assign responsibility to the analyst for "progress," while arrogating to himself the right to drag his feet. It is a seemingly slight twisting of the truth that the patient indeed has the "right" to set the pace, but it is not true that the analyst is "responsible for progress"; he is responsible only for the skilled application of therapeutic principles on behalf of the patient.

"Progress" is a possible outcome of the collaboration of analyst and patient. If the analyst "buys in" to the transferential attribution of responsibility for progress, he is likely either to grow frustrated at the patient's "lack of cooperation" and withdraw or in other ways punish the patient for her behavior. Equally destructively, he might redouble his efforts to try to do the analysis alone. Concern for maintaining the patient's activity would point the analyst toward interpreting the patient's understandable effort to deal with a conflict between staying safely in her neurosis and changing by assigning the responsibility for change to the analyst. It will be useful to refer again to an earlier statement of the principle that the patient is always right.

More About the Patient's Being Right

A most important corollary of Marshall Field's "The customer is always right," is that it is not possible to win an argument with a customer. Even if one manages to make the sale, one is likely to lose the customer, and more likely one will lose both sale and customer. Unfortunately, it is not usually so in analysis. It is only too possible for the analyst to win an argument with his patient and wittingly or not, put the patient down. Sometimes he may win the argument even though the terms of the argument might never have been made explicit and he might not even have been aware that he was involved in an argument. Unlike the salesman, the analyst is not likely to lose the patient after he wins the argument. Out of role respect, the need for help, transference dependency, and masochism, the patient is likely to retire and lick his wounds and, having "learned his lesson," he will subsequently try to avoid tangling with the analyst. But it is not possible for the analyst to "win," certainly not to win consistently, and also to analyze effectively, for he will have given cause for the patient to take refuge in one of the positions of his unconscious fantasy. Here is an example:

> The patient had been musing in a somewhat distant fashion during this session, to which the analyst had arrived several minutes late. The analyst felt defensive about being late and, on arriving, muttered a perfunctory, "Sorry." The patient neither acknowledged the apology nor commented on the lateness, but spoke in a monotone and in a desultory way for some minutes. Finally, the analyst, who was still feeling a bit on edge and sensed that the patient's behavior had something to do with him, said in a tone that expressed some of his annoyance, "You seem to be avoiding some issue." The patient seemed startled and replied, "Sorry." After a brief pause he added, "I just remembered the dream I had last night." He started to relate the dream. The analyst leaned back and listened to the dream in his usual fashion. His tension now gone, he was happy that the analysis seemed to be back on track.

I dare say any analyst could give an example of this commonplace event, if he even remembered so unremarkable an incident. What is there to learn from it? Consider, the analyst ignored the patient's blurting out, "Sorry," implying that the patient was apologizing for having committed the offense of feeling hurt and irritated by the analyst's lateness; he expressed his complicated reaction in his characteristic passive-aggressive way. Instead of taking the opportunity to analyze this character pattern, the analyst, feeling guilty about his lateness and relieved at not having been attacked for it, put it out of mind. He did not connect the patient's sluggishness with his own tardiness and, not recognizing that he had coerced the patient's apology, he was happy to accept it. He concluded wrongly that he had succeeded in getting the analysis back on track rather than confirming his role in one of the patient's transference paradigms. By relieving his sense of guilt for being late in this way, he also reinforced the tendency unwittingly to suppress the patient's muted expression of resentment. Again, we have encountered the idea that the "analytic material" is what the patient does, not just what he says.

The analyst in that example did not realize that he was in an argument, let alone that he had won it. Even though the patient stayed, the question remains to what extent and in what way the analytic situation may have been deformed. It is also possible, of course, for an analyst to lose an argument with his patient. Usually, however, analysts tend to avoid losing an argument by avoiding topics that might lead to losing one, with consequences similar to those that ensue when patients avoid topics they fear might annoy the analyst. These are matters for supervision.

Many so-called impasses can be understood as chronic arguments that have not been made explicit and that neither patient nor analyst can afford to win or lose. Often both parties do not even recognize that they silently have been arguing, and thus they remain stuck, unable to extricate themselves lest they lose the relationship they value. This sort of situation could well be described as a neurosis that has developed in the context of the transference, or, in short, as a "transference neurosis."

The general solution for the impasse requires that both analyst and analysand understand that the analysis has metamorphosed into something like an argument (possibly a silent one) and why. The usual reason is that the analyst has bought into the transference, has lost his analytic split, that is, has perhaps temporarily lost his view of himself as the transference object. By enacting that role, he has become part of the problem (Schlesinger, 1981b, 1989, 1995a). The particulars of the reason must be sought in the same way as those behind the reluctance to associate freely, of which the impasse is a variant. (Analyzing in the transference neurosis, or, as it is often put, the "middle phase," is discussed more fully later.)

The Patient Is Doing the Best He Can

The idea that the patient is always right has a more general significance than to counsel avoiding argument. Putting it as "the patient is doing the best he can" is neither Panglossian nor Pollyannish but is an essential component of the analyst's attitude toward the patient. In effect, it is a restatement of our understanding that the peculiar and painful situation that the patient brings to his analyst is not actually his "problem." He may call it his problem, and, for the time being, out of courtesy, the analyst may refer to it that way too. But it is actually the best way the patient has been able to figure out (consciously and unconsciously) to work around a problem that he is not aware he has.[2]

[2] It is conventional to refer to matters that for the moment are unavailable to recall as "deeper" than matters easily available. I do not follow that usage because it evokes the misleading imagery of a mental geology with stratified memory systems. Such unnecessary structural imagery can easily burden one's technical approach to the patient by implying that there is a necessary order to interpreting content. The notion of the "analytic surface" has altogether different implications and is taken up in Chapter 8.

It is the task of the analysis to figure out what the problem is for which the neurosis is the unworkable solution, but thus far the only one the patient has been able to imagine. By taking this stance, the analyst conveys his respect for the ingenious, if painful and impractical, measures the patient has felt compelled take in order to live with his as yet unseen problem. It will then be possible to help the patient discover the conflicting underlying assumptions that he had to adopt both to construct the problem and to limit the range of solutions. Patient and analyst will inquire into the remarkable way the patient's mind works even now to insist that this impracticable solution is both exclusive and inevitable. The patient will come to understand that at some early time, when his comprehension of reality was limited, it must have seemed the best solution available. He also will discover why these problems and solutions, of whose connections he is hardly aware, have yielded the plan of action, the script, for his current life.

This line of thought may call to mind the witticism attributed to a contemporary of Freud, who joked that psychoanalysis is actually the disease of which it pretends to be the cure. I used to wince at hearing it quoted, but I think, in a certain sense, it is right. We do use the analytic situation to recreate the condition of which the patient complained, and we could regard the treatment as a controlled reliving and working through of it.[3]

Some old-timers may recognize that a radio comedy skit was once built on a similar idea. Steve Allen parodied the popular "Answer Man," who would solemnly answer serious requests for information submitted by the radio audience. In Allen's parody, a panel of "experts" had to guess what the question might have been to which Allen had supplied a punning quip for an answer: for instance, "Panel, what is the question for which 'Nine W' is the answer?" New Yorkers will recall that before the interstate highway system was built, Route 9W was the main north-south highway from the city to Albany, but that was just a tease. The correct question, according to Allen, was, "Richard Wagner, do you spell your last name with a 'V'?" In analysis, too, the task is to discover what the question or problem was to which the patient's odd behavior is the answer or solution. As in the quiz show parody, we presume that the patient's "answer" is correct, but what could the question have been?

It might seem that I should next offer the bromide that, having first discovered the reasons for the problem he has been at cross-purposes to solve, the patient will then be better able to choose a course that makes

[3] Theodor Reik (1959) discussed the religious mass and the criminal trial in the same terms, as controlled repetitions of a crime.

for a less expensive and more effective solution of that problem. Perhaps he might come to see that it is not a current problem but was a problem in his infancy, a problem impossible to solve at that time because it was badly conceived but that, in any event, no longer needs a solution. In the most general sense, the bromide is true; we explain matters to our patients and our students in such terms, and they tend to accept the formulation because it is plausible. But it does not describe accurately how most of the time change actually happens. It is not just that putting things this way places undue weight on cognitive knowing in bringing about change. I have, in effect, just implicated one of psychoanalysis' most hoary questions: Does insight lead to change, or does change lead to insight? But it is not necessary to take an ideological position on the question of whether insight precedes or follows change, for it is an empirical matter, one that can be settled by observation in any particular case.

It has been my experience that most often significant change occurs before insight, at least in the restricted sense of awareness that one has changed, that is, that one is not quite the same as formerly, but without necessarily knowing why. The patient may react with surprise, even alarm mixed oddly with pleasure, on discovering that he is no longer "the same." The change might well be something he has "always sort of wanted," but it is not an unmixed blessing. A fear lurks that "progress" might have come at the expense of "undermining his will." After all, he wasn't asked about having this change happen right now and he didn't will it to happen (Schlesinger, 1993a, 1996).

The systems point of view can be helpful in resolving the paradox that change seems to occur without specific choosing while we maintain that the general aim of psychoanalysis is to promote choice. Recall that it is a characteristic of systems that an alteration in one part of the system can affect another part. A change that surprises, pleases, or worries a patient may be the result of work done in another area altogether, work that had the effect of reorganizing the neurosis and loosening its grip in an aspect that has not been the focus of analytic attention. Insight, in the sense of why did this change happen and what problem has been solved by this now-loosened inhibition, may follow from the ensuing analytic effort to discover why this change occurred just now. Of course, asking what leads to personality change is not necessarily the same as asking how we prefer to explain such change (Schlesinger, 1988, 1996).

The Patient Is Still Right

I may seem to have taken a stance on the slippery issue, whether the will is free. The issue of the free will has, of course, an unavoidable metaphysical cast. But if we stay within the clinic and claim only that psychoanalysis aims to free the will from the bonds of neurosis, and that the freedom attained is at best relative, the ultimate question need not be addressed. In this context Freud's (1923) aphorism, "Where Id was, there shall Ego be," could be rephrased in operational terms as, "Where compulsion was, there choice shall be." In any given case it should be possible for analyst and patient to estimate when a sufficient degree of internal freedom has been achieved, as, say, when considering the patient's readiness to leave the analyst with maximum benefit obtained (Schlesinger, 1990, 1996).

The discussion of compulsion and choice raises again the principle that the general aim of clinical psychoanalysis is to promote the activity of the patient, that is, to promote freely chosen, not anxiously compelled, activity. Freud[4] defined health aphoristically as the ability to love and to work; both are actions. Relatively speaking, we hope our patients will see themselves as the agents of their own destiny rather than as the helpless victims of external forces. We hope they will see that their previous condition of neurotic servitude had to do with choices they once may have felt forced to make, or perhaps made quite naturally, without realizing they had chosen at all.

This is the condition we presume characterized infantile life when expectations about important contingencies were formed before the full development of self-conscious, reflective awareness. The experience of a patient who is suddenly faced with the possibility of choosing may be to find it unwelcome, as a requirement rather than a choice. After all, "Nobody ever asked me before, why do I have to choose now?" Choosing is risky and the patient might prefer to remain unaware that his current situation is the product of having chosen "wrongly" at some much earlier time. The patient may manifest mild incomprehension at being expected to choose, "But that's the way things are; no one made them like that, they just come like that. I don't like the way it is all that much, but that is the way it is."[5]

---

[4] Everyone "knows" that Freud said that to love and to work are the criteria for mental health, but the statement is not to be found in his writings. The closest version is in Freud (1912), where he urged that we be "content if one has won back some degree of capacity for work and enjoyment" (p. 119). Erikson (1959), apparently relying on a personal communication, quotes Freud as offering "*Lieben und Arbeiten*" in response to a question about what a normal person should be expected to do well (p. 96).

[5] Some readers may see an allusion to another vexing issue, the question of "primal repression." Can something be repressed if it was never in consciousness in the first place? The issue is vexing, I believe, because it mixes concepts derived from the topographic model with the structural model. The question might better be put as, Does the unconscious contain only what is repressed? That version of the question might seem clearer, but it is no more answerable.

If we can agree that the general aim of analyzing is to increase the patient's activity and sense of agency, we can derive some implications for analytic technique, not least that the analyst should refrain from doing for the patient what the patient can do for himself. This recommendation, of course, is borrowed from child rearing (Brazelton, 1973) and seems to advocate an abstemious technique. Indeed, it would be difficult to argue with the idea that the analyst should aim to do only what is necessary and to eliminate the unnecessary, but that recommendation begs the question of what we mean by necessary. There is the obvious implication that the analyst should avoid excessive nurturing as he should avoid excess of any kind. But the more serious and more subtle implication for technique has to do with how we frame interventions.

Framing Interpretations so as to Promote Patient Activity

The principle of promoting a patient's activity implies that the analyst should offer interventions that tend to promote the patient's taking an active part in the interpretive process (Schlesinger, 1995a). If the analyst prefers to offer constructions that he has tried to make "complete," if he attempts to give the patient "the whole story," he then requires little of the patient other than to listen and approve or disapprove the whole package. Analysts often put a great deal of thought into the formulation of such constructions, and justifiably take great pride in the ability to generate and articulate them. If only they kept the constructions to themselves and allowed their patients to arrive at them in their own ways and in their own time.

Recall that our aim is to promote the patient's activity in the here-and-now, not just in future life. The "whole story" of a complete interpretation is usually too complicated for a patient to grasp in one hearing. And the longer and more complicated it is, the more ideas it contains, the less likely is it to connect emotionally to the patient's experience, that is, the less likely it is to be evocative. The usual reaction of the patient on whom such a "blockbuster" is dropped is to say or think, "Wow!" Delivered with conviction, such formulations are impressive and produce awe whether they are right or wrong, and they usually are at least partially right.

Less Is More

Would it not be better if the analyst were to *fractionate* complex constructions and offer only a bit at a time, with no more than one idea to any intervention, preferably less than one idea? By less than one idea I mean that, if one offers an incomplete idea that points in the direction one is thinking, the patient might offer something in return that would tend to complete the idea, thus providing a degree of confirmation for the not yet fully proposed construction. Her associations might veer off in an unexpected direction, thus possibly correcting or enriching what the analyst had in mind.

In short, the patient's response to a fraction of a potential construction provides the analyst with diagnostic information as he builds toward an interpretation. From this point of view, long sections of a session, even the work of several sessions, could be considered as the process of building an interpretation, a construction that links events in the session with those in life outside and in the past in a way that offers new understanding.

The view of interpretation as a process conflicts with the older view of interpretation as a construction, perhaps a complicated one, that has arisen in the analyst's mind and is delivered as a package to the patient. We might say of this older view that "interpretation is an event." Another problem with offering a complicated, multipart construction to the patient all at once is that the expectable defensive process it evokes at the outset may deafen the patient to much of its later portions. The patient may not "get" much of it, and the reasons why will not be clear. He may apologize for not fully understanding and appreciating the complicated view of himself that the analyst obviously has worked on to perfection and has presented to him, as it were, on a platter. The bolder patient may ask the analyst to repeat it. It is hardly the way to arouse the emotional as well as cognitive insight to which we aspire when interpreting.

We may take a lesson here from the way enlightened parents try to let their young children in on some of the mysteries of life. When a child exhibits some curiosity or gives other signs of stumbling on missing facts, the parent will not deliver a lecture he has been composing "just in case." Instead he will offer a conjecture about what might be concerning the child and then take his lead about what to do next from the child's response. The adult in psychoanalysis is, of course, not a child, but he deserves the same respect for his readiness to take up a difficult topic and also for his ability to work on it himself rather than to have the "answer" supplied. It is another instance where, as in architecture, less can be more. For example:

> The patient had been ruminating once again about his childhood family constellation, as usual mentioning but not pursuing the odd arrangement that his mother's younger, more attractive, unmarried sister had lived with them for some time. His father worked in the City and often came home for lunch. His mother was away frequently finishing her graduate degree. He had been very fond of his aunt and she of him; she had read stories to him and liked to indulge him. But she disappeared one day while he was at school, never to reappear or even to be mentioned by name again. The

> analyst had noted the patient's repeated sidling around the issue of the aunt and had a story in mind that would have connected all of the dots and filled in some missing ones about the pattern of attraction, avoidance and sudden disappearance. At a moment when the patient had just mentioned her abrupt leaving again, again with no theory about it, he offered a comment. He had considered several ways of intervening and chose what he considered the least leading. He said, matter-of-factly, "She just disappeared."
>
> "You mean Aunt Jane?" the patient said. "I don't recall ever asking why she left or why I never heard from her again. I don't think I was supposed to know—but I was so fond of her." The patient began to sniff audibly and began to explore an aspect of the oedipal constellation that had previously been obscure, had led him to blame himself for her departure, and had also put up a wall between the patient and his mother.

That patient was ready to pick up the thread dropped by the analyst's lead and fill in material that conveniently supported the analyst's theory. Technically, that the intervention led to confirmation was less important than that it facilitated the patient's activity at completing the interpretation. It would have been equally useful, if less immediately gratifying to the analyst, if, given such a lead, the patient had taken off in another direction altogether. It would even have been useful if the patient had come to a dead halt. For that response would have told the analyst that he was on the right track and that he would have to deal next with the patient's unreadiness. If the analyst had thrown the whole construction at the unready patient, he probably would not have received a useful message. That is, if the patient had "stopped cold" after a "complete" interpretation, the analyst would not know which part of the interpretation the patient had reacted to. Clearly, the analyst should welcome a spontaneous and emotionally laden response of any kind, and such responses are more likely to occur if the analyst does not take it on himself to do all the work. I am sure some hunches may have occurred to you about the personal and dynamic (narcissistic?) reasons, in addition to possible technical preference, why an analyst might insist on delivering "complete" constructions, but these hunches are not part of a formal treatment technique.

Framing Follow-up Interventions

How can we put into practice the working principle that the analyst should frame his next intervention on the basis of his understanding of the patient's reaction to a previous one, whether a casually rejected or more directly despised one? Consider the following example:

> The patient had been talking of her failure to get across her point of view to her husband, and how the weekend had been one long frustration. The analyst thought he had heard a metaphoric reference to the same sort of complaint the patient had been making to him about his failure to recognize the legitimacy of her plight at the office and the appropriateness of her discouragement at never feeling validated by her boss.
>
> The analyst suggested, "You seem to be feeling the same way about your husband as about your boss and about me last week. None of us appreciates your point of view, let alone supports it."
>
> The patient sniffed audibly and shifted her position on the couch, turned slightly to the wall, and then remained silent.
>
> Taking the sniff and change of position as implying a rejection of his comment, as if to say, "What should I expect of such a clod?" the analyst continued, "I guess what I just said was another example of the very thing you were talking about."
>
> The patient rose to this comment, saying angrily, "I can't say anything without you intruding yourself. I was talking about my husband, and you won't ever acknowledge that I have a legitimate complaint about him." As she continued in this way, she cooled off a bit.
>
> The analyst inferred from her somewhat halting speech and increasingly uncertain tone of voice that she was losing confidence in the validity of her complaint, at least about him. He sensed also that she was having difficulty carrying on, since she seemed to have caught on that by her behavior she was actually confirming what he had said. And, although she was still too angry to admit it, she was too fair-minded to continue complaining unabatedly.
>
> The analyst used these inferences to propose, "I think you are of two minds about what you have been saying and what you feel right now and that you find it difficult to put it into words." His comment was less specific and also less intrusive than his earlier one, and he did not make use of all he thought he understood about her current emotional position. But he felt a bit chastened by her angry outburst and in the interest of therapeutic tact, and because he did not want to provoke her, he felt inclined to mollify her a bit. He thought that, if he would let her cool off further and not press his total understanding on her all at once, the two of them would be able to work more productively on the character pattern that was emerging.

In that example the analyst began with an ordinary transference interpretation by including himself in the patient's complaint about her boss. He followed up, however, by pointing to something he heard closer to the "surface," the *function* of her response, her efforts to deal with the conflict that now emerged between her insight and her pride.

From this point, the analysis continued in a way that will be familiar to analysts. The example demonstrates (1) that an analyst can respond usefully on the basis of his understanding that what the patient did after his intervention was a response to it and that the form and function of the patient's reaction were part of that response; and (2) that he can make tentative inferences about the meaning, that is, the withheld content, of the patient's largely nonverbal response.

Analytic "Knowing"

A beginning analyst might worry that, as the analyst in the previous example did not really know for sure what was going on in the patient's mind, it might have been presumptuous of him to tell the patient so directly what he thought she was experiencing. Didn't he actually give her a suggestion? Wouldn't it have been even more tactful and less risky to intervene with a question, such as, "What are you feeling now?" rather than to offer a guess?

This objection raises several important issues: first, the nature of analytic "knowing." How certain ought one be before venturing an intervention, even to offer a fraction of an idea? Second, what are the relative dangers of positive and negative errors when analyzing? Third, we can consider the advantages and disadvantages of the questioning form when analyzing.

To begin, let us concede that the analyst is no more likely to have absolute knowledge about the inner world of the patient than about anything else. But should not the analyst be prepared to intervene, knowing that, although he has only partial knowledge of the mind of the patient, he has much more information about the context and the current state of emotional affairs in the analytic session?

Clearly, I have put the question of "knowing what is in the patient's mind" in a way that does not allow a general answer. One can usefully seek an answer only at a particular moment in a specific analysis. But the question implies there ought to be a general answer and, further, that grave consequences would likely follow a misstep. I do not know which state of the analyst's mind is more harmful to analyzing: the absolute certainty that he is right, or the fear of making a mistake. I have had a good deal of experience with young analysts who were fearful of ruining the analysis with a "wrong interpretation." It is difficult to get across the message that the fault, if there is any fault, is less in saying the wrong thing than in saying anything wrongly. And let me remind you once again that, for the analyst, sins of commission are far less serious than are sins of omission. Our patients seem to be much better at listening past our words for our intentions than we are at turning our intentions into words. If you view interpreting as a process, as a succession of increasingly specific interventions, and allow the patient to participate actively, the process is self-correcting. Analyst and patient collaborate in formulating an interpretation and in testing its usefulness.

If we can agree that the analyst has no source of absolute knowledge and that all interventions, however phrased, must be considered tentative, then we can ask how the analyst's appropriate tentativeness is best conveyed. Should he precede every intervention with some formula conveying doubt or uncertainty, such as, "Do you think . . . ? " "Perhaps it might be that . . ." or "The thought occurred to me that . . ." or "Is it not possible that . . . ?" All of us have used such conventional ways of introducing an idea and at the same time indicating by syntax or tone of voice that we are being diffidently modest about proclaiming our absolute certainty, or that we are not so certain as to foreclose all doubt, or that we are ready to disown it if any objection is raised.

My quarrel is only with the routine use of any formula, for soon even an unperceptive patient will mark such formulaic usage as "shrink talk." The patient will sense that the analyst fears that he might be wrong, that he and his ideas will be rejected, and that he hopes to attenuate the expected objection by distancing himself from the idea even as he offers it. Couching most interventions in the form of a question is subject to the same criticism, and more. The way one intervenes, that is, the *form* of the intervention, tells at least as much to the patient as the words one uses, and there is little to choose between brashness and fearfulness. Either attitude suggests that the analyst is displaying a character attitude rather than a considered stance about technique.

The belief that certainty is a requirement for opening an interpretive process might stem from the wrong impression that analyzing is like a military campaign or a criminal investigation, that it is adversarial in nature and the risks of being wrong range from a slight weakening of one's case to disastrous defeat. If the analyst aims to root out the source of resistance as the police might go after corruption, he rightly would be concerned about avoiding collateral damage or breaking down the wrong door.

Many beginning analysts frequently seem to have that attitude. Indeed, they have support from good authority (for instance, Greenson, 1967) to think that their aim is to overcome resistance. Often patients think that way too. One of the reasons young analysts find this attitude congenial is that, to the degree that they have bought into the transference, they tend to struggle against identification with the hateful aspects of the transference figure, against which the resistance seems to be directed. Also, and not totally without reason, they attribute to patients the power to delay their graduation. Hence, resistance seems to be the enemy.

4

Transference and the Process of Interpretation

Implications of Using Transitive Verbs

Our usually laudable preference for direct and clear expression leads us to speak of our activities in psychotherapy by using transitive verbs, implicitly analogizing psychotherapy to the procedures of allopathic medicine. One of the serious errors that we invite by this mode of expression is to think that psychotherapy is something the therapist *does* to the patient, just as surgery is something a surgeon does to the patient. In common usage, we speak of "interpreting a symptom," we "analyze a neurosis," we "reassure the patient."

These familiar usages probably do no harm, provided we understand that they are only a shorthand way of describing the much more complicated way we involve ourselves with patients when doing psychotherapy or analysis. We want to keep in mind that what we call treatment is what happens within the patient intrapsychically as a result, in part, of what is occurring interpersonally between patient and therapist. To put the issue properly, rather than, "I reassured the patient," I should think, "I spoke reassuringly to the patient who then appeared to relax a bit and seemed less anxious." Is this formulation an improvement? It might merely seem prissier.

But consider this possibility: I could have said, "I spoke reassuringly to the patient, and he blew up at me," sadly not an uncommon outcome of a misfired wish to help. If we think of ourselves, unself-consciously as "reassuring the patient," we likely will fail to ask the vital question, What led the patient to experience reassurance or indignation at that moment? The patient's experience of feeling reassured or infuriated must not be taken as the direct and inevitable effect of an intervention labeled by the therapist as a reassurance he "gave" the patient. We cannot give anyone reassurance any more than we can give anyone freedom. From another point of view, we could say that there are no direct effects from psychotherapy, only mediated effects. If we could really "give" reassurance, our patients would always stay calm and never blow up at us. The issues are, of course, the same when we speak of support and interpretation as "things" we give.

I mean by this introduction to lead us back to a discussion of the "structure" of psychotherapy not as a static issue of architecture, but as an aspect of therapeutic communication, as both message and medium and hence a vital part of the therapeutic activity itself.

Does it add clarity to speak of the structure of therapy as being part of the interpretive process or as part of the process through which reassurance or support are experienced by the patient? From one point of view, we can easily read sense into these assertions. It is easy to see, for instance, that a patient could experience support through one aspect of structure, the evidence of constancy conveyed by the regularity and frequency of sessions and the relative uniformity of the therapist's attitude of uncritical and empathic attention. We can see that our therapeutic intentions, our sense of what helps people in pain, are built into and expressed by the seeming "architectural" elements of structure. Thus, we could say in our shorthand way, that the structure itself is supportive, and indeed it is. We could also assert paradoxically that, while psychoanalysis is the "most expressive" of the therapies, it also is likely the "most supportive" by virtue of the frequency of its appointments and constancy and regularity of its procedures.

A Deconstruction of the Interpretive Process

Let me take this deconstruction of the therapeutic process a step further. One could think of an intervention, for instance an interpretation, as made up of two portions: one, relatively invariant; the other, quite variable. The variable portion is what we usually think of as the interpretation proper, such as when an analyst, referring to something emerging in the therapeutic process, intends to augment its meaning. In contrast, we usually do not consider the relatively invariant portion, the part we might think of as structural, as part of the interpretation itself.

Perhaps an analogy will make this point clearer. It is a quite simple matter, conceptually, to purchase a theater ticket or to park your car in a public garage. You have done these simple acts many times, probably without realizing they have "structural" aspects. Next time you go to a movie, look at the back of the ticket and see what you have agreed to by accepting it. Notice, too, that on your parking stub is a patch of "legalese" in fine print that tells you about the rights you have agreed to surrender, rights you may not even have known you had. Most of us have become inured to this pettifoggery and never read the fine print. We find out what it means only when our car turns up missing or when the theater owner decides to refuse admission.

The point of this digression into the banalities of consumer law is that there is fine print also in the therapeutic contract. The fine print is, of course, *not* the arrangements about hours and fees; those appear, as it were, in bold type. For we know, and patients sometimes remind us, that, whatever else happens or does not happen, appointments and fees are assured. If I were to make explicit the usually unstated but essential preconditions that form the general context of an interpretation, the preamble of "boiler plate," put in legalese might look like this:

> WHEREAS, we have come together because you have sought my assistance in understanding certain self-defeating patterns of behavior in consequence of which we have established a therapist–patient relationship in which you expect me to offer conjectures as to the possible meanings of your statements and behavior, and
>
> WHEREAS this understanding of our mutual expectations still obtains, and
>
> WHEREAS, you have just described to me an instance of that behavior that reminds me of what you told me yesterday, and also many times in the past, and
>
> WHEREAS, it seems similar in form to ways in which you have imagined yourself treated as a child, and
>
> WHEREAS, you seemed earnestly troubled by this latest expression of difficulty, and
>
> WHEREAS, I sense that you are not only telling me about it "out there" but are also sort of feeling it right now with me, and
>
> WHEREAS, you now have an uncomfortable sense that there is something a little odd about the way you are telling me all this . . ." and

And here follows the interpretation proper.

The first of those "clauses" is the essential aspect of structure. It alludes to the therapist's understanding that at this moment he and the patient agree that a therapeutic situation exists and that he is therefore "privileged" to begin an interpretive process. The remaining clauses refer to the therapist's sense that the time is ripe for a particular interpretation. They rest on his preconscious awareness that the structural elements of the first clause are in place and permit him to make the kind of intervention he has in mind. Of course, any or all of the clauses after the first one could be included in the "variable" portion, in the "interpretation proper," but they can be left out if the therapist believes the patient understands them as "givens."

Communicating Through Structure

Recall that this excursion into "legalese" was intended to help the therapist who just had his head handed to him when he "reassured" his patient. Such events are, of course, not uncommon in psychotherapy or analysis. The therapist feels at sea, disconcerted; something is going on that he does not understand, and he senses intuitively that nothing that is coming to mind would be right to say. Consider that at those uncomfortable moments the therapist is at least implicitly aware that he is no longer in a "therapeutic situation." That situation, from which he derives his moral and therapeutic authority, somehow has metamorphosed into some other kind of situation, one he cannot name, but the "rules" of which do not privilege him to make an ordinary therapeutic intervention.

At such times, rather than wondering, What did I say that was so wrong? the therapist should direct his attention to the nature of the situation in which he currently is with his patient—just as when one returns to the public garage to discover one's car is missing and suddenly has reason to review the back of the claim check. How and why did the formerly therapeutic situation change into some species of nontherapeutic situation, one that does not support the therapist's intention "to treat"?

What to do? To restore the therapeutic situation requires that the therapist identify the elements of structure that, at least for the moment, have ceased to support an ordinary, that is, content-focused, intervention. But at this point my digression ends, for we have circled back to the ordinary business of analyzing, which, as I have reminded you repeatedly, must take into account the form as well as the content of communication.

So, how to analyze, if that is what it takes? First, consider what elements of structure might have changed. Generally, the procedural elements of structure will not suddenly have changed; the frequency or times of appointments or fee will not have changed—or perhaps they did. Sometimes, when the therapist finds himself on shaky ground, he or the patient may have been tampering with these arrangements. The therapist may have been coming slightly late or may have cancelled some sessions. Or the patient may have been coming slightly late for a while, or may have missed a session, or is being slow in paying a fee, or the therapist may have ignored the patient's quiet wish to have a session extended. Recalling any of these "minor" events might inform the analyst that he or the patient may have been trying to say something important but conflicted, a message that was not ready to be put into words, and that the patient or analyst was doing so by jiggling elements of structure. The example in Chapter 3 of the analyst who unwittingly won an argument with his patient is of this kind.

But there are elements of structure other than the procedural arrangements to consider. They include the role definitions of therapist and patient, which, though seemingly as fixed as the appointment schedule, are quite malleable under the pressure of transference. Transference, after all, has to do only with the remodeling of patient and therapist role definitions. The patient acts toward the therapist as if he were a different figure altogether or as if he had suddenly acquired unacceptable attributes. And the therapist feels that he has indeed become that unacceptable other; hence the feeling of impotence, implying that nothing the transference figure could do now would feel comfortable to the therapeutic ally. With this subtle shift in role definitions, the orderly and predictable structure of the psychotherapeutic situation has become a messy affair of an altogether different order.

It is now up to the therapist to understand how this state of affairs came about and to engage the patient in an interpretive process to restore the therapeutic situation.

Transference as "the Surface"

A technical principle all of us were taught is that we should respect the analytic "surface" and work from the top down. The version I was taught specified that I should address feelings before contents. Later, I was taught to respect the integrity of metaphors rather than immediately pointing out the less conscious referent they contained. The idea that much of a patient's discourse could be understood as metaphor, that is, a way that the patient could include allusion to the analyst in comments that ostensibly referred only to others, and that these indirect references expressed transference, proved to be most valuable notions. These several bits of advice stood me in good stead. As I recall, however, the advice was cautionary, intended to keep us from plunging immediately into the depths of The Unconscious, our notion of the proper venue of analysis. But other than the cautions about how to avoid going too deep, I don't recall being told how to recognize the surface if I came upon it. I don't recall that anyone stated the obvious—that the transference is the surface.

In addition to that advice, the systems point of view implies that the analyst should register the form in which the patient casts his communication, for example, by crying, asking a question, or making a proclamation, and its function. But attention to function should be primary, for it is the key to transference. I have found that it is easier to keep the primacy of function in mind when listening by asking myself, Why am I being told this now? Or, to put it in the form of a mantra, "Why now?" The implication is that transference is always tendentious, intended to act upon the analyst. So we may ask about anything the patient says or does, what is its immediate purpose, what is it doing here now? The difficulty in keeping this seemingly simple point in mind while analyzing occupies much of what follows.

It may seem odd to advise attending to the surface in discussing psychoanalysis, the quintessential "depth psychology." The term surface obviously contrasts weakly with the term depth, and the spatial imagery evoked by the contrast is unfortunate and misleading because it places greater value on what is less clearly seen. It leads to the easy assumption that what we are unaware of (even unconscious) lies underneath what we are aware of. Hence we are brought to the facile adopting of archeological imagery and the associated operations of "digging out" the truth or "undermining" resistance. But attending first to matters that are easier to observe does not commit us to becoming preoccupied with superficialities and does not at all detract from our concern with matters and processes less accessible to immediate attention. In fact, it is the way into these matters.

What do I mean by "transference is the surface"? Analysts will agree that transference is the single most important concept in clinical psychoanalysis. The discovery of transference and its capacity both to impede or to facilitate treatment was probably the most important step in the development of psychoanalysis as a systematic psychotherapy. Freud (1914), at one point, was willing to grant the name psychoanalysis to any psychotherapy that recognized the unconscious, transference, and resistance. The analysis of transference, rather than its exploitation, is still the hallmark of psychoanalytic treatment.

There are in the literature countless references to transference from the economic, dynamic and structural metapsychological points of view, but few from the adaptive point of view. Indeed, part of the usual definition of transference is the pejorative "inappropriate." It is paradoxical that this should be so, since clinical experience, to say nothing of common sense, tells us that much of the time transference is quite adaptive. The very invention of the psychoanalytic situation derives from the need to contrive a circumstance in which the maladaptive and inappropriate aspects of transference could be highlighted.

We might say that it is the "responsibility" of the synthetic function of the ego to assure that transference and other residues of early life are homogenized smoothly in the course of everyday functioning. For most of us, most of the time, transference and reality testing function synergistically. Transference plays a large part in our everyday behavior. Much of the way we behave in unfamiliar or strange situations is based on our relevant earlier experience. Our inclination to view strangers as either well intentioned or potentially malevolent draws from infantile experience and unconscious fantasy as well as from recent experience and logical inference. The templates, Freud (1912b) called them "stereotypes" (p. 100) we carry with us into new situations not only orient us cognitively, but also prepare us emotionally with the feeling tone we will need to engage socially. One could say that the human propensity for emotional contagion and for reciprocity owe their readiness to transference. We constantly construe the present and future in terms of the past. To do otherwise would be to abrogate memory. But I must add, lest I seem to want to redeem transference totally, that to the extent one's expectations are governed by transference, one is less able to learn from current experience.

It follows that it would be an unwarranted limitation to restrict our view of transference in a clinical situation to what might be called pathological transference, transference that obviously clashes with consensual reality. But does it not, in effect, deprive transference of all distinctive significance to insist that transference is ubiquitous in life and in treatment, that it can be adaptive as well as maladaptive, that, like air, good or bad, transference is always there? I believe instead that it sharpens our view of transference by depriving us of the comfortable stereotype that transference is invariably pathological. We should not assume that, when transference intrudes conspicuously, it is necessarily more "pathological" than transference that seems to harmonize better with the patient's sense of reality. In some sicker patients, it is just the lack of apparent conflict between transference and reality testing that indicates the extent of pathology.

The view of transference I am proposing requires that the analyst continuously define and redefine the nature and the function (or purpose) of the transference the patient is manifesting now—that he view transference as a process. The analyst must maintain a diagnostic attitude with regard to transference as to all other matters in the analysis. By "diagnostic" I mean something quite apart from the categorizing of the *DSM* and something additional to the analyst's ordinary concern for characterology. I mean particularly that it is the analyst's constant task to understand what the patient is doing, what his momentary purpose is, how he is trying to maintain the status quo of his personality system, all matters commonly subsumed under "the state of the transference." We can describe the analyst's activity as biphasic, alternating between diagnosing, in the sense I have just described, and treating, in the most general sense. We diagnose by observing (mostly listening to) the patient, and we treat by feeding back to the patient a tiny, selected portion of what we observe. Then we diagnose again by observing the patient's response to our intervention, and so on.

We may think of the alternating of listening and feedback as the early stage of an interpretive process. At this point, the feedback can be directed most usefully to facilitating the patient's story telling. Rather than prematurely constructing links to the remote past, the analyst can point recursively toward the immediate past. As the patient adds details to the story, the analyst may have the opportunity to offer a clarifying remark such as, "What you just said makes sense of something that puzzled me earlier . . . ," in that way possibly discovering if the patient was aware of one of the implications of his story, enriching it, and finding out if the patient can continue the story if he understands more fully what he is saying. It also might be useful for the analyst to comment on his understanding of the function or purpose of the patient's telling his story in just that way. I refer to this aspect of the interpretive process as interpreting "upwards," to distinguish it from the later phase, when it would be more useful to make explicit the genetic linkages that the analyst may also be aware of at this early point. Other senses of interpreting upwards are discussed in Chapter 14.

Transference as a Process

In this brief introduction to the broad topic of transference, I sneaked in a term that needs definition and discussion. The term process is central to all that follows. Process implies that time is a major dimension of whatever is under consideration. To refer to transference as a process says, at the very least, that it does not stand still. Change in transference can be expected, change that implies development, growth, and unfolding. "Process" implies a history, a past, and a future.

How to reconcile the view that transference is a process that develops and changes over time with the observation, sad to say, made by all analysts and therapists that transference seems fixed and unyielding to all pressures and blandishments. While the patient's character leads to a prevailing transference readiness, we all have noticed that transference changes, that is, transference attributions change. By change, in this context, we mean that the category of content changes, the transference paradigm changes.

It is customary, if not particularly useful, to speak of "mother transference" or "father transference," for instance, or of "good objects" and "bad objects" in the transference. These crude labels do imply shifts in a person's repertoire of transference. All analysts soon learn to recognize these gross changes. The question commonly asked by supervisors, "What is the transference? " sounds as if it requires such a categorical answer. As candidates soon find out, that question is shorthand expression for, What is the nature of the transference now? Where has it been and toward what is it developing? Who are you and the patient in the transference? What aspect of the unconscious fantasy is being reenacted? What does the patient seem to want from you and what prevents him from getting it? What does the transference evoke in you? Clearly, the answer to such a barrage of questions will have to be a process also.

I wonder if you noticed that, in my expansion of the question, What is the transference, something important was omitted. I guess not, for it is not a question that is usually asked. A supervisor does not usually transfix a hapless candidate by asking, What is the *function* of the transference? What is its purpose right now? We are not used to thinking of transference as having a function or purpose, and we certainly don't expect to be quizzed on it. I hope, though, that you find the suggestion plausible.

Freud (1912b) suggested that the general function of transference is resistance. But retaining or restoring the "familiar," resisting change, and preventing new and potentially painful experiences could be discussed from the adaptive as well as the defensive points of view. That is, We should ask what the behavior in question is doing *for* the personality system. Another function, broadly speaking, of transference with both adaptive and defensive implications is that it serves as a medium of communication, a way for the patient to reenact fantasies, wishes, fears, and dilemmas that he cannot express in any other way. Analysts are constantly faced with immediate and practical questions that fall within the general functions of transference as a medium of communication. For instance, why is the patient communicating with me through this particular bit of transference right now? Why is it uniquely suitable, and what is its purpose?

The overall "purpose" of transference, of course, is conservative, to preserve the neurosis, to protect the unconscious fantasy from the intrusion of reality, to bar disconfirming information, in short, to resist change. Transference works to assimilate reality to the neurosis. Transference usually works quietly, in the background, as long as the neurosis is not excessively challenged by the requirements of adapting to reality. The patient resorts to more insistent transference claims when he senses anxiously that the analyst is failing to fulfill the conditions of the unconscious fantasy. Then the analyst sees a mixed picture of direct expressions of (or derivatives of) infantile fears and wishes together with defenses against them and defenses against recognizing the degree to which the patient is caught up in them (Gill, 1982). The complicated and painful emotional state may feel, to the patient, like an emergency.

The picture may also be complicated secondarily: if the patient has had enough analysis to be familiar with how his neurosis works, he is likely to feel embarrassed for being "out of control," so wrought up with emotions that seem excessive, even ridiculous, but that nevertheless are happening—he can't help it. And, at the same time, he may be angry and resentful at the analyst, who seems to have inspired these feelings and thus caused the embarrassment, leading to a wish to reproach or punish him. And he is likely to be embarrassed at the painful sense that this thought, too, is absurd. In short, this medley of painful feelings actualizes the various aspects of the patient's unconscious conflicts that were stirred up during the preceding moments of the session.

To repeat, the transference is "the surface." The analyst didn't have to dig for it, and he didn't have to wait for it to develop. It is important that the analyst be able to recognize when the patient suddenly shifts from another mode of communication to transference. He must understand that the patient's suddenly behaving like a "sulky child" is only a more obvious expression of transference that was quietly present earlier. And the analyst should realize that the sudden increase in peremptoriness is probably a reaction to something the analyst has just said or done.

Why was it necessary for the patient to respond in that way and through the medium of transference? The process point of view encourages us to look at the contingencies that affect the way transference is expressed. When did the patient shift from words to tears? When did he change the subject or change the way he talked about the subject? To what did the patient react as he shifted from one topic to another or from one medium to another? These are not rhetorical questions. They must be addressed in any analysis. They are diagnostic questions; by attending to these shifts, you can diagnose progression or regression in the current state of the therapeutic process and the state of the transference. To put the issue in more classical terms, these shifts tell you about the state of the patient's libidinal organization and the state of his ego.

Messages couched in the language of transference are always, if not always clearly, tendentious. They are intended to do something to the therapist or to get the therapist to do something to, for, or with the patient. They contain more or less subtle expectations, demands, threats, ultimatums, pleas for pity, or cajoling. But even more important than noting what they require of the transference object is to understand why they occur when they occur. When the patient shifts from relatively pure symbolic communication, from telling a story, to becoming a whining brat or a threatening bully, the question the analyst should ask himself is, Why now? What is the function of this eruption of demand in the transference? Thus, a complete expression of the diagnostic point of view includes attending to *what* the patient is trying to say (content), the *way* in which he says it (form), and to changes in both content and form, particularly *why* the patient says what he says in the form he says it right now (function). Recognizing that the patient is involved in transference is not the end of the diagnostic process but is only a beginning. For example:

> A male patient in his 20s was talking in an unusually animated fashion about some expansive business plans, plans he hitherto had been too inhibited to conceive of, let alone carry out. The analyst responded with interest, he thought, hoping the patient would find encouragement to move ahead. Suddenly the patient broke off, looked away, shrugged and lapsed into a sullen silence.
>
> The analyst commented on the change in stance and supposed the patient was experiencing some trouble. The patient seemed irritated and became even more sulky. The analyst recognized that the patient suddenly had begun to act like a hurt and sulky child.
>
> This position was a common one into which the patient would slip with little provocation, but it had not been present for some months. The analyst wondered why the patient had suddenly retreated into this once familiar funk. He recalled that the patient would slip into this stance whenever he caught himself being unusually active and hopeful, overextended beyond his customary cautious, timorous manner. When he noticed that he had overextended himself, he would pull back and sulk, as if to say, "There is no use in wanting to be a man. I don't dare to be one. Father is the man and there can only be one in the family. He caught me trying to grow up, and I am not going to let him put me down again. I'll become an even smaller child and show him."
>
> Why was the patient acting out this old story once again? Suddenly the therapist remembered his own well-intentioned grunts of approval in response to the patient's enthusiasm about his plans. He said, "Something happened just now that made you suddenly behave differently."
>
> "No, I just don't feel like talking. It wouldn't do any good."
>
> "Sounds as if you felt you couldn't win, so why try."
>
> "Well, I never do. What's the point!"

"I don't know about never, but it must have hit you just a minute ago when I asked you for more details about your plan."

"Yes, I felt angry and scared and almost sick. I knew you were going to laugh at my puny plan."

"Yes, and too scared to tell me about your fear. Instead you reacted as if your father had ridiculed your plan and you knuckled under once again, biting your tongue."

After a thoughtful pause, the patient said, "That's silly. You didn't challenge me, but I sure felt you were getting ready to."

Here the shift to a more recognizable expression of transference can be seen both as the patient's resistance to confronting the analyst directly with his fearful expectation because of anxiety and rage, and also as an involuntary expression of the very feelings he was defending himself against but in a regressive mode, in action language. As the patient began to change and permitted himself more risky behavior, becoming more active and assertive than was comfortable for him, he became hypersensitive to the analyst's behavior. His sudden retreat could be understood as a highly compressed bit of play-acting, punishing himself for becoming once again the impertinent child who ought to be punished and, in fact, has already been put down for his temerity.

The analyst's intervention acknowledged the patient's anxiety-driven need to express himself regressively; and, although it referred to the past, it did not specifically direct the patient's attention to the distant past but, rather, to the present, to what the transference was an immediate response to and why it was necessary. The patient alluded to the past by saying, "I never do [win]."

Note that, while one could think of the patient's behavior as resistive in that it was designed to hide and forestall, clearly it displayed much more than it concealed. The analyst focused not so much on what was withheld by the transference behavior as on what it conveyed. Note also that, although we speak of the "emergence" of transference at such moments, we do so only for convenience. It is important to remember that the transference is there all the time and, when it seems to jump out at us, we are seeing only a change of form.

If we consider transference to be a medium of communication, a language, not just a content, we may be prepared to abandon the notion of interpretation as mere translation of content and focus first on the patient's immediate purpose in shifting to another medium of expression or language. We might analogize to trying to understand international politics. When an editorial in a foreign newspaper calls the American president an imperialist lackey, the content is clear. There is nothing new to be learned unless one takes into account the context, the occasion that gave rise to the familiar denunciation. So it is with our patients. The more severe and chronic the neurosis, the narrower is the repertoire of responses available to the patient. It takes only a little skill to know that one is seeing transference and only little more skill to know what the transference says. It takes much more skill to discover why the shift to a more open expression of transference was necessary at this time. The information gained from this vantage point is especially useful for formulating interpretations.

Transference and Metaphor

It is worth noting that the key concept in clinical psychoanalysis for Freud was *Übertragen* (a German verb literally translatable as "to carry over"), for which the standard English translation is "to transfer." The more familiar, but not more correct, usage refers to "transference," a noun that surrenders the sense that the concept properly refers to an action. In stressing that transferring is invariably enacting, I mean to return to the original, and clinically more useful, usage.

To transfer, of course, is a common English verb with Latin roots and also means to carry over or carry across. It is also worth noting that the word metaphor is a noun with Greek roots and has the same literal meaning as "transference—"that which is carried across." I suppose this brief etymological exercise may help to justify the prominence that I give to "metaphor" in this presentation. In any discussion of clinical matters, transference must carry a heavy burden. I hope that using the term metaphor when I mean to emphasize a particular aspect of transference (or, better, transferring) lightens its burden and enhances clarity. I use metaphor and its derivative forms, metaphoric and metaphorical, when I want to emphasize the *formal* similarity between an ancient relationship paradigm contained within an unconscious fantasy and an emerging relationship paradigm being forced on the analyst.

Whereas the nominal medium of communication between patient and analyst or therapist is words, we understand that the words must also be understood as rhetorical, not just lexical. The patient has an important story to tell, commonly a story rooted in current reality, and he will try to tell it as objectively as he can. But, to the extent that the patient is driven by an unconscious fantasy, the words of the story will unwittingly become the vehicle to express unconscious fantasy; and, as they do so, they will be spoken persuasively, tendentiously, intended to influence, not just to inform.

As the story unfolds, the analyst will hear allusions to past situations with the same formal structure and also will feel tugs and pushes to behave like the most significant figure in the patient's past. Soon the positions of figures from the past begin to seem interchangeable with those in the current story; the analyst as transference-figure begins to feel himself cast as chief among them. The analyst begins to understand why this story is being told just now and why he is being drawn to act as he now feels compelled to act. The current story, while having new characters and details, has the formal structure it needs to continue the transference theme that has been developing in recent sessions. By similar formal structure I mean, for instance, that there is in each instance an authority figure and a powerless other in danger of being victimized.

The patient's speech shifts gradually from objective narration as he warms to the subject. Certain events in the story are repeated with increasing salience. The patient's tone of voice becomes persuasive, imploring, cajoling, threatening (or a mixture of them), as he tries to convince the analyst (that is, the transference figure of the moment) of some personal truth or to get him to do something to, for, or with the patient or to prevent him from taking some undesired action. The patient's story has its own locale and set of characters, but, in the story-telling, the patient has metaphorically expressed how he feels involved with the analyst/listener as well as with the characters of the story. Past and present and outside and inside the session seem to have merged. For the analysis, the metaphoric allusions in the story are the main points of interest.

This sort of transferring, which permits understanding the patient's story of an external situation as metaphor, is a common experience in analysis and psychotherapy. The technical handling of such material is the topic of much that follows. My purpose here is to focus on the formal nature of such communications from any of several points of view. One can think, conventionally, that the patient's behavior expresses resistance. This position is likely to be the recourse of a beginner who wonders fearfully, as he grasps the transference implications in the telling of the story, How am I going to convince this stubborn patient that he is dramatizing his current relationship with me?

Leaving aspects of this problem for later discussion, let us now note only that in fantasizing a battle that he believes he is likely to lose, the analyst has already been induced to take a stance in the patient's enactment of the fantasy for which the story was the vehicle. We might well question where the "resistance" is located. But, to be fair to the beginner, the story telling does indeed express resistance. For whatever reasons, the patient is unable to tell the analyst directly that he feels threatened, seduced, disrespected, or ignored by him. He cannot say it directly and he cannot drop it. He does the best he can by allowing the forbidden ideas to infuse his view of the events of his day, which, no surprise, seem to have the same formal structure, the same pattern of temptations and prohibitions. The act of resisting always reveals more than it hides. An image that may capture this is of a person surprised in the nude, with only a wash cloth in hand—he or she may choose what to hide but in doing so will expose all the rest.

5

Transference and Countertransference

Countertransference

The usual discussion of transference seems to hold that transference flows only from patient to analyst. Yet we can hardly believe that the traffic is only one way, for transference is ubiquitous in all human relationships and affects all parties. So, to begin with, we must touch on the obvious: the analyst, like the patient, has "an unconscious," with unacknowledged needs, wishes, and fears that may, and likely will, be mobilized in the analytic situation. The involuntary participation of the analyst, as Menninger and Holzman (1973) put it, like that of the patient, may involve a variety of attitudes. Some we can understand as direct expressions of residues of the analyst's infantile experiences; others, as attitudes that may be best understood as defenses against these residues and against the resonance of them evoked by the patient's transference.

Many writers now seem to prefer to lump both sources of transference feelings together with other emotional attitudes that do not necessarily originate in the analyst's unconscious as countertransference (e.g., Racker, 1968; Kernberg, 1987). Those who advocate this view at first called it the "total view," but in the best sense of *carpe diem*, they have recently adopted the name "contemporary" for it. I may be forced to accept the designation "old fashioned" for the point of view I propose.

As both a theoretical and a practical matter, it is worth distinguishing between the two classes of involuntary contributions on the basis of their source. The attitudes and emotions that are characteristic of the analyst as a person, and that emerge in the analytic situation relatively independently of the transference of the patient, should properly be considered the transference of the analyst. Common examples include an overly nurturing attitude, a strong distaste for the direct expression of hostility, and the inability to witness another's pain. These examples are exaggerations of civilized attitudes one hopes to find in an analyst, but when the attitudes are both strong and obligatory, they might well intrude on the analysis. The major rationale for requiring a training analysis is to familiarize the would-be analyst with these tendencies and to mitigate them.

The other class of involuntary participation of the analyst—the ad hoc feelings or defenses against feelings that are evoked in the analyst by the patient's transference—are the only ones that I believe deserve the label countertransference. Among the most important reasons for distinguishing these classes of involuntary participation is that we expect the analyst to deal differently with them. The analyst's own analysis is expected to help him come to terms with the way his character gives rise to transference. The intrusion of countertransference is usually detected first in supervision, perhaps when the supervisor observes that the candidate resorts to defensive maneuvers to ward off certain kinds of transference attributions or to block certain communications from the patient that might arouse too much discomfort. It is not usually useful, and generally not tactful, for the supervisor to attempt to distinguish whether the intrusion is based on transference or countertransference; it is usually sufficient to call to the candidate's attention that his responses to certain kinds of patient communications seem idiosyncratic, or that certain kinds of patient material that call for an empathic response seem instead to reach a deaf ear. We expect that, when the supervisor has alerted the candidate to the problem and its effect on analyzing, he will bring the issue back to his own analysis.

Part of the supervisor's responsibility is to help the candidate to distinguish between "errors" that may result from matters being insufficiently understood, those we might call "dumb spots," from those which derive from unconscious factors and lead to defensive avoidance, or "blind spots." One of the supervisor's functions is to help the candidate learn whatever he needs to understand to fill in his "dumb spots" and also to help the candidate become aware of any tendency to avoid or collude, on the basis, presumably, of unconscious factors. We presume the candidate will take up such matters in his own analysis. But that is not the end of the story, for the supervisor has additional responsibilities with respect to countertransference.

Even if we were to assume that the candidate has analyzed his own sources of transference so that they intrude minimally on analyzing, he still would remain vulnerable to countertransference. The term vulnerable has the unfortunate and unintended implication that the analyst should be *in*vulnerable to countertransference. Clearly, that would not be desirable, for such invulnerability would render the analyst deaf to important messages the patient has no way to convey other than through transference. The analyst must remain open to messages expressed in transference and must appreciate the temptations and fears they arouse in him. He must not be so defended against his own wishes or fears about the patient's coercive invitation to join in the enactment of transference that he fails to hear them or rejects them. To do so would defeat the patient's efforts to communicate with him in this way and would defeat the intention of the analysis.

The analyst must be able to participate deliberately in the patient's effort to remember through reenactment. After all, the patient has no other way to get at these memories. As the analyst lends himself to the patient's purpose in this way, he will experience himself, to a greater or lesser degree, becoming the transference figure of the moment. At the same time, by maintaining the therapeutic split (Sterba, 1934), the analyst will continue to be able to experience himself as the patient's therapeutic ally. The analyst will thus feel freer to allow his partial metamorphosis into the transference figure to develop, to recognize what is going on, and to be able to empathize facultatively with each of the characters who have entered the room (Schlesinger, 1981a). The supervisor can help the candidate allow himself to experience the countertransference in signal quantities, to tolerate it, and to use the experience to inform his interpretations.

Once the candidate recognizes that, as it were, with one hand he has been encouraging the patient to say all and with the other hand has indicated that he would prefer him not to, it takes only a little supervisory encouragement to help the candidate experience the anxiety directly and withstand the risk. Candidates sometimes must be reassured that following this advice will not lead them to become so intensively involved as to lose themselves in the reenactment. Indeed, to be able to tolerate transference attributions, even distasteful ones, and to recognize them as split-off aspects of the patient's personality and be able to empathize with them, while maintaining one's position as analyst, are essential therapeutic skills. It takes much practice to develop these skills and much help from supervision as well as one's personal analysis.

As with transference, the common varieties and the more flagrant examples of countertransference hardly need illustrating. But there are more subtle varieties, some of which may not be recognized as such. Here is one:

> The patient, a woman in late middle age, presented for treatment with "depression" following a divorce requested by her former husband, who, after more than 20 years of marriage, had found a

more desirable companion. She filled her sessions with unrelenting complaints about how badly she had been treated, how her social position had been degraded, how she had been stigmatized, how her standard of living had been diminished. In fact, as the analyst reported, she had won a very generous settlement in the divorce and had suffered no lowering of her standard of living. At any rate, it was at least an order of magnitude higher than that of the analyst. She did not mention any feeling of loss of the husband as a person, but only as a fixture who functioned to support her social position.

The analyst was concerned that he had come to dislike the patient, and while he clearly recognized her narcissistic pathology, he found himself regarding her as a social parasite, one no socially concerned person should have to put up with. He could not empathize with her in her self-described "misery." Indeed, he could hardly stand seeing her and, when he did, could respond only minimally and then only to the "unreality" of her complaints. He hoped the patient would leave as soon as the acute disturbance about the divorce had subsided.

As the analyst and I discussed the case, several aspects of the situation became salient. The patient's complaining was repetitive and unchanging, as was her whiny tone. Inasmuch as the analyst refrained from responding to her, one might wonder that the patient persisted. She was not unintelligent and surely had registered the great difference in economic status between them, yet she never commented on it or on any of the other differences between them or on the possible effect that her unrelenting complaining might have on the analyst. The patient seemed to be treating the analyst as she regarded the former husband—not as another person whose individuality, interests, and feelings might be considered, but as a receptacle in which to deposit her grievances. In short, the analyst's distaste for the way the patient presented herself and the way she used him kept him from appreciating that her behavior might also have a transference component. And his revulsion also kept him from realizing that his own negative feelings, feelings the analyst knew were interfering with his ability to treat the patient, might have been evoked in him by her transference. He was not free to consider that it might have some utility for the patient to have him react as he did.

With these thoughts in mind, the analyst changed his approach to the patient. He used some of the observations we had noted to comment about one of the patient's complaints that she surely was aware that the economic situation she was complaining about was far better than anything the analyst could hope to achieve, but she never had alluded to this knowledge. After a brief pause, the patient muttered, "Miserable as I am, I want you to be envious of me." The patient was startled to hear herself say this and was chagrined and apologetic.

Before long, she could let herself associate to her wishes to revenge herself on her ex-husband (and his surrogates) and to punish him for his selfishness in removing himself from her life; she would make him hate her if he would not love her. She would rather sacrifice her life if she could but become a stone in his shoe, a painful reminder of his treachery, so that he would never have another happy day. The revenge motive began to alternate with thoughts about getting on with her own life, and the transference shifted to envy of the analyst, who "obviously" had gotten it all together. The analysis continued in expectable ways once the analyst came to understand that his "politically correct" repugnance for the patient's "unabashed materialism" had been partly scripted by the patient.

Transference from the Point of View of Technique

The prime fact to keep in mind with regard to transference, from the point of view of psychoanalytic technique, is that, whereas transference is to be understood theoretically as an expression of infantile memory, particularly a recollection of unresolved early conflicts, the clinical phenomenon of transference is, in essence, enactment. Transference is expressed in what the patient does, not only in what he says. If a patient were to say, "You look just like my father," that statement ought not to be taken as prima facie evidence of transference; the analyst might well resemble the father sufficiently to justify the comment. On the other hand, the analyst might infer accurately that the patient's readiness to see a resemblance to his father might arise from transference. It would unmistakably be transference if the patient acted toward as if the analyst were his father or if he expected the analyst to treat him as if he were the father of his infancy. This observation touches on the more general point that all important messages in analysis—and these mainly are expressions of transference—are presented in the language of action, actions that include spoken words, but far more.

It is commonsensical that, when we are in a new situation, we tend to deal with others in terms of expectations based on previous experience.

Transference derives from expectations based on (mostly repressed) childhood experiences, and the unconscious memories of these experiences or fantasies about them color expectations drawn from contemporary experience. One could say that these ancient experiences, as well as more recent ones, have molded our character, that is, the ways we deal with self and others on a daily basis (Schlesinger, 1992).

While transference is ubiquitous, its manifestations vary considerably, depending on the context of observation. Ordinarily, unless one is quite disturbed, when one has a clear task to perform, or when one has a relatively well-defined social role, expectations derived from early as well as recent influences will permit expressing individuality without violating consensual reality. Unless the current situation resonates overwhelmingly with infantile experiences, or unless one is very regressed, the various sources of inner and current social expectation tend to blend synergistically into socially appropriate behavior, and transference, although present, does not "show" as such.

Nonetheless, the main technical purpose for establishing an "analytic situation" is to make transference "show," to allow it to become salient. In the psychoanalytic situation, the social arrangements are fixed. The role assignments of patient and analyst are clear but not controlling, and they are more binding on the analyst than on the patient. The duration of a session is set, but the duration of treatment is open ended, so that time is effectively unlimited. The "task," free association, seems simple enough and seems undemanding, but it is not a task that can be completed in any final sense. The setting of the analysis holds few constraints other than on mobility. Under these repeated and unvarying conditions, recent experience offers little guidance other than support for the analyst's assurance that it is safe for the patient to say what comes to mind. Then transference comes front and center and is more readily identified as such.

As the patient tells about events in outside life, the balance in the narrative between fidelity to reality and the requirements of unconscious fantasy tends to shift toward the latter. As the analyst listens to the developing story, he will hear metaphoric references to the analytic situation and to the relationship with the analyst. The question becomes one of analytic understanding and skill (tact, dosage, and timing) to determine whether it would be more useful to continue to facilitate the expression of transference by allowing the "story" to develop until the patient detects the underlying drift and speaks to it, or to interpret the transference. As the patient is defended against recognizing that he is saying more than he intended to say, it is not likely that he will address the transference spontaneously. Instead he will break off telling the story or will change the subject when he gets uncomfortably close to noticing that he is getting into hot water. If the analyst fears that "it will get away," he may be tempted to interpret it, "to strike while the iron is hot." And, if the patient's defensiveness is not too high, he may be able to use the analyst's summing up. Alternatively, if the analyst empathizes with the patient's presumed attack of discomfort that led him to break off, the patient might become curious about it and be able to collaborate in completing the interpretation.

According to the oldest version of our theory of neurosis, the most important infantile memories, those which are represented in the patient's unconscious fantasy, are not available to conscious recall. But, although not themselves recallable, they color the expectations brought to all new experience. In even a moderately severe neurosis, transference may color a patient's expectations so completely that he may construe any potentially new emotional experience as something painfully familiar; every occasion with presumably new possibilities devolves into a replica of an ancient one with an inevitably hurtful outcome.

As Santayana (1905–1906) put it, "What we cannot remember we are condemned to repeat." A person in the grip of a neurosis is constantly trying to solve the insoluble problem posed by an unconscious conflict. Having only a rigidly preformed and inadequate grasp of the problem and seeing only a couple of impossible solutions, he is distracted also by feeling impelled to do something now to quell mounting anxiety. The history of the patient's attempts to resolve the conflict as they were laid down can be read in fantasies that also are more or less unconscious but that are expressed in symptomatic behavior and in his characterological stance. Every current situation that stimulates or rearouses the conflict will set the scene for a replay of the fantasies in a version adapted more or less well to current circumstances.

The analytic situation, with its relatively unvarying conditions and few distractions, allows both participants to discern the degree to which the patient's thinking and behavior are driven by unconscious fantasy. The situation makes it clear that neurosis makes a mockery of the axiom that consciousness is continuous. Both parties soon can appreciate how much effort it takes for the patient to preserve even a semblance of continuity (free association) under the restrictions that prohibit telling a continuous story. Inevitably, the story veers into a forbidden area, and, when it does, the patient must interrupt it. The patient may go silent, may change the topic, or may resort to euphemism or to using pronouns with no clear referent. The patient may be aware that he is too embarrassed or too anxious to go on, or that he has come to see that the whole exercise is pointless, but he is not generally aware that forces unknown to him forbid him to go on.

To repeat, then, transference is repetition in behavior, an expression of memories that cannot be recalled but that exert influence, compelling some thoughts and actions and prohibiting others. Transference is always expressed directly in action, including language suffused with action, though it may be referred to metaphorically in terms closer to symbolic language. Generally, of course, the patient is, at best, only partially aware of the extent to which his behavior is inconsistent with current reality.

We can also view transference in terms of newer versions of the theory of neurosis that stress the centrality of relationship. We can sharpen the definition by emphasizing that not only are expressions of transference in action, they also invariably are tendentious. A patient immersed in transference (perhaps better put as a patient who is engaged in transferring) is not simply telling a story or conveying a message or imparting information to the analyst, he is attempting to induce the analyst to join him in replaying the unconscious fantasy. Through transference, the patient invites (or, perhaps better, coerces) the analyst to join him in "remembering by being once again" a self the analyst never was, but a self the transference figure once was, or is believed to have been, according to the current version of the patient's unconscious fantasy. And the reenactment includes a version of the way the patient was, or fantasies he was, as an infantile avatar. The analyst will experience himself being molded by the patient, as if he were made of clay, in an attempt to personify the other side of the conflict, the side opposite to the one the patient feels forced to take at the moment.

Transference Is Not Unitary

The foregoing description might make it seem that the patient is both unitary and univocal in transference. Actually, transference is multifarious. A little reflection will confirm that it must be so. After all, its source is the patient's conflict-ridden unconscious fantasies whose elements were laid down over a period of time during early development. Usually, the first glimpse we get of the fantasy is a compressed or condensed and distorted version of it. As the analysis progresses, that first glimpse will expand in depth and complexity and will be revealed as a layered history of that fantasy or, if you will, of the infantile neurosis. One might think of unconscious fantasy as a fantastic history of early childhood.

Consider further why it must be so. The patient was and is divided within himself. The memories, verbal and nonverbal, that make up each layer of the unconscious fantasy reflect the infant's emotional understanding of his relationship with his significant figures at the time. While during infancy his sense of reality was age appropriate, the sense of reality present in unconscious fantasy is also of that time but now is anachronistic. During the course of childhood, such patterns were laid down successively, and each may be expressed in the multiple relationship paradigms that are enacted in the transference. In each, the infantile self reaches out toward a projected figure in order to reconnect with an internal object of desire, fear or hatred, the one salient at this moment in the analysis. Each of these transference couples, or dyads, corresponds (both in actuality and in fantasy) to a significant moment (or period) in the patient's history when an important, that is, affect-laden, memory was laid down. Bowlby (1973) called them "working models of attachment," and his theory of attachment attempts to account for how and when they develop.

Interpretation versus Abortion

Beginning analysts find transference difficult to work with because they wrongly assume that the complementary positions of transferee and transference figure are stable, even fixed; so that one could speak sensibly of the analysis being in a phase of "mother transference," or "father transference" as if there were only one of each kind. The beginner may be bewildered if he attempts to attune himself to subsequent developments while holding to the misleading assumption that the patient's transference repertoire includes only one or two roles. For, as I have described, as soon as the analyst interprets in the transference what is or was going on between this couple in that time, the transference paradigm will change.

If the analyst does not expect that change, he might not notice it and thus will continue to relate to the patient as if he had not made a mutative interpretation and as if the patient had not responded to it by changing. Unaware that the interpretation no longer is apt, he might even repeat it. On the other hand, if the analyst notices the change but did not expect it, he might fear that the change presages disorganization. Indeed, Kernberg et al. (1989) have described such shifting self- and object representations in the transference as characteristic of the treatment of borderline patients. Certainly, unstable relationship patterns and shifting transference positions are more characteristic of these poorly organized patients, but the transference paradigm's changing in response to interpretation neither is restricted to any one diagnostic category nor is an indicator of severe pathology; it is an expectable phenomenon when an analysis is proceeding normally.

To an unprepared analyst, the shifts in the transference might seem kaleidoscopic, but they are not random rearrangements of fixed elements as are the patterns in that optical instrument. The kinds of change the analyst should be prepared to notice following an interpretation include that the patient who had been acting out memories of himself as a child may change sides in the conflict and take on the voice of the censorious parent. Or he might turn to appeal to another face of the transference figure, the kindly side rather than the harsh side. Or the transference focus might seem to be given up entirely for the moment as the patient shifts attention to some other aspect of current or past life, seeming, as it were, to come up for air. The analyst should be prepared to view the seemingly nontransferential material as related metaphorically to the transference, but coming at it from another side. This last possibility is especially noteworthy for it requires a "diagnostic" assessment of whether the patient is turning away from the transference defensively or is momentarily released from the bonds of transference by the work of interpretation. The latter occurs more frequently than is commonly recognized and if the analyst recognizes it, he might usefully empathize with the unusual sense of freedom the patient is experiencing for the moment.

As the analyst gains experience with his patient, he may notice that the transference paradigms tend to succeed each other in an orderly fashion. As the aspect of the neurosis being expressed is worked through, the current pattern of transference attributions will seem to lose salience as another aspect of character, with its transference patterns, gains prominence. As he becomes familiar with this process, the analyst may come to understand that the sequencing of the successive transference paradigms would make sense if, in his own mind at first, he interpolated between them such conjoining phrases as, "Yes but . . ." or "That was because . . ." or "You don't understand, I had no choice but to. . . ." As the analyst becomes comfortable with the idea that, with these interpolations, the sequencing makes sense, his awareness of the tentative linkages can nourish effective interpretations.

For other patients, the transference patterns may follow upon each other as do the musical themes in a rondo, A, B, A, C, A, D, and so on. Each time the patient seems to have worked though a new issue to a useful degree, he seems to go back to "Go," as if compelled to begin the weary round once again. If he does not despair, the analyst might see the return of theme "A" as a signal that, for the moment, the patient is finished with "B" or "D," and the analyst might wonder why. Perhaps some bit of analytic "work" has been completed, or perhaps the patient has run into a block and has been freed to, or forced to, "go back to Go."

In what may be experienced as dreary repetition may be much useful information hidden under a blanket labeled "nothing worth looking at under here." As the analysis progresses, the analyst may come to see that there is a "higher" order being revealed by the sequence of transference patterns. The analysis of one aspect of the unconscious fantasy leads to a particular and logical successor, so that, in time, the analyst may be able to "read" the patient's march through the "stations of the transference" as a narrative of the governing unconscious fantasy, one the patient ultimately can use to understand why he is the way he is.[1]

The rate at which these aspects of the transference succeed each other in response ultimately to interpretations by the analyst, or by the patient himself, provides information about the patient's readiness to separate from the analyst. Early in the analysis, it may take weeks or longer for the unconscious fantasy to run through its protean changes. Toward the end of the analysis, a truncated version of the sequence may play out in days or less, even within a session.

With transference, the patient works on the analyst to make him into the object the patient needs to play out the particular conflict he is compelled to repeat. The patient is not fully aware that he is trying, in the manner of the director of a play, to find or imagine within the analyst/actor the qualities he needs to play against in his opposite number. The analyst is required to submit to being cast in a series of specific roles in the reenactment of the patient's unconscious fantasy. As the analyst helps the patient to understand the nature and necessity of that complicated reenactment, the patient is enabled to "remember" some of the emotional content of his childhood.

The process of interpretation begins when the analyst recognizes that he is observing transference and then directs his initial efforts to facilitating the fullest possible expression of the fantasy contained in it. The commonest error made by young analysts is to rush that process and "interpret it," that is, "translate it," before the patient has had a chance to express "it" fully. The premature translation generally carries little conviction and generally also aborts, for the time being, the patient's narration of the transference fantasy. Done in that way, "translation," in effect, says to the patient, "Stop what you are doing and pay attention. I know better than you what you are about to tell me."

---

[1] You can check on the plausibility of these ideas by observing how, as a consequence of the softening of defensiveness as a function of your interpretations, the transference shifts in a way that ultimately proves to be predictable. In that way you can evaluate the effect of your interpretation. Once you have grasped the order of the shifting, you will have an additional way to locate yourself within the analytic process.

The Therapeutic Split

To facilitate the expression of transference, the analyst must be able to sense that the patient simultaneously is telling him a story and is reenacting that story with the transference figure. By virtue of allowing himself to "split" therapeutically, the analyst will be able to experience both himself as the objective listener and as the opposite figure in the reenactment. He then will have a choice to speak either in the voice of the analyst or in that of the transference figure. For many beginners (and not only beginners), at this point matters get "sticky." It may be much more comfortable to speak only for the objective listener, even though one may have noticed that the effect is jarring on the patient and diminishes his interest in continuing to express the fantasy. Analysts who have worked with young children have an easier time speaking for the transference figure; a child who is engrossed in play-acting a fantasy and has assigned the role of wicked witch to the therapist will not tolerate the therapist's failure to play along. Sadly, our adult patients have learned better manners and do not generally express their irritation or discouragement so directly. Here is an example of speaking in the voice of the transference figure:

> The patient is a painter of some reputation who entered analysis because he felt he was not able to fulfill his talent; he could not paint what he could almost see in his mind's eye. Despite wide recognition, he felt dissatisfied with his own work. As a child he was quite fearful and was babied by his mother, who was acutely sensitive to his distress and would reach out to take his hand when she anticipated he might be uncomfortable, as when they were flying on a family vacation.
>
> The session in question occurred several weeks before the annual vacation break. The patient, increasingly invested in the analysis, had been making efforts to apply his insights in his life. His painting was going better. Concerned that the pace of the analysis might be compromised by the impending vacation break, the analyst became increasingly uneasy; the patient's sense of dependency was palpable, and yet he had not mentioned any wish to stay in contact during the break. The analyst was tempted to offer a way for the patient to stay in touch or to ask the patient why he had not himself proposed a way to stay in touch.
>
> As he pondered these choices, he realized that the tug he was feeling to offer his continuing presence to the patient was being evoked in him as the transference figure and that, as such, he was supposed to offer support solicitously, as had the patient's mother

when he was a child, without waiting to be asked. But how to use this insight? If he asked the patient why he had not asked to stay in touch, his question would sound like a corrective, implying that the patient should have asked, feeling as dependent as he did. But this was a transference fantasy about what the patient's infantile mother would do for him, and this too was the feeling the analyst recognized had been evoked in him.

The analyst knew why the patient could not or did not want to ask, for the fantasy-enforced yearning was for unsolicited support. Inasmuch as his immediate purpose was to encourage the fuller expression of that fantasy to advance the interpretive process, the analyst decided to speak as the transference figure. His first impulse was to propose to the patient that they set up regular phone calls during the break. But if he did that, he would simply be enacting the transference fantasy, not advancing the interpretive process. After considering several alternatives, he offered, "I feel I should be offering to call you during the vacation." The patient fell silent, his eyes tearing. With a mixture of reproach and relief he said, "I've been feeling so alone, so abandoned, I didn't know where you were." Unexpectedly, the patient's associations led to a time when his mother was taken to the hospital with an infection and was parted from him for several weeks. It was then easy to make explicit the way the traumatic events had found repetition in the transference; the patient had all but done it himself.

By beginning the interpretative process by facilitating the expression of the transference fantasy, the analyst helped the patient to experience the transference fully. Then the patient was helped to appreciate the current and genetic implications of the reenactment, that is, that both sides of the transference reenactment, both the ordinarily solicitous mother and himself as a child, "belonged" to the patient. Only when both sides in the fantasy were, so to speak, placed "on the table" was it possible for the patient to distinguish memory from perception, the central task of testing reality. By phrasing his intervention in terms of what the patient's transference had evoked in him, the analyst also encouraged the development of a therapeutic split in the patient so that the patient could feel both the ancient sense of desperation and the wish to force his mother to return and observe himself objectively both in the current and ancient situations.

A major problem analysts may have when working with transference comes from losing the therapeutic split. When analysts become suffused with any emotion, but chiefly anxiety, in more than signal quantities, the split can become rewelded and analysts then find themselves coerced into an "action mode." They feel themselves drawn into a position where their options have been reduced to either going along with the patient's reenactment or refusing to go along with it. And they sense, uncomfortably, that both choices, as actions, are equivalent and equally unacceptable. Suddenly feeling a loss of freedom both arouses anxiety and leads the analyst to defend himself against the patient, who now seems "in control." Whether he complies reluctantly or digs in his heels anxiously, the analyst has been drafted willy-nilly to perform in the cast of the patient's repertory company. He has been impelled by his own anxieties into counteracting.

Another way of looking at this phenomenon is to say that at work here is a principle known to economists as Gresham's Law. Gresham observed that, when two currencies of unequal negotiability are circulating, the better currency will tend to be hoarded while the less negotiable one will be spent. Thus the expression, "Bad money drives out good money"; that is, bad money drives the good money out of circulation. In psychoanalysis and psychotherapy a parallel observation is that lower level communications, or actions, or action-loaded communications tend to drive out higher level, symbolic communications.

Transference tends to provoke countertransference; actions provoke counteractions just as in "ordinary" life, being hit tempts one to hit back. It takes special effort to lower the level of tension by raising the level of communication from action or action language to symbolic speech. It takes time to develop the skill not to do "what comes naturally"—to allow oneself to feel molded to respond in action, to be able to step out of oneself to observe that process, and to be able to speak electively from the positions of any of the parties in the fantasy. This essential skill is central to a worthy conception of psychoanalytic technique (Schlesinger, 1981a).

The more flagrant instances of transference-provoking-countertransference or action-provoking-counteraction are familiar enough not to need examples. But the more subtle varieties may escape notice altogether. Here is an example of how an analyst responded to the bid of a patient to join her in playing out a message typical for her:

> A young attorney, because of her obvious brilliance, was being considered for partnership in a medium-sized law firm. She sought treatment for episodic spells of unaccountable difficulty getting her work done on time. What she produced was outstanding, but the senior partners were worried by her inconsistency and had let her know that they were deferring their decision.
>
> She also complained of an inability to form a satisfactory relationship; all the men she met were either unsuitable or boring.

About a year after beginning analysis she impulsively married a man who had long been interested in her. Also a professional, he was devoted to her. He was steady and placid, and he did not excite her.

As her analysis progressed, she was able to see the pattern of her life, she would provoke her boss to worry about her whenever she felt she had succeeded sufficiently to be taken for granted. Then work would become boring, and she would let things slide until the atmosphere became tense again. During the year, her marriage had become less rocky, but the couple's sexual life had dwindled.

Prior to this session, she had returned from a vacation with her husband; she reported that it had been so-so. She went on to document how she had done the best she could to have fun under the great handicap of her husband's lack of interest in the active sports she adored. He was not up to dancing the night away; he had even brought with him several books he had saved for vacation. He did not even seem to mind her seeking other company to join her in energetic pursuits. Having met a man who enjoyed the same sports she mentioned in passing that on the last evening she "had sort of kissed him." The analyst noted the odd construction of this phrase and asked her what she meant. She became flustered, defensive, said it was nothing. She didn't do anything, and she became obviously resentful and remained sulky for the rest of the session. The analyst was puzzled, for while she was often annoyed by his inquiries when her account of events had been ambiguous, her annoyance had never been so intense.

As the analyst and I discussed the event, it became clear that the patient had set him up to do just what he did, to intrude himself into the story. He felt that he needed to know precisely what had taken place between the patient and her friend, and he justified his intervention as dealing with her vagueness as resistance. Probably feeling guilty about whatever she had done, she experienced his question as a demand to explain and justify what she had or had not done. Although her behavior could certainly be viewed as resistance, the analyst addressed it in a way that neither reflected awareness that she might have been unclear for a purpose nor suggested that he was tempted to respond to her as the transference figure might have done. Her response suggests that she saw him as a person who, like her husband and other historical authorities, would pay no attention to her until she got into trouble; and then they would only disapprove of her wishes and actions. If he had been able to "look over the patient's shoulder" and see the transference figure as she did, he might have focused on what she had been doing in relation to the transference figure, that is, anticipating his criticism and then defending herself against it through vagueness, rather than focusing on her failure to make her thoughts clear to the analyst.

We can consider the patient's behavior as a compromise between wanting to be open with the analyst and wanting to conceal, more or less, her wishes from the transference figure. In this context, her use of "more or less" implies that her behavior also represented her annoyance with and resentment of her husband, who "forced her" to live out her passions elsewhere and thus incited her desire to "rub his nose" in his inadequacy.

The analyst might have been able to sense that the patient's way of telling the story was tendentious in these several respects, staying purposefully unclear so as to draw from him an intervention that would justify her feeling that he was blaming her for the husband's unmanly failure. From that perspective, the analyst's intervention was a counteraction, and the patient responded in action as well, resentfully defending herself and retiring sulkily under his perceived disapproval.

The essential technical issue rests on the distinction between becoming involved in the story, that is, centering interest only on the *content* of the story, on the relationships being described by the patient, as opposed to being equally attuned to the *way she tells* the story to the analyst. Of course, attending to the story and to the telling of it need not be exclusive alternatives; the analyst ought to be able to attend to either. But if the analyst is not able to maintain his therapeutic split, he is likely to be drawn into counteracting and becoming a character in the story. Plausible interventions to illustrate a focus on the telling of the story might include suggesting to the patient that she seems not to want him to know too much about what she has done or what she thinks about it, or that the way she is telling the story suggests that she might be concerned about what he thinks about her behavior.

In the next supervisory session, the candidate said he had thought about our discussion and had resolved to avoid asking questions, as he realized he was often tempted to do. He was gratified to hear confirmation of our thinking when the patient continued the story of the unsatisfactory, passionless state of her marriage. It was comfortable and pleasant but without excitement, boring. She mentioned that she was preoccupied with a fantasy, a plan to get out of the marriage, but rejected the plan as untimely inasmuch her husband had just begun to remodel their kitchen. At this, she supposed that the analyst must be appalled by her cold-blooded wish to exploit her husband. The analyst remained silent.

Toward the end of the session the patient noted that the analyst had not said anything. He responded that she might have some idea about what he had been thinking. She did but wanted to hear from him. He suggested that she might have been thinking that he believed it was possible to have both passion and security in a marriage. Snorting in disbelief at the absurdity of "his position," she affirmed that it was just the sort of thing her husband would propose, but she knew such a combination wasn't possible. The analyst interpreted her attribution to him of a wishy-washy, indefensible position and then began another episode of working through an important aspect of her neurosis. The analyst did not, at this point, pick up the theme of "cold-bloodedness," which he felt was too hot to handle at that time. At the same time, he recognized that it represented an escalation of the patient's efforts to involve him because of his silence.

At a later point, the analyst again felt stymied, this time by the patient's tale of how badly things were going at work. Clearly, her troubles were, as usual, self-inflicted, and he had all he could do to keep himself from pointing this out. He sensed that he had been put into a position in which he either had to bite his tongue or say something he knew would be perceived as critical. The patient gradually became more despairing at seeing no way out of her difficulties, and, feeling unsupported by the analyst's silence, she began to cry.

Just as suddenly, the analyst felt free to act; the patient's tears seemed to give him permission to be helpful, and he found himself offering suggestions about what the patient might do to remedy her situation. On reflection, he could identify the intense pull he felt to intervene as having emerged when he sensed she was slipping into a masochistic enactment. He was also able to see that his leap into "helpful" action had been provoked by the patient and that, by "doing something," he was able to alleviate the painful state of impotence that he had been experiencing. The intervention also fit within the transference paradigm that was salient at the moment; she forced solicitous attention by threatening to "fail" when she felt she was being "taken for granted," or ignored, after having achieved some measure of success.

Note also that in his worried imaginings, the analyst had lost sight of the metaphoric function of the story. For, while transference is invariably expressed in action, as an enactment or a dramatization, its purpose is to communicate something the patient cannot say in any other way because he cannot remember; the fantasy is unconscious. It is not the analyst's business to convince the patient of anything, but merely to facilitate the patient's telling the story as fully as possible so that he can come to understand it, in both its current and past instances.

6

Resistance

In Defense of Resistance

As a longtime libertarian, I have found myself from time to time supporting unpopular causes, taking up the cudgel for some concept unjustly maligned as a public enemy. "Resistance," for example, is blamed everywhere for thwarting the good works of the analytic establishment; its very name has become pejorative. Not only do I want to defend and rehabilitate this misunderstood concept; even more, I want to have its heroic side appreciated so that it is recognized as among man's best friends. Unfortunately, my efforts on behalf of my beneficiary-elect have hardly affected public opinion. So once more into the breach.

Why defend resistance? It is certainly not an underdog; some clinicians seem to believe that, if left unchecked, resistance might take over psychoanalysis and psychotherapy entirely. Is it not true that, if it were not for resistance, psychoanalysis would take no time at all? Is it not the case that, but for resistance, analysts would never feel their efforts to be futile and care managers would smile on psychotherapy? Is not resistance to blame for all that is difficult, painful, unpleasant, and expensive about psychotherapy? Are we not entitled, even obligated, to "break through," undermine, avoid, or hypnotize away resistance? How could we treat a patient without "neutralizing" his resistances (Fenichel, 1941)?

What therapists commonly call resistance is behavior that manifestly opposes what the patient believes the therapist wants to do or wants to happen. Obvious examples are a patient's prolonged silence, refusal to talk about what the therapist wants to hear, or coming late to sessions or not at all. But these flagrant "misbehaviors," though they certainly involve resistance, are not the most common forms of resistance or even the most important ones. Resistance is not a sometimes thing, not an event. Resistance is a continuing process that usually operates in ways that do not call attention to it. These more subtle forms of defending are far more important in shaping the process of psychotherapy than are the more egregious forms.

What do we mean, then, by resistance? A nonpejorative definition is that resistance is defense expressed in the transference. This simple definition, which we owe to Gill (1982), has several technical implications. It implies, for instance, that, whereas issues of drive and fear of punishment may inspire defensiveness, resistance is a form of coping with these dangers. The usual understanding is that, when defense is expressed in transference as resistance, the patient is externalizing one side of an unconscious conflict, appoints the therapist to stand for that extruded side, and then acts out the conflict with the therapist. The patient reenacts the unconscious fantasy rather than remembering it. At such times, the therapist may seem to the patient to be his enemy and the process between them adversarial. The situation becomes even more complicated when the therapist yields to the temptation to play out the role created for him by the patient, for then the therapist misses the opportunity to bring to the patient's attention what the patient is doing.

But defense is not always expressed in transference in noisy and flagrant ways. Nor is the only pattern of interaction between patient and therapist in transference an adversarial one. The motive of defense can be expressed subtly in behavior in such a way that it does not call attention to itself; it can operate synergistically with other motives subsumed under adaptation. The therapist may be led to acquiesce in the more subtle forms of defense expressed in transference either by colluding with the patient or by unwittingly acting out some complementary, though not necessarily adversarial, role in the patient's unconscious transference fantasy. The therapist might, for example, take an approving maternal role or bask in the patient's idealizing fantasy.

What, then, do we do about resistance? I put the question in a misleading way by suggesting that we must take a stand and, as Fenichel (1941) proposed, prevent resistance, get it out of the way, undermine it, or in other ways confirm the transference position given us by the patient to serve as a threatening enemy. But recognizing that the patient is resisting should, at the very least, tell us that he is doing the best he can, even though he is frightened. Something has just happened that intimates threat. Thus, to the therapist, resistance should be no more a nuisance or inconvenience than is pain to a physician when it occurs in the course of a physical examination. Both the resistance and the pain tell us that something important is going on in that area. Resistance, therefore, is of interest to us, and we would like to know more about why the patient needs to behave in that way.

Note the paradox: although a resisting patient may be attempting to thwart us, to withhold information, to deny cooperation, or more subtly to avoid collaborating in the therapeutic task, he is also conveying a good deal of information and, in a larger sense, is fully cooperating in the treatment. Since our major premise is that the patient does not fully know what the problem is and is forced to repeat what he cannot remember, we must recognize that the behavior we call resistance is part of that repetition and is part of his way of communicating through reenactment.

The resistance is an expression of the patient's need to protect himself against what, for the moment, appears to be a worse danger, one represented by the analyst and his well-meaning intrusions. If the analyst views matters in this way, he will have a broader range of options for intervening. He could empathize with the patient's feeling unsafe *at the moment*. He could suggest one of several reasons why it might make sense for the patient to feel unsafe *at the moment*, and thus "normalize" the patient's reaction. I have stressed "at the moment" because such resistance, what has been called "minor resistance" (e. g., Greenson, 1967) tends to pass quickly, its presence marked by a momentary pause or change of expression, suggesting that the patient is watching his step, rather like stepping carefully through a barnyard or a mine field.

I introduced a new term, normalize, but it does not refer to a new idea. Normalizing describes one of the ways the analyst expresses his understanding that the patient is doing the best he can and that his, perhaps odd, reaction is understandable.[1]

Rather than being dismayed by resistance, the therapist might well welcome it. The technical problem is how to help the patient communicate more effectively, whether through resistance or otherwise. Certainly all therapists are prepared to empathize with patients' feelings of anxiety and hence with their need to resist. It is only a step further, but a most important step, to desist from feeling, "I suppose the patient feels it necessary to act that way, but I do wish he would stop it," to feeling, instead, "Since he has to act in that way, perhaps I can help him communicate with me through this odd and painful behavior so that we can come to understand it better." I call this stance "going along with the resistance." For a simple expression of this stance, consider this example:

> During an initial session, the patient, who had been complaining of inhibition, told her story freely. But when approaching what was going on with her boyfriend, where the current trouble seemed mostly expressed, she became obviously uncomfortable, spoke vaguely, and looked pleadingly at the analyst. The analyst, who had been listening quietly and empathically, said, "I think you are getting close to the matters that trouble you the most, but you don't yet feel comfortable enough to talk about them."

---

[1] You may have heard some resonance with the teaching of Hellmuth Kaiser in these thoughts about resistance. He was a remarkable teacher and had important things to say. Sadly, he is little referred to these days. His collected papers are worth careful study (Fierman, 1965).

> The patient started to cry and, after a few moments, said, "I was afraid you would make me talk about it, and I can't. But, if I don't tell you about it, how can you help me?"
>
> The analyst looked thoughtful for a moment and agreed, "Yes, that could be a problem."
>
> With that, the patient straightens up and haltingly began to describe her boyfriend's demands and her qualms.

That example is an illustration of ordinary therapist tact. But, if we deconstruct it from a formal point of view, we might note that the analyst interpreted her behavior; he put her behavior into words. His underlying assumption was that she was doing the best she could under the circumstance, that she was in conflict, and that he could assume the conflict had unconscious roots whose conscious expression was that she felt unable to do the very thing she had come to do. Speaking to that conflict, he respected both her wish to tell and her feeling that it was as yet unsafe to do so. He neither played into the transference expectation that he might force her to tell nor excused her from telling. In this instance, dealing with the issue "on the surface," that is, in transference, for the moment made defending less necessary.

Resistance and Neurosis

Like resistance, neurosis too can have pejorative connotations, but it need not. If we were still using old-fashioned nosology, most of us would be happy to be consigned to the "normal neurotic range." In addition to reassuring us that we are not too crazy to be analyzed, that lamented term has the further propaedeutic significance of implying that conflict is part of life and not necessarily pathological.

In my parlance, "neurosis" is present when a significant portion of one's personality resources is devoted to defending against unrealistic and anachronistic dangers. From the systems point of view, neurosis, like personality itself, can be thought of as a conservative organization. We recognize, sadly, that any bureaucracy is concerned first with its own preservation, even though its purpose for being may no longer exist. Likewise, the neurosis looks out for itself first, even though long ago the apparatus designed to ward off infantile dangers ceased to serve any useful function. All bureaucracies resist change, and so does neurosis. The prospect of change itself, of whatever kind, seems dangerous. Although I may seem to belabor the obvious I must note that we would not be made aware of a conflict if a ready solution for it were available and that transference and resistance reflect the expedient turning away from that failure by externalizing one side of it. Conflict, transference, and resistance—and the tripping over one's own feet that we call neurosis—are all part of life, not just of psychopathology.

Although a patient brings himself to a therapist believing he wants help, his concept of help is generally not the same as the therapist's. The patient wants relief from pain, from inconvenience. He does not essentially want to change or to give up the neurosis and most often would be happy to pay off the therapist the way he pays off his superego to let him retain the primary and secondary gains of illness. Much of the course of any treatment can be viewed as a patient's effort to bring the treatment into the neurosis: to force the therapist to play a role in the "scenario" of the patient's unconscious fantasy and thus to reduce the danger that the therapist's ability to act independently might, like the proverbial bull in the china shop, threaten the continuation of the patient's neurotic, but familiar, style of life. It is only the uncomfortable portions of this style of life that the patient is willing to recognize as his "illness." This process of attempting to include the therapist and therapy in the neurosis, what we call transference and acting (out) in the transference, is also, clearly, resistance.

The patient tries to present the neurosis as something he has, whereas the therapist's objective is to try to show the patient that it is not something he *has* but something he *does*. A neurosis is not an albatross hanging around the patient's neck; rather, it is something the patient recreates constantly, day-by-day in his life, and minute-by-minute in the therapeutic situation as well. Paradoxically, it is this recreation of the neurosis in the therapeutic situation, that is, in transference (this so-called resistance), that gives the therapist his major leverage to help the patient think, feel, and act differently. The field of the treatment is the therapeutic situation, chiefly transference.

Recall, although transference is an expression of resistance, primarily resistance against change, it is also the only way in which the patient can communicate what he cannot remember. As he repeats and reenacts his conflicts and his history of failed solutions to them, he provides himself and the therapist important information about why he feels it is necessary to do so. The transference repetition, motivated mostly by the patient's need to defend himself and resist change, also sets up an in vivo situation in which the therapist can make a difference in the patient's life because he has become part of it. Thus neurosis is best thought of not as a static entity but as a process, a way of relating to oneself internally and, through transference, externally to others.

In neurosis, the personal past is constantly being recreated and repeated. Of course, it is characteristic in life, and usually highly economical, that we construe the present in terms of past experience and that we repeat old patterns and old solutions, when possible, rather than invent new ones. Repetition is not necessarily pathological any more than is transference, but repetition is of the essence of neurosis when it distorts current reality and, in the service of living out the conditions of an unconscious fantasy, substitutes fantastic rewards and punishments for realistic opportunities and gratifications. From this point of view, the therapist must allow the transference attributions to settle on him sufficiently so that he may participate in these acts of continuous recreation and by judicious intervention help the patient realize that he has been compelled to act as he does, and why, and thus to open for him a wider range of choice than he has experienced.

Resistance as Process

To discuss resistance as a process logically requires that we first discuss transference as a process, as in Chapter 4. To recap the main points, transference, like the neurosis it expresses, is not a static condition but a constantly changing one. Its function, however, does remain constant, to retain or restore the familiar, to resist change and ward off new experiences that might challenge the premises of the neurosis, that is, of the unconscious fantasy lived out in the neurosis.

If resistance is defense expressed in the transference, is there anything we can say about resistance that we could not just as easily say about transference? Indeed, a discussion of the therapeutic and technical issues involved in transference would also be a discussion of resistance. Although there is great overlap of transference and resistance as concepts, the terms are not fully interchangeable. To maintain clarity, I prefer to use these terms not to describe kinds of behavior or categories of phenomena, but as points of view toward behavioral phenomena. Thus we could describe the behavior of a patient both from the point of view of transference and from the point of view of resistance. At times, the two discussions might overlap a great deal; at other times they might be different enough to be mutually illuminating.

The overlap is greatest when we are considering gross transference disturbances: transference crises, episodes of acting out in the transference, flagrant examples of oppositional behavior, and the like. But recall that transference can also be adaptive and that much of the time transference and reality testing support each other. The self-preservative needs of the neurosis as a system can often be accommodated without calling attention to them through flagrant display and without egregiously disrupting smooth, reality-oriented functioning. There are times when the function of defense expressed in the transference, the "resisting," is accomplished without its being at all obvious what, if anything, is being transferred. If a therapist were queried at such a time, he might respond that at the moment "the alliance" seems dominant and the therapy is proceeding smoothly "without resistance."

One of my articles of faith, or at least a heuristic assumption, is that in psychotherapy defense and transference, and hence resistance, are always present. To draw an analogy from the late-night TV reruns of WWII movies, when the "Resistance" wants to prevent an enemy train from reaching its destination, they do not find it necessary to blow up a bridge. It may be enough to throw a switch the wrong way, to bribe the conductor, to mislabel some cars, or to uncouple them "accidentally." The most economical way for the underground Resistance to function was to achieve maximum disruption of the enemy with minimum exposure. The best resistance is the one you do not see. So it is in psychotherapy and psychoanalysis: resistance can most effectively prevent change by subtly interfering with just one of the operations that serve changing. Most of the clinical examples in this book illustrate resistance operating subtly to maintain the status quo.

The Modalities of Resistance

In psychoanalysis, psychic change—which, broadly speaking, corresponds with changes in the meanings of the major events of one's life, in the significance of relationships, and in ways of solving problems—is the hoped-for outcome of an interpretive process. The analyst will observe the patient's response in the course of the interpretive process to see if the hoped-for result is occurring: Have the nature, direction, and patterning of the patient's associations changed? Has his mood changed? Has his behavior inside or outside the therapeutic situation changed in other ways? These are the three expressive modalities or realms to which the analyst must attend: cognition, affect, and action. A complete response by the patient must involve all three. It follows, then, that resistance may operate in any or all of these modalities. The relationship among the modalities, or the forms in which communication can be cast, is complex. Although classical theory favors the sequence interpretation → insight → affect → action, that is, behavioral change, in actuality any of the three may lead.

We soon learn to be suspicious of a patient's reaction to an interpretation that is only in words. Words without feelings are likely to imply the defenses of intellectualizing or isolation. We tend to be less suspicious of a wordless affective response, at least at first; but we soon learn that affectualizing can also be a formidable resistance. Words with appropriate affect carry greater conviction, as well they might, for they generally lead to appropriate action, which may or may not follow. A therapist's attention following any intervention should, then, turn to the patient's response and be "diagnostic" in the broadest sense of the term, to assess the need for immediate further intervention, that is, for follow-up interpretation. One of the factors that should determine what the analyst does next is his sense of the completeness of the patient's response to the earlier interpretation.

Resistance in the Cognitive Realm

Resistance operating in the cognitive realm may be harder to detect than resistance against affect or action. In the cognitive realm, defense is most often accomplished by subtle acts of "isolation"—breaking the connection between the words that might otherwise convey a dangerous idea (Freud, 1894, 1926). When the connection among them is broken, they can remain in consciousness since their noxious implication is no longer obvious. This phenomenon can be demonstrated clinically material to show that the work of defense and "synthesis" can go hand-in-hand so that the content of thought does not look as if it was censored. Unlike in a letter that has passed through military censorship, there are no gross blackouts, no scissored phrases. The continuity of thought may seem largely undisturbed. Subtle shifts in emphasis and the obscuring of relationship accomplish the work of defense merely by separating the elements of a pregnant sentence with time, a brief pause, or by interpolating indifferent material. A censored series of associations could be diagramed as A ___ B ___ C ___ A , and so on, the blanks standing either for a brief pause or for defensively inserted "filler" material. Recognizing this defensive strategy, an analyst could interpret merely by repeating what the patient said as a continuous phrase, omitting the pauses and filler material. For example:

> The patient's major wish was to see himself as a "good person." His major symptom was an exaggerated fear of hurting or offending anyone. He also had an explosive temper that was easily triggered by the feeling of being imposed upon. His childhood was a generally deprived time, since his mother was bed ridden and his father had deserted the family.
>
> On this occasion he spoke in a roundabout way, with many interruptions, of an unusual day in his boyhood: It was sunny and beautiful, his friends were playing ball outside, his mother was in bed with a wasting neurological disease; his place in the family

was as caretaker. He told all this in a way that gave very little sense of why these recollections had emerged at this time. The analyst thought he heard the patient trying to present himself as "good" but was not clear about why a special point had to be made of it just now. The analyst ventured, "I think you are trying not to tell me that you were out there playing ball with your friends while your mother was suffering in bed." The patient slumped and after a pause reports that his head had started to spin.

And then the rest of the story came out: how he suddenly realized with a pang of guilt that he had been enjoying himself playing ball for perhaps half an hour and had forgotten about his mother. Fearing she might have died during his neglect, he rushed back into the house.

This historical material then connects with his current fear that the analyst has been encouraging him to enjoy himself too freely, that he could not "just have fun," for he certainly would then be neglectful of duty and his delinquency would expose him to punishment; perhaps the very illness his mother suffered from would be visited upon him. Indeed, he had a sample of it in the somatic sensation that was his immediate response to the intervention.

Another common method of isolation is to remove the conjunction that would join two phrases and thus reveal their connection, or to substitute a less indicative conjunction that would tend to soften or blur the connection. The analyst could go about interpreting by summarizing the patient's set of isolated ideas but suggesting what the missing or replaced conjunctions might have been. Thus, he might say to the patient in the diagrammed sentence A ___ B ___ C ___ A, "I think you are telling me that you feel A *because of* B and *instead of* C and therefore are quite justified in feeling A."

Here is an example of the defensive use of an indifferent conjunction:

A patient returned from a long-planned and eagerly anticipated trip home in a distant state and began to speak of it in a matter-of-fact, dreary tone, listing the people who had attended the family reunion as if they were of equal and indifferent importance to her. After listening for a while to her unvarying recital and recalling the excitement of her planning for the trip, the analyst commented on the blandness of her recital. Summarizing the sequence in which she had enumerated the guests, he stressed the "and" that linked them: "You told me that cousins Mabel and Hannah were there AND your aunt and uncle from Toledo were there, AND Charlie was there, AND your other aunt from New Mexico was there, as if they all meant the same to you."

He paused then to recall that her excitement in planning the trip was built on the hope that Charlie, her childhood sweetheart, might turn up. "I believe you went home mostly BECAUSE you wanted to pick up again with Charlie, but one couldn't gather that from the way you put him in the middle of the crowd." The patient started to cry, "I didn't want to remember, and I didn't want to tell you about it. It was awful. I feel so humiliated for telling you about my childish wishes. Charlie came with a girlfriend, and there I was with my new dress and new hairdo, looking as if I had gone to the prom without a date."

In general, the work of interpretation in the face of resistance operating in the cognitive realm involves restoring the sense of relatedness that has been removed by defense. The most common way to begin the interpretive process is for the therapist to summarize his understanding of what the patient has been telling him. In summarizing, the analyst condenses the patient's verbiage. In the therapist's boiled-down version, the patient's key ideas are much closer together. Their relationship thus becomes more obvious and their collective impact correspondingly greater. When the patient hears the therapist "say the same thing" (but without the padding), the ideas seem more real, and more "objective." Hearing them through the external ear, spoken by another, is an altogether more powerful experience than hearing them through the internal ear, as when one only thinks them or when one says them to oneself. Another factor, one not often mentioned, is that, since some time elapses between the patient's first statement and the therapist's summary, the passage of time itself may diminish the patient's defensiveness,—what is being heard and considered is now not totally new; the surprise element is gone. Even a brief elapsed time may permit sufficient processing to lower the threat of the unexpected.

There are, of course, other ways for resistance to operate in the cognitive realm. The whole range of cognitive abilities can be used for purposes of defense. In general, these methods deal less with the content than with the formal aspects of the patient's communication. Doubting and reasonable weighing of alternatives can easily serve resistance. As each side of a conflict is given judiciously balanced expression, the net movement averages out to zero. A move in one direction is countered by a move in the opposite direction, a yes by a no, a wish by a fear, a promising idea by a doubt. There are instances when these modes of defense seem obviously pathological, as when a paralyzed obsessional becomes blocked or a schizophrenic patient shows classic ambivalence. With most of the patients we see in psychotherapy such flagrant examples do not occur; the intrusion of defensive purpose is gentler, and the need for defense is synthesized with the requirements of adaptation sufficiently to make up what Shapiro (1965) has called "neurotic styles." Thus, unless the therapist is especially attuned to them, he is likely to overlook these expressions of resistance, though he may feel put off, or become bored, or otherwise made to feel ineffectual without knowing why.

Resistance in the Affective Realm

Resistance operating in the affective realm is displayed when a patient betrays the presence of conflict by the lack of fit between what he says and the way he says it. Speaking with an affective tone that does not fit the content gives a mixed message that permits one to say something and to unsay it at the same time. We speak of the most extreme form of this kind of resistance as patients' showing inappropriate affect. We call milder forms irony or sarcasm. In the previous example, the patient who was reporting a disappointing visit to her family home also spoke in an affective tone that signaled the presence of conflict to the analyst. The patient resorted to that form of resistance as an ad hoc measure. The following example is drawn from the treatment of a patient for whom it was a characteristic form of defending:

> The patient, a woman in her late 30s, had several children. She presented for marital discord and intermittent child abuse and also carries the clearly unwarranted diagnosis of schizophrenia for which she had been overmedicated. In the course of psychotherapy, she began to show a pattern of externalizing conflict in a way that also aroused anxiety in the therapist. She spoke at a very rapid pace, seeming to require very little response from him, and described events in her life of vastly different levels of significance for herself, for others, and for her treatment as if they were all of the same importance.
>
> As the therapist listened and tried to grasp what the patient was telling him, he found himself becoming irritated and anxious, feeling controlled as he heard the patient run down her laundry list of daily events interspersed with allusions to having pulled her daughter's hair or having struck her son. The affective "leveling" of these communications, reciting them as if one were no more important than any other, enabled her to hide from herself the significance of her actions while evoking in the therapist the anxiety and guilt that the patient had to defend herself against feeling.

One could say here that the patient was resisting awareness that she had a problem or that she was trying more or less unconsciously to avoid awareness of it by concealing from the therapist her relationship to it. We could also say that she was resisting changing her ways, which might come about if she were to allow herself to be fully aware of how she felt about what she was saying and to take responsibility for her actions. We could consider that she was resisting reinternalizing the conflict and resisting experiencing the pain that would surely be present if she faced the consequences of her actions on others and the effects on her self-esteem.

A therapist can help such a patient express conflicted feelings in ways less destructive to herself and to her relationships by first of all, helping her to slow down her pace of talking so that she can listen to herself. Also, by helping her see that keeping him in the dark served an important defensive purpose for her, the therapist might put to therapeutic use the anxiety he experienced when he found himself unable to grasp what the patient was saying. Such issues may be approached in any number of ways once the therapist grasps the function of this behavior, that is, what the patient is doing for herself by thwarting him and how she is going about it.

Following the principle that the patient is always right, the therapist must attempt to discover the legitimacy on which her way of communicating with him rests, what she is trying to do for herself by speaking in this odd, affectively discordant way. He must go with the resistance, that is, help her understand that, for reasons no longer present, she has been compelled to defend herself in this expensive and off-putting way, and to consider that there might be alternatives. Of course, often while doing so, the patient will come to realize that the apparent need for defending is anachronistic.

It is important that the therapist observe carefully what the patient does about a new awareness (or a new affect, for that matter) to see whether the patient intends it to lead somewhere or is content to have it remain complete in itself, to admire perhaps, but not to use. These antinomies are never complete; it is never totally one or the other. If the therapist is alert to these possibilities, he will sense whether an interpretation leads to a complete response and to continuing change or has merely forced some temporary accommodation from the neurosis.

This matter of heightened awareness that seems to lead nowhere has often been discussed as a flaw in the insight. Insight may be disparaged as "pseudoinsight" if it is not accompanied by appropriate feelings or seems to serve resistance by not leading to action. The terms pseudoinsight and intellectual insight wrongly fault insight because it is only insight. The fault is not with the insight but in the failure to act on it.

When analyzing this state of affairs, it is important that the therapist not fall into the trap of considering the insight "ungenuine" because the patient, while agreeing with the reformulation of his behavior then does nothing about it. It is far more useful to recognize that the patient has again accomplished a neurotic solution and has managed to have his cake and eat it too by stopping his response short of action. This solution draws on a capacity that was highly useful in early childhood, when good intentions, or saying, "I understand," were enough to put an end to a state of tension between parent and child.

The idea that a promise is the beginning of a process of performance rather than the equivalent of an apology that puts an end to an unsatisfactory state of affairs is a later developmental achievement (Schlesinger, 1978). It is a task for follow-up interpretation to help the patient see the ways in which he tries to ignore that he knows better and is quietly sabotaging the possibilities of change. The therapist must interpret the ways in which the patient tries to include the new within the old, or makes an empty concession by saying "Yes, but," or makes room for the insight in the neurosis rather than seizing the implication that the neurotic system itself could change. What I am proposing also fits with the concept of interpretation as a process rather than a one-shot affair. The therapist should also consider that the patient's inaction may be a form of acting, a way of saying no quietly without taking responsibility for open defiance.

A therapist must be ready to diagnose a patient's response to an interpretation and be ready to interpret that response both in its positive and negative aspects. That is, the therapist must interpret the ways in which the patient makes use of what he has learned and the ways in which he tries to ignore what he has learned, to say, in effect, "There is nothing new to that, and I, therefore, need do nothing about it." By approaching the art of interpretation in this way, as a continuing process, the therapist will avoid making the mistake of damning the insight as ungenuine or intellectual. Instead, he will see that the problem is one of a neurosis struggling to survive, as any system does, and thus of a patient's needing help to extricate himself from old self-defeating patterns while being fearful of the new.

Resistance in the Realm of Action

One of the general goals of all psychotherapy is to promote a patient's activity within the therapy. By "activity," in this sense, I mean, first of all, a conscious effort by the patient to become active in relation to the interpretation, to grapple with the new idea, to test its truth, and to make it his own or modify it or reject it. A major style of resisting is to avoid becoming active in this sense. A major task for interpretation and follow-up interpretation is to promote the patient's active responding.

A common resistance takes the form of the silent refusal to become active in this way, masked by a willingness to assume the truth of the interpretation; e.g., "I suppose you're right, Doctor . . ." The therapist must be prepared to follow up his original interpretation to include the resistances the patient erects to avoid taking account of the interpretation, to avoid having any feelings about it, to avoid acting on it, or to avoid letting it act on him.[2]

The analyst ought to understand that the patient prefers to leave the interpretation "on the table" as an interesting, perhaps even plausible, idea but has declined to engage with it or to test its truth for himself (Schlesinger, 1994b). We could say that the patient has declined to become active in relation to the intervention, because, we presume, if he were to entertain it actively, he might have to make any truth in it his own. We hope that, in response to an interpretation, the patient will stop for a moment, the pause reflecting at least that he now is aware that two ideas are competing in his mind, his own line of association and that of the analyst. The content of the interpretation alters some meaning the patient has depended on. It may remind the patient of other matters he would rather not think about but that now seem uncomfortably compelling. The patient also has to deal with the mixed sense of confusion and enlightenment, of anxiety and relief provoked by the interpretation. The analyst's next intervention should deal with one or another aspect of the patient's initial response.

If you have patients who are themselves psychotherapists, you may have noticed an interesting sidelight to the issue of action in response to interpretation. Frequently such "professional patients" manage to put their insights into action through their own patients. One of the first signs that something is getting through to such a patient may be the report that his patients unaccountably are getting better. Sometimes the professional patient is aware that he is serving as a "middleman" between his analyst and his own patients; he is trying out the analyst's advice on a guinea pig, as it were, before using it himself. Other professional patients may treat their analyst's interpretations as "export goods," not intended for domestic consumption. Here the pattern of resistance is clear: wisdom is allowed to skip a generation, and the patient's patient is nominated to be the surrogate actor. The interpretation, "You seem to be able to help your patient to do what you yourself find impossible" can have considerable impact.

Another common form of resistance in the realm of action is a patient's willingness to derive a suggestion to act in his life from an interpretation

---

[2] I do not want to be understood as making an unqualified plea for action in psychotherapy. Although I believe it is axiomatic that insight must be confirmed through action and that action is essential to test out the truth of insight, I realize that action can also serve the purpose of resistance; a patient's "flight into health" is one example.

that refers to behavior within the therapy. The patient seems eager to act on one of the perceived implications of the therapist's words before (or instead of) actually understanding and evaluating them either to test their truth or to see if they fit his circumstances. Such behavior implies, "I do not want to understand and thus be responsible for that idea as my own: I would rather follow your 'suggestion' and let you be responsible. And if it doesn't work, it will be your fault."

Since resisting implies holding back, it may seem paradoxical that leaping ahead or acting prematurely can also serve the purpose of resisting. But, if resisting can be said to have to do with preventing change by inhibiting or exaggerating one of the three components, cognition, affect, and action, then perhaps it should be understandable that by leaping ahead, by acting prematurely, the patient can prevent a full response for which he might then have to feel responsible.

Consider the following example:

> A patient responded to a therapist's interpretation with increased tension by saying, "You mean that the reason I am so cool to my wife when I get home from work is that I resent her easy life, the kind of life my mother used to have, and that it reminds me of how exploited my father used to seem. She hasn't had to suffer fools all day at the office. She just waits around for me to come home to take care of her needs. Well, if that's the way it is, it's silly, I don't have to behave that way. When I get home this evening I will be nice to her."

That brief vignette could be used to illustrate resisting on several counts: (1) The patient treats the idea as still belonging to the therapist. It is not his idea but someone else's. (2) He does not reflect on it to see if it fits with his own experience, if it makes sense, and if, therefore, he could make it his own. (3) Instead, he prefers to assume it to be true, a kind of hypothesis. (4) Yet he declares his willingness to act on the untested and unproven idea as if the idea, if true, could of its own power change things.

The patient thus leaps ahead to put into action, at least in fantasy during the hour, an idea whose implications he has not stopped to examine. He has explored neither its cognitive nor its affective significance though he seems to become more tense. We might assume that the therapist's interpretation made him anxious and that he dealt with his anxiety with seeming compliance, making of the interpretation an order or suggestion to do something different "out there." His rushing ahead in fantasy to apply the therapist's idea thus expressed his resistance to testing the idea fully, making it his own, and acting accordingly if it turned out to suit his purpose. A premature decision to act in this way also serves resisting by saying, in effect, "Now that's settled. We don't have to talk about it any more."

The therapist could intervene at this point and make use of any portion of this deconstruction of the event as it has thus far been laid out. I do not mean that it does not matter what the therapist does at this point but rather that there are insufficient indications given in the example to select among a range of possible interventions. Interventions could include, for example, "Something about what I just said made you anxious," or, "It seems easier for you to put that idea into action than to consider it long enough to see whether it makes sense to you."

The usual advice with regard to characterological defenses and styles that seem to serve the purpose of resisting is to "confront" the patient with his (mis)behavior. Confrontation, used in this way, connotes an adversarial relationship. Unrequested information is to be thrust on an unwilling recipient. It is natural for the therapist to want to make the patient aware of what the therapist has just discovered, for example, that the patient is using his intellectual resources and characterological habits more or less unwittingly to "sabotage" his treatment. And so the therapist might say something like, "Have you noticed that every time I offer an idea about what might be going on, you shrug it off?" Or, "Each time you consider a plausible solution to the problem, you find a reason to doubt it would work."

Such "classical" confrontations of resistance not infrequently "work"; that is, if the patient's anxiety is not too high, he may be intrigued enough to stop and look at his behavior. But this description of the process conceals the problem contained in this approach. The confrontation stops the patient. He is now expected to attend to the therapist's observation that he was doing something he may have been unaware of, the implication being that he should not have been doing it and therefore should now desist. Of course, the state of the therapist–patient relationship and the way the therapist words and expresses a confrontation make a huge difference in how a confrontation will be received. When the manner and tone of making the intervention convey little hostility or condescension, and the state of the relationship is largely trusting and cooperative, such interventions can be quite helpful. These conditions, however, are essential. Certain inherent tendencies in this technical approach must be overcome before hand by the therapist or the patient (or both) if this kind of intervention is to "work."

We can take an alternative approach by considering resistance and interpretation as processes. We already assume that the patient's behavior is serving some needed purpose and that the patient is doing "the best he can" in the conflicted circumstances in which he finds himself. But to point out what he is doing—with the inevitable implication that he should not be doing it—does not make effective use of this way of understanding his behavior. A better way would be for the therapist to make use of his awareness that the patient's defensiveness is being expressed in the transference in order for him to control the behavior of the therapist, that is, as the transference object.

Often it is the therapist's discomfort at being in this position that impels him to resort to a confrontation. Consider that the patient is reenacting an unconscious scenario in which the therapist also is assigned a distasteful role. If the therapist is not aware that he is experiencing transference, he may try to relieve the sense of impotence that results from feeling forced to play a role not of his own choosing. I believe the therapist's motive in confronting the patient may, at least in part, be to try to break out of the assigned transference position, usually an uncomfortable one of ineffectuality (although other painful positions are not uncommon). Of course, in doing so, the therapist abandons the opportunity to help the patient understand the perceived necessity to cast the therapist in that helpless role.

The key concept underlying that alternative approach is the "therapeutic split" between transference object and therapeutic observer. It will be useful to review the main ideas. The therapist must continuously cultivate the split in himself. He must be able to allow the patient to communicate his problems by molding the transference-object aspect of the therapist as he needs to. Only in that way can the patient reenact his conflicts in the transference to a useful degree.

At the same time, the therapist must keep part of himself split off, uninvolved in the transference reenactment, and thus able to observe the interaction between the patient and the transference figure compassionately from various vantage points. Chiefly, the therapist will attempt to view the interaction from over the patient's shoulder, as best he can, in order to view the transference figure as the patient sees him. From this vantage point, the therapist can empathize with the patient's fears and his need for the defensiveness he expresses in the resistance. Since the patient who is resisting is preoccupied with defending himself against threat, the therapist will want to assist him by empathizing with him in his difficulty with the transference figure, not by educating, cajoling, or scolding him out of his "unreasonable" attitude (Schlesinger, 1981a).

The alternative way I am proposing—to go with the resistance rather than oppose it—may sound paradoxical, but it is derived from the larger view of psychotherapy as a process and the general principles that "the patient is always right": to begin where the patient is, to facilitate the expression of what the patient is trying to say, to work from the surface, to deal with defense against affects and with affects before everything else, and to encourage the patient to be as active as possible in his treatment. Going with the resistance answers each of these requirements and permits a sympathetic exploration of the resistance, its sources in unconscious transference fantasy, and its precipitants in the proximal events of the psychotherapy. In the course of this process, the patient also will have an opportunity to test the current reality of the unconscious fantasy and the necessity for his defensiveness. It is thus an advantage that much of the interpretive work in this approach can be done by the patient, and much of it can be done while remaining in the patient's metaphor (Schlesinger, 1981b).

Transference and Metaphor

Let us examine the strategy of going with the resistance when defense is couched in metaphorical communication that also expresses the patient's resistance against recognizing his involvement in transference. From the vantage point of the transference, the advice to "go with the resistance" could be paraphrased as "Stay in the metaphor." For example:

> A therapist described an incident near the beginning of the treatment of a young man whom he did not regard as particularly "psychologically minded" and who was getting progressively more dissatisfied with his treatment. Although the therapist believed he was being very active in helping the patient, the patient did not experience the therapist's behavior that way and felt he was expected to "do all the work" while the therapist "just sat there." The therapist felt that the patient had one foot out the door, and was afraid the patient might become so irritated as to quit.
>
> In the course of this hour, the patient lapsed into a disgusted silence. After a while he said that he had to tell the therapist a story about something that happened to him just the other day.
>
> At his job he has been very angry with his boss, who pushes him and everyone else around. He feels he wants to speak up to his boss, but, after all, the guy is the boss and he has the right to act like one. But he sure would like to tell him off.

Later the therapist told his supervisor that he tried to "interpret" the patient's story and succeeded in showing him a series of correspondences that finally led the patient to agree that he probably had been trying to say something about the therapist, although this grudging acknowledgment had no particular effect on his mood, attitude, or anything else.

In presenting this case, the therapist did not notice that the differences between the "story" and the patient's overt feelings about the therapy and the therapist were even more impressive than the similarities. Whereas he was complaining that the therapist was inactive and silent and made him do all the talking, his complaint about the boss was that he was so authoritarian that the patient was afraid to speak up at all. Although it seems a safe assumption that the patient's story expressed and made use of transference, a direct correspondence is not all that obvious.

One might infer that the patient would like to make the same complaint about the therapist as he does about his boss, that he feels pushed around; but the therapist's behavior does not seem sufficiently to justify this complaint. Perhaps that is why the patient is so silent. Perhaps this "story" permits the patient to make his complaint without violating his sense of reality.

To follow the advice implied in this analysis of the situation, it might have been useful for the therapist, first of all, to facilitate the patient's willingness to express his irritation with the therapist, verbally within the metaphor about his boss. He could then empathize with the displaced expression of transference rather than attempting to "interpret it" in the sense of "translating it," that is, rather than removing the disguise as a first step. Note that this advice is based on the premise that the patient is always right, that the therapist's first task is to facilitate what the patient is trying to say, that the therapist should address the affect and defenses against expressing it, and to stay on the surface. If the therapist had been able to use all this advice, the interchange with the patient might have gone as follows:

T: It must be galling not to be able to tell your boss what you think.

P: Yes, I get so mad I feel like quitting, and I would if I didn't need the job. Sometimes I feel it's not worth it. A man shouldn't have to put up with that.

T: If a man can't speak up when he wants to, he may not feel like a man.

P: That's right! I quit the last job I had when I began to feel that way. I wish I could afford to do the same thing now. [Patient looks pensive and is silent, his thoughts seeming to be elsewhere.]

T: Something about what you just said makes you a bit thoughtful.

P: Yes, I was just wondering about another job that was offered to me, but I didn't take it because that boss also looked like he might be trouble.

T: I guess each time you get into a new situation you have to wonder whether the boss will make trouble for you. [Patient looks thoughtful again but not withdrawn.] I guess you could hardly help but wonder if the same thing might happen here in your therapy.

P: Yes, I have—I do. I am irritated and worried. It hasn't happened yet, but I feel it is going to and I can hardly sit still expecting you to land on me. I am so jumpy.

This constructed continuation of the example demonstrates that the patient can be helped to communicate through metaphor that both defends against and expresses transference. In this instance, as is frequently the case, the communicative possibilities of the metaphor and of transference, and their adaptive significance, are more impressive than their resistive implications and are essential to the therapeutic process. As the patient is helped to communicate about his "bosses" through the metaphor, he also has the opportunity to hear himself and thus to begin to wonder about (that is, to interpret) the meaning of what he is telling the therapist. At the end of this constructed example he is much closer to being able to tell the therapist directly about his fears about what might happen in the therapy situation.

The constructed example also illustrates a useful technique in working with metaphor. The therapist couched his interventions in what I call "umbrella" statements. These are empathic statements that do not repeat exactly what the patient said but are slightly more general in their construction. They can be taken to refer to a class of persons that also includes the analyst and are just general enough to include events beyond the particulars of the patient's story. This approach has several advantages. The main one is that it facilitates the patient's telling of the story and encourages elaboration. Moreover, it has diagnostic value: by listening to what comes next, the therapist can discover how ready the patient is to consider the transference implications of his story. Where does the patient go next? Does he come up with more instances from his daily life, or do his associations perhaps turn to the past? Does the patient pause and look uncomfortable and perhaps change the subject, suggesting that he suddenly sensed that he has been saying more than he had realized and might be expressing feelings about the therapist in his story? Therapists who work with young children will appreciate the parallel between this advice and how one helps children continue to tell their stories through play.

The commonest reason for a patient to lapse into metaphor is the presence of more or less unconscious transference feelings against which he is defending. In general, it is a sound technical stance for the therapist to facilitate the patient's communicating through metaphor as long as the patient seems to be able to communicate more freely in that way and as long as the metaphor seems capable of bringing in the therapeutic situation allusively. By listening to and facilitating the expression of the metaphor—another version of going with the resistance—the therapist can also learn more about the nature of the transference that is hinted at as well as the reasons for defending against it. Thus, he may arrive at a much better position to help the patient understand what is going on.

To put it another way, imagine the transference and metaphor to be on more or less parallel paths. But as long as the paths are only a little distance apart and continue parallel with each other, there is no great advantage in insisting that the patient use one path if, for some reason, he finds it easier to use the other one. As he continues down his preferred path, that is, as long as he can avoid recognizing the allusions to the therapist, he is able to communicate indirectly while also maintaining the measure of defense he needs. Sooner or later the patient will notice that what he has been saying in metaphor also applies to the therapist. Thus, by his speaking metaphorically, the patient's tolerance for more direct communication may improve and his defensiveness may lessen. Usually, however, as I have illustrated, the patient's increased readiness for more direct communication is signaled first by a more open expression of defensiveness.

7

Dreams
Royal Road or Scenic Route?

The Use of Dreams in Psychoanalysis and Psychotherapy

The meaning of dreams has been identified almost entirely with psychoanalysis. Hardly any other form of treatment (including the therapies derived from psychoanalysis) pay special attention to dreams. But even psychoanalysis, which in its earliest years laid heavy stress on dream analysis, seems to have put it aside. More recently, there has been a mild revival of interest in dreams in psychoanalysis (e.g., Fliess, 1953).

Before considering the potential use of dreams in psychotherapy, let us look briefly at the history of the use of dreams in psychoanalysis. We may then be better able to understand the early, deep, and widespread interest in dreams as the "royal road to the unconscious," the later falling off of interest, and the more recent revival of interest. Several catch-phrases can serve as landmarks in this brief review. The first I have already mentioned—"the royal road to the unconscious." The second is "ego psychology." And last is "the widening scope of psychoanalysis." Each of these phrases encapsulates a piece of the history of our field. Each can also help us to map the shifting pattern of interest in the dream.

The Royal Road

The sweep of the image of the "royal road" tells of its centrality in early psychoanalysis. The royal road, the king's highway, led straight to the seat of government. Similarly, dreams were viewed as the most direct and the easiest way to the unconscious. If one knew the "secret of the dream," one knew everything worth knowing. The earliest examples of cure by psychoanalysis included many accounts in which dream analysis figured but only a few in which the analysis of dreams was the chief mode of therapeutic activity. But, remember, it was one of Freud's major discoveries that dreams (1900), jokes (1905), symptoms (1894, 1895b), and parapraxes (1901) all had a common structure. Each could be understood as "the return of the repressed," the expression of an unconscious wish, its disguised fulfillment, and the ensuing consequences. The first flush of enthusiasm about these discoveries was fueled by early therapeutic successes. Interpreting wishes seemed to lead to the removal of symptoms. Sadly, or happily, depending on your point of view, it was not always that simple.

The secret of the dream had been revealed to Freud and with it much of the secret of neurosis. But human personality turned out to be terribly complicated, and much of psychopathology, whether of neurosis, character, or the major psychoses proved resistant to therapeutic effort. It often seemed easy enough to understand a dream wish or the meaning of a symptom, but that was not enough to change the chronic recycling patterns of behavior, the deep disturbances of affect, and the slippage in the structure of the personality itself. Perhaps all that dreams can tell us about uniquely is the underlying wishes, a discouraging thought.

You will recall that the earliest popular notion of dream analysis made almost exclusive use of Freud's (1900) discovery of the difference between the latent and the manifest content of a dream. The manifest content, the story of the dream as the patient told it, was to be cracked like the shell of a nut in order to expose the valuable kernel, the latent content. The latent content, the dream thought, contained the wish. But the wish, as we have seen, turned out to have only limited therapeutic significance when taken by itself.

Recall also that this earliest conception of the therapeutic use of dreams made use of only part of Freud's initial discoveries. I believe it was Freud's most important insight that what is significant about dreaming is not the wish but the dream work, the complicated processes by means of which the unconscious wish, in disguised form, finds hallucinatory gratification. The metamorphosis of the wish and the consequences of attempting to gratify it, resulting eventually in the dream story as we come to hear about it, are far more important than the wish itself. After all, how many different wishes are there?

At the level of wishes, we are all more alike than different. But the reasons that make any wish especially salient right now, and that make it unacceptable right now to some other aspect of our personality are potentially differentiating. How we recognize the conflicts inherent in the dream, how opportunities are made for concealment, disguise, and expression, why we remember this dream rather than another, and why we tell it just now—in these matters lie our individuality.

But there was reason even in those heady days to look under the lamppost for what was lost in the darkness. It is much easier to find the wish than to unravel the dream work. Often, when a task proves more difficult than anticipated, pride may suggest that perhaps it isn't worth doing. But there are other reasons to consider that the arduous task of so-called complete dream interpretation might not be worth doing.

Recall the "dream-specimen" of psychoanalysis, the "Irma" dream (Freud, 1900). Freud's associations went off in all directions and each association had the capacity to give rise to new lines of association (Erikson, 1954). To protect his privacy, Freud told us only a portion of his associations. Recall also how much time even this incomplete analysis took and that Freud was eager to plumb the mysteries of the dream. Some of our patients also begin with such eagerness but soon seem to lose interest in pursuing the dream further when they find their privacy too much compromised. We may wonder, therefore, in the interest of cost-effectiveness, if this kind of exploration of a dream in depth is worth the patient's time and money. Are there perhaps easier ways to achieve therapeutic movement?

As the time requirements for thorough dream analysis became clearer, in part because of the recognition of resistance and transference, and as it became clear that dream analysis is no shortcut, the primacy of dream analysis tended to diminish. And so dreams came to be seen not as a royal road but, rather, as a twisting byway, interesting for those who prefer the scenic route but not suitable for through traffic. Dreams seemed to lose their status as a special and the most important way for the unconscious to reveal itself and became just one more way.

The earliest of the developments I described were paralleled by other important and painful discoveries about the durability of neurosis. With the discoveries of transference and resistance and the problems of character and secondary gain, psychoanalysis came to be seen not as a time-limited venture that could be accomplished during a summer vacation by walking around the lake a few times with Freud, but as an increasingly lengthy process requiring daily attendance and going on indefinitely, perhaps even interminably. And paying careful attention to dreams did not seem to speed up matters. These sad discoveries were also paralleled by the growing awareness that insight did not always seem to be enough to guarantee "cure."

Ego Psychology

To augment our understanding of the changing place of dreams in psychotherapy, we have to alter our view of some basic psychoanalytic concepts, including resistance, transference, and interpretation. We commonly hear these and other concepts that are essential to psychotherapy used in static ways that are alien both to the clinical facts and to the spirit of psychotherapy as a process. We hear resistance spoken of as something a patient *has;* that transference is either present or not; and that interpretation is an event, the act of delivering a translation of psychic contents to the patient. As I have argued in the preceding chapters, I think it essential to redefine these concepts as processes, in terms more congenial to an overall view of psychoanalysis and psychotherapy as processes. And, recall, the term process implies that whatever is under consideration has time as an important dimension.

Viewing interpretation, including dream interpretation, as a process implies that achieving understanding or insight and structural change occurs as one works with a patient's resistance, not simply against it. As one does so, one facilitates the patient's working-through and assimilating the material of interpretation. This general working principle in psychoanalytic and psychotherapeutic technique derives from Freud's (1900) early recognition of the importance of the dream work but was not generally well appreciated until the advent of the school of thought we now call ego psychology. It is a point of view as applicable to dreams as to any other kind of patient material.

The major implication for changes in point of view that are summarized in the term ego psychology is that interpretation is not an event that takes place all at once, occupying only the time it takes the analyst to voice his conviction about what the patient "really means." Rather, interpretation consists of augmenting or enriching the patient's understanding of his own behavior, including his intrapsychic behavior, his thinking, feeling, imagining, and dreaming. Interpretation is not merely a matter of translation, of substituting one meaning for another, reductionistically telling the patient, "What you really mean is . . ." Rather, interpretation says, in effect, "In addition to *x* you also feel *y*," and, not infrequently, "It is hard to feel both *x* and *y* at the same time."

The process of interpretation has come to involve not just *what* the patient thinks and what he also means by what he thinks, but also *how* he thinks and *when* he thinks it, that is, What is the *function* of thinking "x" *right now*? Interpretation is not something that the analyst does to or for the patient but, rather, something he does *with* the patient. The patient's activity is essential not only for its own sake but also because the patient's response to the analyst's activity provides important information to the analyst that helps to guide his next intervention. It follows that interpretation is never finished, never complete. There is no obvious end to the interpretive process. One can always add more to one's understanding, and by the same token, one can be satisfied for the moment with less than full understanding—whatever full understanding might mean.

Thus the model of an interpretation as delivering an ultimate truth in the form of a blinding revelation is foreign to the concept of interpretation as a process. By looking at interpretation as a process, we can be content to deal with small portions of insight—partial versions of an alternative way of looking at things. As one offers a single idea to the patient and the patient hears it, reflects on it, possibly objects to it, and associates to it, he eventually adds to it. The analyst, in turn, observes this process of working-through the new idea and is then in a position to modify it or add to it himself. It thus may well be that the patient is the one who offers the final—that is, final for the moment—version of the interpretation. From this vantage point, one can see how the processes of interpretation and working-through overlap considerably.

The Widening Scope

This brings us to the third catch-phrase, "the widening scope of psychoanalysis." Even before psychoanalysts seemed to run out of "classical" neurotics to treat, some of the more venturesome of them began to realize that it was not only the neurotics, categorically defined, who could benefit from psychoanalytic treatment. If psychoanalysis could admit us to the deepest recesses of human beings, would we not have access to people's most mysterious activities, the acts of creativity, and to the bizarre experiences of the most tortured among us, borderline and psychotic persons? And what about children? Could we perhaps not prevent neurosis with proper educational methods, or at least prevent adult breakdown by treating the "infantile neurosis" the first time around? And what about the miserable masses who could never afford the attention of psychoanalysts even if there were enough analysts to go around? Could we not, as Freud (1919) suggested, "alloy the pure gold of psychoanalysis with the copper of suggestion" to produce an effective therapy at less expense?

Thus began the application of psychoanalytic principles to the development of psychotherapies suitable for children, psychotics, borderlines, and addicts that has led to the scene we have today. At last count there were reported to be something close to 200 brand-named psychotherapies, mostly derived directly or indirectly from psychoanalysis (though a far smaller number admit it). But even those derived explicitly from other traditions, such as reflexology, would soon come to discover that their patients require them to rediscover what Freud discovered, the ubiquity of transference (1912b, 1915a) and resistance (1912b) or, to put it briefly, "the unconscious" (1915b).

Each of these therapies makes a claim for its right to exist on the basis of some improvement over psychoanalysis, typically greater cost-effectiveness by shortening duration of treatment or requiring less frequent visits or by abandoning free association. Since time and free association seem essential to dream (or any) interpretation as we know it, one might well ask the fateful question, "Is there any room for the use of dreams in a practical therapy?"

Let us consider the place of working with dreams as a practical matter in psychotherapy. Psychotherapy covers a wide range of activities from crisis intervention to something approximating psychoanalysis. What we can say about psychotherapy in this regard certainly applies as well to psychoanalysis. We can deal with that end of this continuum by stating that the closer a psychotherapy is to psychoanalysis in intent and procedure, the more that working with dreams will approximate what one would expect to find in a psychoanalysis. I have just begged the question, of course, for the proper place of working with dreams in psychoanalyses these days is not at all certain. At the other end of the continuum, crisis intervention, the issue of working with dreams hardly arises except when a dream itself precipitates the crisis.

But what about the more usual psychotherapy in which the patient is seen once a week or perhaps twice and in which the patient occasionally dreams, reports them, and is interested in working with dreams. Notice that I have begun to use the expression, "working with dreams" rather than "dream interpretation." I mean by this alternative formulation that there are useful things one can do with dreams in addition to, or instead of, interpreting them, that is, in the narrowest sense of identifying the wish. Dream interpretation, according to the technical model developed by Freud (1900), is based on his theory of dreams. In brief, Freud's view of the "purpose" of dreaming is to be the "guardian of sleep." If access to motility is blocked by sleep, disturbing unconscious wishes can safely be allowed hallucinatory fulfillment. The purposes of defense are maintained by requiring that the fulfillment of wishes be disguised. Thus, the manifest content, the dream as told, conceals within it latent dream thoughts, and within these can be found the dream wish, the representative of an instinctual impulse. The unfinished thoughts of the day, the day residues, fragments of which form the material of the dream, are seen somewhat like a ladder on which the dream wish can climb.

The dream work includes the processes of transformation and disguise that cloak the dream wish in a mantle of respectability. Thus, for Freud, the most successful dream is the one that is not remembered; it has served its purpose by preserving sleep. It is only the less successful ones that we hear about; the least successful are the ones from which the patient wakes up with anxiety. Dream interpretation was seen by Freud as not an end in itself but as a way of advancing the analysis when resistance is not too high. It does not pay to attempt a thoroughgoing analysis of a dream unless the patient's collaboration is assured, which implies that resistance is relatively low or, better, that his perceived need to defend himself is low

Depending on the talent and interest of the patient and the goals and timetable of the therapy, there is no reason why this model of dream interpretation would not serve for a time-limited psychotherapy about as well as for psychoanalysis.

Working with Dreams

The distinguishing feature of working with dreams is that its goal is not necessarily to discover the dream wish. As Freud (1900) noted, many aspects of dreaming are of high interest in addition to the dream wish:

1. The latent dream thought is a thought like any other, and, if understood, it can be placed in the continuity of consciousness, that is, of waking thought.
2. The day residues are particularly interesting because they represent "unfinished business," incomplete tasks, issues that would disturb sleep were they not permitted harmless quasi-discharge through the dream. The mechanisms of dream work, like ways of defending, are multifarious. But individual patients have a fairly narrow repertoire of them, and one soon comes to recognize the kinds of disguises used, the modes of representation, and the typical personages of the dream even if one is not always sure of what the play is about.
3. Working with dreams also can make use of such formal properties of dreaming as why this dream is remembered and told rather than others, and why it is told at this point in this therapeutic hour. That is, what is the told dream an association to, or what other story is the telling of a dream interrupting?

This contrast between working with dreams and classical dream interpretation is a matter of emphasis or degree. The operative word, classical, implies perhaps that the search for the dream-wish ought to be the central concern. In every other sense, working with dreams can be understood as classically interpretive in the best sense of the term, as enriching the meaning of the patient's experience.

Dream analysis, conceived of as the search for the dream-wish has more historical than practical importance. Now, more than 100 years after Freud's initial discoveries, we have a fair idea of what dream-wishes ordinarily are about. It may be less important in a practical therapy, for instance, to discover that a dream-wish involves homosexual submission to the father, for instance, than to know what the patient is experiencing and doing about it at this phase of his treatment. As in most other areas of treatment, it is the patient's relationship to his innermost wishes and fears, rather than the wishes and fears themselves, that define health and illness, adaptation and maladaptation, mastery and submission or vitiating avoidance.

Perhaps an example will make these issues clear and provide a springboard to consider such basic issues as the uses of both manifest and latent content, and reliance on incidental (free) associations as well as elicited ones.

> The patient, a woman in her early 30s, was in twice-a-week psychotherapy. Though she had not been explicitly encouraged to do so, the patient easily slipped into free association, so that from time to time the treatment has closely resembled a psychoanalysis. She had come because of a vague dissatisfaction with her current second marriage and "unexplainable" temper outbursts. She felt she had just about everything she had asked for from life, but it had no meaning.
>
> The dream occurred during her husband's absence from home on business. She had been surprised to receive a telephone call from a man she had not seen in many years. In grade school, she had a crush on him and, after a while, in a juvenile way, he had reciprocated. They had not seen each other since high school. Now, 20 years later, her "dream man" had reentered her life. She arranged to see him at his hotel to "renew acquaintances" and spent most of the night with him.
>
> She reported that she had felt shocked and thrilled at the phone call, apprehension and excitement as she planned to meet him. She was deliriously happy during their encounter. What is more, she felt no guilt, which surprised her inasmuch as fidelity in marriage has been an important moral commitment for her. Her first reported dream occurred several days after this event.
>
> She related the dream as follows:
>
> "I was at home at night. The children were asleep. I had the vague sense that somebody was trying to get in. I was alarmed, cautious.

I tried to remember if I had locked all the doors and windows. I wondered if I should wake my husband but wasn't sure he was there. She wasn't sure what "they" might be after. Money they could have, along with anything else, as long as they didn't hurt the children. There was a vague feeling of apprehensiveness that remained after I awakened."

The patient was interested in the dream and could see in it elements of her recent experience. She was alone then; she had felt apprehensive about what she might do when reunited with her old boyfriend. Her associations then ran to the rapid play of thoughts that followed the telephone call: What would happen if she actually let herself have an affair? Suppose her husband found out. It would hurt the children; she might even lose the children. But, if nobody knew, would she ever have to tell her husband?

These were thoughts she had not reported previously. Only as associations to the dream could she tell the therapist of her temptation and apprehensiveness. Her associations suggested to the therapist that perhaps it was he, as well as the husband, who had been betrayed by the affair. The therapist, in his own associations, recalled incidents from the patient's childhood that the patient did not allude to at this time. As the patient worked with the dream, she clung to the idea that its main value to her was to demonstrate her glorious sense of having been free of guilt, which she was happy to attribute to the success of her treatment and the skill of the therapist.

Only gradually did it become clear that this was not the whole story. She kept returning to the dream imagery of the unknown potential intruder; her concern about whether or not she should alert her husband, if, in fact, he was even there; and her thought that it didn't much matter what happened to her as long as the children were not harmed. She began to see how, in her dream, she had converted an escapade in which she had engaged willingly, if in conflict, into a fearful scene in which she might have to sacrifice herself to an unknown intruder in order to save the children. If her husband had only been at home, they would all have been saved, her transgression would never have happened.

The major use of the dream at this point in therapy was to help the patient see what she had done with her experience, to see how she had dealt with the issues of blame, responsibility, guilt, and self-indulgence. Thus, although the therapist was aware that the dream also alluded to ancient events in the patient's life, he believed that the main therapeutic usefulness of exploring the dream was to focus the patient's attention on her present commitments rather than on the influence of old conflicts and patterns of resolution on her current life. The allusions to the transference, to the therapist as an intruder in the marriage and also as one who was betrayed, came into focus only after the patient was able to reconstruct her complicated effort to have her cake and eat it too.

Presenting a vignette of that kind risks telling too much and yet too little. Any imaginative clinician will read far more into the text of the dream and the context in which it occurred than I have presented. You will see far more that could have been done with the dream than I have offered. I mean only to illustrate that what, from the point of view of classical dream interpretation, could be called merely a "partial interpretation," was, from the point of view of this patient and her therapy at this time, all that might be necessary. One could say that the patient remembered the dream and told it to the therapist when she was ready to fill in the gap in her experience represented by her delighted freedom from guilt, until she was ready to enlarge her awareness of what the events had meant to her and was readier to take responsibility for her life with its pleasures, costs, and pains. There is, of course, no reason in principle why the interpretation of the dream could not have gone in other directions. But, in a practical therapy, whether psychotherapy or psychoanalysis, the governing principle is to do what best serves the treatment at a given moment rather than what might serve the theory.

It is also useful to recognize the similarity between working with the manifest dream content and working with metaphor in general. All clinicians are used to understanding the experiences patients describe as not only reflecting the events reported but as containing allusions to other events or even to character traits. Thus, in that patient's dream, the sense of being alone in the house at night and exposed to an external danger can be seen as expressing metaphorically her half-conscious awareness that, when her old friend called, there was no one to protect her against her own wish to fly to him.

The example also illustrates that we have an alternative to the idea that the "real analysis" of the dream would have to be a relentless search for the dream-wish. Rather, there are many possible approaches to the multiple meanings available. For instance, at one point, the major meaning of the dream to the patient was to see how she had dealt with her anger at her husband for being away at that critical time—it was his fault that she could not resist temptation. At another point, the meaning was that, if he had only been there, she could have awakened him and had him reassure her that there was "nothing outside" so that she and her infantile wishes could go back to sleep. At still another time she ruefully became aware that it was her dream and "she didn't have to dream it," keeping her husband not at hand. On the other hand, if he had been present in reality, she might have had to tell him who the telephone call was from and would not have had the chance to live out a childhood fantasy.

The opportunity to use our understanding of metaphoric communication is as applicable to working with dreams as to working with waking thoughts. In earlier chapters I stressed the importance of going with "the resistance," staying within the patient's metaphor as long as it is useful, a principle that now can be extended to working with dreams.

The ways in which the patient dealt with the dream material illustrates two other uses for working with dreams. First, the patient was reluctant to acknowledge during this phase of treatment that she had any feelings about the therapist other than being grateful for his help. She regarded him as a person who had a professional interest in her and nothing more. She could not understand patients who "fell in love with their analyst."

Working with this dream and associating to the various meanings of "the intruder," on one hand, and the missing husband, or "guardian" on the other, she became aware of feelings toward the therapist. She recalled with some embarrassment little "fugitive thoughts," such as wondering what the therapist was like when he was with other people, specifically other women, wondering what it would be like to be his friend, and, in one unguarded moment, what it would be like to be married to him. On the other hand, she recalled wondering in the moments following the exciting phone call and the rapid play of fantasies about what might happen, how she could possibly tell the therapist about it. For a moment, that thought had almost dissuaded her from going ahead. Thus, telling the dream and working with it also served as a means of coming to terms with the idea that the patient was involved with the therapist in multiple ways. It is as if the dream "told on" the patient. Of course, it did not do that until the patient was ready to tell on herself.

Another use of the dream was to help the patient recognize that, whatever else the dream was, it was a product of her imagination, though she felt as if she were the passive observer and possible victim of its events. The dream was her construction, and she ultimately was responsible for its content and the way it was put together. Assuming responsibility for the dream also was a step toward assuming responsibility for her other behavior. Thus, working with the dream also helped her integrate her wishes, fears, temptations, and prohibitions and led to her accepting the consequences of her behavior as an aspect of her continuing development.

In the circumstances of a dynamic psychotherapy a dream can be an additional—and a potentially valuable—means of external communication between patient and therapist and a means of internal communication between the patient and herself. Dreams are neither "the royal road" nor a bumpy detour. But do they have no special significance at all?

While dreams can be understood as consisting of thoughts like those of waking life, they differ from ordinary waking thought, fantasies, and daydreams in that they occur to the patient during sleep and seem to occur without conscious control. The dreamer is not usually aware of a dream's authorship as he is when fantasizing or daydreaming. Because dreams are silent about authorship, as are metaphors and as the example illustrates, working on dreams can be a fruitful avenue to exploring a patient's sense of responsibility for his wishes, actions, and inhibitions.

A dream as first told is generally not a definite construction. While the first account of a dream is generally fairly coherent, as the patient repeats the telling or reflects on it, it generally becomes obvious that in the dream, as initially recalled, all its aspects were not quite clear and the dream not well connected. As the patient tries to recreate the continuity of the dream story in successive retellings, he will generally add elements or indicate that certain parts were not as clear as he first thought or that something has just occurred to him that was really there in the first place. These added elements and areas of doubt speak to the operation of shifting resistance and often point to the more important elements of the dream in concealing the latent content and dream wish.

Another use of dreams is that, for not quite psychologically minded patients, it can provide a training ground for demonstrating the value of thinking about an "inner world" and of exploring it. Patients can be helped to become curious about themselves when they first come to see something about a dream that makes sense to them. In the same way, working with dreams helps patients to focus not only on *what* they think but on *how* they think, and it can be instructive, making plausible the idea that events can have several meanings, something to which an account of the day's events may not easily lend itself.

As illustrated in the foregoing example, dreams and the inferences drawn from them can have a kind of evidentiary or confirmatory function for a patient. The dream he relates may have the same structure as events he has been looking at in his life, the implications of which he is unwilling to accept. Seeing the same formal arrangements in a dream may help a patient gain conviction about the meaning of a persistent pattern of behavior. In this connection, the question of "compliant" dreams must be considered.

As noted, the opportunity to take responsibility for one's own productions is particularly striking when a dream, which first seems to be a visitation from outside, must be accepted as one's own creation. The general strategy of working with dreams in this way stems from the basic axiom of this book—that consciousness is in principle continuous. When we see gaps, ellipses, or interruptions, we know that the work of defense or censorship has been operating. One can construe the work of psychotherapy or psychoanalysis as understanding the nature and functions of an individual's modes of censoring, resisting, or defending in the service of restoring the continuity of consciousness. Thus, working with dreams in this way, as in working with other kinds of mental contents, has the basic function of filling in the gaps in waking thought.

In summary: A therapist's activity with regard to dreams consists, as with all other kinds of mental contents, essentially of listening, understanding, and conveying portions of his understanding to the patient at appropriate times and being guided in his next interventions by the patient's response to the earlier ones. The therapist's questions (that is, to himself) with regard to a dream as a mental content are "diagnostic" as I have been using the term and not different from questions about other forms of thought, such as:

1. Where does the dream fit in the patient's experience? At what point in the hour was it told?
2. What seems to be the reason for remembering this dream and for telling it when it was told?
3. What is clear and what is doubtful about the account of the dream? Which elements remain fixed and which shift during retelling and elaboration?
4. After the dream is told, what is the patient's attitude toward it? Is he eager to go on to something else? Is it left to the analyst to figure out if he wants to understand it? When the patient's attention wanders from the dream, where does it go?

In general the therapist will make the not unreasonable assumption that everything that occurs both before and after the telling of the dream can be regarded as an association to it. In the same way, the telling of a dream must be understood as an association to what has just preceded it in the session; that is, the dream was told when it was told because it "fit" with the material in which it was embedded.

8

From Listening To Interpretation

I once proposed (Schlesinger, 1995a), somewhat hyperbolically, that it does not really matter what an analyst says; it only matters what he says *next*. I intended this as a plea to view interpretation as a process rather than a unitary act. I hoped to stress the importance of following up by including the patient's expectable efforts at defense in the next step of the interpretation. This book, in many ways, is an extension of that plea.

Of course, what goes on in the analyst's mind prior to beginning an interpretive process also matters a great deal, and one might suppose that he would select judiciously what to say first from among the myriad possibilities that might come to mind. Actually, it is not at all that way. As most analysts will agree, while we may speak about the myriad possibilities after the fact, if one is attuned to the patient, only one thing comes to mind. Overstated as the mock advice might be, it does capture the essential idea of interpretation as a process rather than as an event. Before one interprets, one has to listen, and analytic listening is not a simple matter.

Hearing versus Listening

Freud's (1912a, 1913) instructions about listening were few, mainly an admonition to maintain an evenly hovering attention. Ferenczi (1919) detailed the complicated mental work demanded of the analyst as he gathers and sorts through information that could lead to the formulation of an interpretation.

Over the years, glosses drawn from the emphases of the times have been added, as from developments in the philosophy of science, leading to what might be called an "objectivist" position about listening (Ramzy, 1974), on one hand. On the other hand, we have a narrative or relational point of view, leading to what might be termed a "constructivist" position (Spence, 1982, 1984). Out of self psychology, Schwaber (1979) and Stolorow (1991) have focused on empathic listening and intersubjectivity. Object relations theorists have emphasized the importance of listening for themes of the unconscious fantasies of the patient and their power to shape countertransference. Some, such as Spence (1984), have rejected the ideal of "free floating attention" as theoretically wanting, not merely difficult to attain. In contrast, some others have insisted on the necessity of an even more rigorously controlled state of mind, complete emptiness.

Surface versus Depth

Many theorists give primacy to the "deeper," more unconscious, less accessible, and less determinable sources of information, which they consider properly psychoanalytic. But focusing on the depths, to the possible exclusion of the surface, carries with it the danger that what is distinctive about a person and the interaction of the moment with the analyst will be missed. For at the "deepest" level we all are more alike than not. My focus, therefore, is on processes closer to the surface of experience, but without detracting in the least from what is distinctively psychoanalytic about our interest in listening. What is importantly unconscious and determinative *at the moment*, though it may derive ultimately from sources far from consciousness, will generally be represented in more superficial manifestations that are accessible to the knowledgeable observer

Any social situation, including the analytic situation, permits manifold possibilities of understanding, depending on the nature of the parties involved, their hierarchy of long-range purposes, and their immediate intentions. One does not have to be an analyst to grasp the intricacies of relationship and intention displayed at a cocktail party. But the enjoyment of social complexity, and the delicious sense that one understands much that the speakers intend to stay safely hidden in the open, is available mainly to the casual, uninvolved observer. Being involved tends to focus one's attention. For the analyst, the paradoxical problem is how to be involved and remain uninvolved at the same time.

Before we consider how the enormous range of information available to an analyst condenses into a single line of understanding, and perhaps into an interpretation, it will be useful first to describe how information enters the analyst's mind. We may assume that information arises from three sources: first, from background knowledge the analyst has about life in general, psychopathology and psychoanalysis in particular, and from specific knowledge about the patient; second, from what the analyst currently hears from the patient (and sees); and, third, from what the analyst senses from his own cognitive, affective, and somatic reactions to the patient's conscious and unconscious communications and demands.

These three sources, while conceptually distinct, are not generally experienced separately in the moment of analyzing when things are going smoothly, but each may be focused on when the analyst is less than certain about what is going on, especially when information from the several channels seems discordant. The relative importance of these three sources will vary from time to time, but all three will contribute to every interpretation, as one only may be able to see in hindsight. Before we take up how these streams of information flow into an interpretation there are some other issues to consider.

The Position of the Analytic Listener

To capture the truth that an analyst gets only a second-hand view of a patient's psychological reality, Freud (1913) analogized the analyst to the passenger on the inside seat of a railway carriage who listens to his fellow on the window seat describe the passing scene. One could imagine the analyst/passenger remarking, "We seem to be on an odd voyage. I believe this is the third time you have described passing that church." Come to think of it, that is not a bad opening for an interpretive process.

But the analogy misses the special position of the analyst as an object of transference; that is, he is both audience for the story and part of the "view" being described. Neither does the analogy consider the purposes the patient might have in relating the view as he does or the kind of response he might expect from his seatmate. It does not take into account that the patient is compelled to describe the view in just that way.

Literature provides many examples of listener–actor pairs. Consider the loyal squire Sancho Panza, who accompanied Don Quixote on his adventures. He knew full well that the windmills were no more than that and that his Dulcinea had long since given up any pretense at maidenhood. But despite his clearer view of matters, he accepted his role as the Don's assistant and did not intrude his superior sense of reality on the Don's quixotic quest. To our everlasting gratitude, he permitted the story to be told in full. We might well recommend his attitude to the analyst, for the temptation to abandon the position of listener and intrude on the patient's futile quest so as to straighten him out can sometimes feel irresistible.

The Several Modes of Listening

To begin at the surface, then, listening is, in essence, a process of construction. Though we are trained to expect surprise and to listen also for what we don't expect to hear, we generally listen expectantly, which is to say, we listen from our previous experience as it informs the current context. When we listen in everyday life, we tend to take the context for granted as given by obvious external circumstances. For example, the shout, "Fire!" will have different, and instantly understood, meanings depending on whether we hear it in a crowded theater or on a target range. Most of the time, listening this way is highly efficient.

When parties in conversation know each other well, shortcuts develop that serve both to maintain contact and to transfer information efficiently. A kind of allusive, private language also may develop between analyst and patient who have been together for a while, and the analyst may understand, or may think he understands, which "him," "her," and "it" the patient is referring to.

The analyst/listener preparing for interpretation must learn to listen in several modes at once. For instance, he must listen "contextually," that is, in the ordinary mode of one familiar with the events so often described by the patient. It is a way that supports the patient's expectation of shared understandings so that the patient does not feel compelled to dwell on what should be self-evident. But consider, if the analyst remains in this mode and relies totally on the sense of familiarity, his mental set will facilitate the communication only of what is already at least partly known. The expectation of familiarity will tend to reduce the likelihood that he will hear elements new to that context or discordant with it. Such discordant items, of course, could be markers of change emerging in response to interpretation, on one hand, or of resistance to change, on the other hand. If the analyst listens only in the contextual mode, much of what is essential to analyzing might be missed. To follow up an interpretation requires that one has heard a new element in the patient's response, a marker of change or of resistance to change (Schlesinger, 1995a).

It is essential, therefore, that the analyst be able to listen in a way complementary to listening contextually. Perhaps we might refer to it, accurately if ungracefully, as listening decontextually. Or, since ordinary listening inevitably involves construction, this alternative mode might be thought of as listening deconstructively. Perhaps more usefully, it could be described as listening naively, attempting to listen without preconceptions, or listening literally rather than figuratively. When teaching, I try to capture the sense of this mode of listening by urging students to "cultivate stupidity," to try to listen simple-mindedly. Most would-be analysts have a difficult time not thinking ahead, not trying to "get there" before the patient does. It takes considerable experience before one becomes comfortable listening from a position a half-step behind the patient.

The analyst must also be able to listen for intention rather than for content, to listen for the patient's purposes in telling the story, as revealed in the way he tells it. He listens for, and experiences in signal quantities, the effect the patient wishes to have on him. In this third mode, one listens for transference as opposed to listening for content.

Listening contextually bears some relationship to what has been called listening empathically, but it is not a simple equation. Empathy is not defined by having the good feeling that one is "in tune" with a patient (Schlesinger, 1981a). Empathy can be considered the experiential midpoint of a dimension that has alienation at one pole and identification at the other. Empathy must therefore be thought of as particular rather than general in its application. We recognize that the patient is a complex system whose personality, by virtue of the "lytic" effects of the analytic situation, is "decomposed" to some degree. In the analytic situation, the patient is usually in a state of conflict and therefore speaks with several voices. The patient generally attempts to resolve the pain of feeling divided by externalizing at least one of the contending voices, the object of his inner dialogue in the analytic situation.

Thus, to listen to that patient empathically, we would first have to define the position from which we intend to listen. Do we mean to listen from a position slightly behind the patient, looking over his shoulder at the transference figure? Or do we take our position behind the transference figure looking toward the patient? Both vantages belong to the patient, of course, so it is not a matter of taking sides against the patient. We might also take a position equidistant between them, looking down on this odd conversation, as it were, and marvel at the mess "those two" have gotten themselves into. This is the position from which the "therapeutic ally" usually observes matters. One can speak empathically from any of these positions,

The desired state of "free floating attention" is one in which the analyst drifts effortlessly among the several modes, attending now in a mode dictated by transference expectations, and then in a more detached mode to appreciate the tug of transference without yielding to it. At another moment, he senses from his gut reaction what it feels like to have metamorphosed transiently into an unpalatable transference figure.

Theodore Reik (1949) popularized the notion of the psychoanalyst's "third ear." Reik meant, of course, an informed ear, one sophisticated at divining unconscious meanings. The analyst, of course, must be familiar with the ways the unconscious expresses itself in symbolism, allusion, opposites, metaphor, and the like, which was Reik's idea, and also familiar with the signs of mixed intentions that appear in the formal structure of language. The analyst should listen for these formal characteristics with a "second ear," while listening empathically with both of his natural ears, as well as to the "voice of the unconscious" with a metaphorical third ear.

The analyst must also attend to the process going on between himself and the patient. He will notice the "march" or progression of the successive positions he and the patient occupy in the unconscious fantasy, and he may also notice a rhythm that emerges as the patient alternates between unself-conscious story telling, or narrative, and self-conscious reflection, and perhaps directly addressing the analyst. We might think of the patient as alternating between free association and resistance, but that would give reflection a bad name and might imply that it would be better if the patient never came up for air, as it were. The interruptions of the narrative mode may signal that the "story" brushed against an aspect of the transference and aroused at least a signal of impending anxiety. Or the patient may have come to the end of the incident being described, and so the momentum of the story telling has slowed. I merely want to suggest at this point that, among the phenomena that deserve the analyst's attention, are the pace and the rhythm of the discourse.

The Hazards of Listening Too Intently

The foregoing points may seem obvious when put as a general argument, but they are far from obvious when one is in the analytic situation. The analyst must learn to tolerate a degree of ambiguity and, while recognizing that for the moment he is at sea, not feel impelled to do anything about it, such as reflexively ask the patient to clarify matters. The operative term here is "reflexively." Of course, there may be times when asking for clarification is entirely in order, just as there will be times when, having asked for clarification, the analyst then realizes that he has put his foot in it, that he had been invited or seduced into intruding and that, as an expression of transference, had complied.

Particularly when the analyst is fearful that he has gotten lost and does not understand what the patient is saying, he may tend to compensate by listening more closely. As the patient becomes vague or lapses into ambiguity, the anxious analyst may be carried along by the rhythms of speech and the superficial intent to communicate; he may follow the patient down the garden path and overlook that what the patient is saying has long since stopped making ordinary sense. He then will be unlikely to realize that this "non-sense" is a part of the message to the transference figure, who, perhaps, is not expected to understand. If he had managed to cultivate naiveté, he could have avoided falling wholly into the trap. He could have recognized that he (as transference figure) was "as usual" not understanding or perhaps should have become suspicious that the patient was withholding something in order to have him insist on finding it out.

When listening too intently in a contextual mode, the analyst may lapse into identification with the patient. Since he "knows" what the patient means to say, he may even jump ahead to get there first. The analyst should not want to get ahead of the patient; the possibility would not even occur to him as a naïve listener. The same moral applies to meanings that the patient leaves unclear, and elisions that beg to be filled in. As he drifts into identification with one of the conflicted sides of the patient the analyst may lose himself in the patient's story, wanting to take his part against the unfriendly outsiders, the uncaring "they" who habitually misunderstand him. Regressing with the patient in this way, the analyst may sample the gratifications of a maternal idyll. Enjoying a spurious sense of oneness with the patient, the analyst may feel that he understands the patient completely, in spite of the patient's vague communications.

Or the analyst might drift into a sort of "paranoid" transference if he feels alienated by the patient's "failure" to be clear, and yet he may be reluctant to interrupt and demand clarity lest he provoke the patient into justifiable rage. A full catalog of such hazards would be lengthy, but the governing principle is simple: if one listens uncritically from only a single vantage point, one may fail to notice that one has surrendered one's therapeutic split (Sterba, 1934) and risk colluding in the patient's defending.

From Listening to Interpretation

If listening is this complicated, we might suppose that planning to make use of the results of listening would be even more complicated. This deconstruction of the process of listening might lead one to expect that, if the analyst were able to shift ad lib among the several modes of listening, he would then be able to choose a highly discriminating approach, could arrive at a precise estimate of what is on the surface of the patient's experiencing, would have a sure grasp of the thrust and intensity of transference expectations, and could also assess the patient's readiness to make use of an intervention directed at the proper target. Possibly, but I have never met an analyst who claimed to be able to do it.

As I noted at the beginning of this chapter, this kind of involved cognitive process does *not* occur when we are with a patient. The misleading supposition arises from the artificial distinction I made between listening and understanding and the technical use of understanding in interpretation. While the distinctions are artificial, making them is heuristic. In supervision, for instance, having such a framework can facilitate making a conceptual and sequential post hoc analysis of the processes that might have led the analyst to propose to the patient the one (usually right) thing that came to mind as a "conjecture" about what he observed (Brenner, 1981) or to figure out how an unfitting thought came to the analyst's mind and why he was or was not able to inhibit it.

But, once again, more important than saying the one right thing is the ability to listen to the patient's response and then to shape the subsequent interventions to take account of that response (Schlesinger, 1995a).

The borders among the operations in listening are hardly as visible as my dissection of them might lead a novice to expect. In practice, the process generally is seamless; we slide from one mode of listening to another, shifting attention effortlessly and without deliberation from aspects of the patient's recital to observation of our own inner state, to the patient's genetic history. While I have referred to these processes collectively as the analyst's mind "at work," referring to the process as the analyst's mind "at play" would capture the sense more accurately. For, from time to time, the experienced analyst is able to approximate the state of freely floating attention that Freud (1923a) recommended to us. We may recognize this state as the free exercise of a natural function of the mind when it is not occupied with a task. But this capacity, seemingly as easy as falling off a log, is generally achievable only after extended practice designed to help us to unlearn the way we were all socialized to listen to each other in ordinary conversation (Schlesinger, 1994a).

An Aside on Analytic Listening

It might have seemed, from this discussion of listening, that a would-be analyst would need several more than the two ears nature gave him. Indeed, it is much easier for the supervisor who is once removed from the fray to attend to the multiple facets of the process. In part, of course, it is much easier to see the larger pattern of things than when one's nose is close to the ground. But, more important, the supervisor has the advantage of hearing about the process through the analyst's oral report, especially if the report is impromptu, not a reading of a written notes. While a good report will be a reasonably true reconstruction of the session, it is a condensed reconstruction and, like a sieve, presents in about five minutes the "solids" of the 50-minute analytic session. As a supervisor, I am continually amazed that, after presenting a beautiful summary of a session in which everything important has been laid out and the connections with previous sessions and the resonance with previous supervisory sessions is clear, the candidate will look blankly at me and wait to be told what is going on. How is it possible that the person who was there and communicated so well about it seems unaware of the significance of what he just said?

This phenomenon is quite dependable, but its full exploration belongs in a book on supervision. The main point for us to consider here is that the phenomenon is the same one we experience with a patient who tells us everything we need to know without being aware of its significance. Transference dumbs down both. The analyst must be at ease with the patient in order to split into transference object and therapeutic ally and observer and to allow his attention to fluctuate freely even as he has enjoined the patient. It is a skill that can and must be learned, and it is equally important for an analyst to recognize that the skill is essential also to learning in supervision. The analyst can be helped to understand that vulnerability to anxiety leads to projecting to the supervisor the power to understand. The candidate can recover his own ability to observe, listen, and understand as he tells his story to the supervisor just as he learned to do by becoming available to his patient.

9

The Process of Defense

Freud (1923) placed the responsibility for defense on the ego and described some of the methods by which the ego could defend itself, mainly from eruptions from within. Anna Freud (1936) assembled a list of the methods that seemed stable enough to be considered mechanisms of defense. This work became a major statement of what came to be called ego psychology, a departure from the earlier approach that focused mainly on the presumed operations of the id and stressed the power of drive and instinct.

Later writers have expanded on the manifold ways in which defense may be accomplished and have questioned if a short canonical list of defense mechanisms is a useful way to describe such complex matters. In that tradition, I propose that it is essential that the personality be able to defend itself from awareness which could range from inconvenient or unpleasant to dangerous, and that this purpose may make use of any of the talents and capacities available to the person. Some of these ways are so commonly used for defending that they have come to be identified as defense mechanisms. As this usage has hardened, many clinicians have overlooked the many other subtle and sometimes idiosyncratic methods through which defense and self-deception may be accomplished.[1]

The Role of the Intellect in the Process of Defense

To expand the argument that there are no "mechanisms" that are used solely for defense, I want to show how our ordinary intellectual capacities, particularly language skills, are used for defensive purposes as well as

[1] While browsing a used-book stall, I came across an article by Joseph Jaffe (1966) in a privately published volume. Jaffe discussed several of the ways in which the structure of language may be used for defense, including some I cover here, and I wish to acknowledge his priority.

for adaptation. When we think of how the intellect might be used in the service of defense, we probably would think first of "intellectualizing," and that pejorative term would likely call to mind talking extensively and boringly off the point or at a level of abstraction far from emotional significance. This most obvious use of the intellect for defensive purposes is by no means the most common, or the most useful, since any defense that calls attention to itself is to that extent less effective as a defense. As I mentioned when discussing resistance, the more subtle forms of defending, the ones that tend to escape our notice, operate synergistically and effectively with adaptation. These more subtle forms are more interesting from a clinical point of view, as well as more informative about how the mind works in general (Schlesinger, 1981b).

To lead into how we use for defending the cognitive functions that serve language, a review of some of the assumptions that underlie ordinary discourse is in order. These assumptions are so ingrained that we do not even think about them unless communication fails. Consider the initial moments of an encounter between doctor and patient. As in all social encounters, the first moments will be given over to establishing who the other person is and to establishing that the common language and the ordinary "rules" of discourse will be used. The clinician will want to determine initially whether the new patient is "cooperative," at least that he is willing to use language communicatively as opposed to tendentiously or defensively.

These same issues arise in social conversations, but unless our partner is "off the wall," we will overlook minor departures from expectation in the interest of promoting a relaxed interchange. In the consulting room, however, the analyst wants to discover quickly if the prospective patient is fearful and wants to avoid contact. Or perhaps the patient wants to shock, repel, attract, seduce, or charm the analyst or get the analyst to arouse such feelings in the patient. Ideally, the patient will be eager to tell his story so as to be better understood and thereby better understand himself, and then the initial process will hardly differ from an intimate social conversation.

We do not expect even the most cooperative patient to be able to communicate fully and honestly with the analyst any more than he can with himself. The analyst will listen and watch for the ways that the patient, while trying to tell his story, grossly or subtly alters the (more or less) agreed to premises on which the discourse began, including the very rules of language. Thus, the defensive purposes of the patient may be accomplished not only by (consciously or unconsciously) withholding or distorting information but, more commonly, less obviously, with less effort, and hence more effectively, by subtly changing the "rules", that is, the premises of discourse.

As I noted in the previous chapter, these defensive operations may go undetected if the analyst listens "too closely"; that is, if he is so intent on following the patient's story that he fails to notice the subtle changes in tense, or grammatical mode or voice, or violations of logic, or shifts in "rules" that reflect a momentary change in the patient's relationship to what he is saying or to the analyst, or generally to both (Schlesinger, 1994a).

To recap the argument advanced in Chapter 4, ordinary discourse can be viewed as consisting of two portions, a fixed portion and a variable portion The fixed portion embodies an "agreement," largely unspoken, about (1) the language to be used and the meaning of words; (2) who the parties are, their respective statuses, and their expectations of each other; and (3) where and when the discourse is expected to occur.

In ordinary discourse, the fixed portion can generally be assumed from the context. For instance, when we enter a shop, we assume, usually correctly, that the salesperson will listen to our request and attempt to complete an exchange of goods for money in a way that yields satisfaction for both of us—the salesperson hopes to make a sale in a way that creates or sustains good will. Many of you have probably seen the TV show "Candid Camera." Its humor comes from our seeing the discomfort of an unsuspecting person who unwittingly has been led into a situation in which one of the unstated, but essential, assumptions of discourse has been violated.

In one show, a shill posing as a customer used "double talk" in what seemed like a patient, careful, and even forgiving effort to explain his apparently simple request to the baffled salesperson. The salesperson increasingly felt incompetent and stupid, totally unable to grasp what this seemingly friendly customer was pretending to want to buy. The salesperson's error, of course, was to make the natural assumption that the "customer" was using language in a normal way, intending to communicate rather than to baffle.

A similar situation, but without the sadistically humorous overtones, occurs in the consulting room when the patient suddenly shifts from wanting to be understood to fearing that he will be understood. Rather than giving voice to that fear, he seems to continue to tell his story while becoming increasingly distant, vague, obscure, even incoherent. The baffled analyst may feel at sea, frustrated and angry, reluctant to interrupt to demand clarity because he believes he ought to understand, while sensing that the patient is becoming increasingly tense. Gradually, he becomes aware that the patient is desperately trying to defend himself against mounting anxiety: The clinical situation that was supposed to help the patient has begun to feel dangerous to him, and so he acts to reduce the anxiety by reducing the flow of information to the analyst-become-enemy. By his lack of clarity, he both defends himself and informs the analyst about this shift in the transference.

When we go to a doctor with a complaint, we are presumed to understand and agree to the sort of arrangements we will be expected to adhere to in order to obtain the service we need. These arrangements are part of the culturally defined role definitions of doctors and patients. The usual expectation is that these arrangements will hold unless changed by explicit and mutual agreement. For most of us, most of the time, both parties expect that appointments will be kept, that the fees charged will be paid, and the doctor will do as professionally indicated. The instrumental character of the professional relationship is an essential part of the arrangements, and by culturally sanctioned understanding, these arrangements are dissolved when the service has been given and paid for.

As I discussed in Chapter 4, the issues that pertain to the professional aspects of the analytic relationship are usually placed under the rubric of the structure of the treatment. In psychoanalysis and psychotherapy, the arrangements about money and time may seem settled by agreement at the beginning of the treatment; but soon the "structural" elements of money and time take on something of the character of a primitive "language," one that many patients find convenient for expressing matters of central concern themselves.

To return to my premises about ordinary social discourse, in addition to the "fixed" portion, which often enough comes unstuck, there is the properly variable portion of discourse, which consists merely of *What the patient chooses to talk about.*

It will seem obvious, if only from the relative amount of attention I have given to them, that I attach more weight to the fixed than to the variable portions. Indeed, for the purposes of this sketch of a formal analysis of the psychoanalytic situation, it does not matter what the patient chooses to talk about. It is not that the content of clinical discourse is unimportant—far from it. But we can generally depend on dynamic forces to assure that what is bothering the patient will be revealed in what he says and in the way he says it, no matter what he "chooses" to talk about. Unconsciously motivated contents can be counted on to emerge openly or in disguised form, and they will betray their presence reliably in disturbances of the patient's efforts to communicate within the stipulations of the "fixed" portion.

The "normal" expectation in ordinary social conversation, as well as in analytic conversation, is that a major aspect of the fixed portion, the nature of the relationship itself, as reflected in language, will remain fixed. When it does not remain fixed but is altered unilaterally, a disturbance of some kind will be evoked in the listener. Confusion, bafflement, bewilderment, anxiety, or mistrustful alerting are common responses.

Take, for example, the discomfort of a young woman who has been chatting casually with an older and unattractive man at a cocktail party. She fails to read correctly his shifting intentions until, newly emboldened and thinking he has "softened her up" sufficiently, he starts to make his move. From the young woman's point of view, the old man has unexpectedly altered the premises of the social situation.

Humor, especially that based on absurdity, makes extensive use of the device of altering premises unexpectedly. When invited to become the audience for a joke, of course, one prepares for a pleasant surprise. But humor encountered en passant, especially if one is the butt of it, can produce the jarring effect commonly described as "having the rug pulled out." A similar phenomenon occurs when a patient who has been harboring an unspoken wish that the analyst would "do something" becomes unbearably frustrated and, turning on the analyst, accuses him of misunderstanding, or of forgetting something, or of some other largely fancied malfeasance. The analyst may have been listening too closely, that is, taking the patient's words too literally. He therefore failed to pick up the signs of aggrieved discomfort that surely were present in subtle disturbances in the formal (that is, fixed) portions of the discourse, disturbances in application of the rules of language.

It is worth mentioning that the effect of a violation of the rules of discourse depends on the context. It depends on the persons and the situation. Take for instance the classic one-liner, "How many people work here?" The answer, "About half," is ironic and amusing when told in adult company, particularly among those cynically aware of the stereotypes about the working habits of some employees in organizations. If the questioner were a child, however, the answer would likely be heard as smart-alecky and a hurtful put-down. The assumption of a common base of experience and understanding is essential to the experience of humor. Without that common base, the joke falls flat and may be felt as cruel.

The Defensive Use of Intellectual Capacities

In most of the interesting and effective defensive operations, our patients make use of ordinary cognitive capacities required for spoken communication. Far from offering a new idea here, I take my theoretical departure from the earliest psychoanalytic writings. Recall that Freud (1894) offered his first psychological theory of psychopathology, one centered on the idea of defense.

While not stated in so many words, Freud's original idea of defense involved a process that he described variously as separation of ideas, dissociation of ideas, or splitting of consciousness in order to accomplish repression, which could be understood descriptively as unavailability to awareness (Herzog, 1991). Historically, the earliest use of the term splitting referred to a psychopathological process to account for "repression-defense." More recently it has also come to be used to refer to the capacity for simultaneously observing and participating in the clinical situation, whether by analyst or patient.

Until a better and more acceptable term appears, we will have to risk the confusion caused by the use of the term splitting to refer both to pathology and to an essential capacity the analyst must cultivate and encourage in the patient. I shall not dwell on the other face of the issue of defense that occupied Freud at that time, the fate of the charge of affect of warded-off ideas and the role of this affect in symptom formation. While Freud was attempting at that time to create a general psychology within the then contemporary view of normal science in which affect would be represented as "quantity," he made it clear that psychologically, or experientially, the intensity of an idea is reflected in its ability to command or demand associations. Freud realized that the presence of conflicting ideas, or of ideas of great intensity, is not always sufficient in itself to lead to symptom formation or to the outbreak of neurosis. He noted also that the ability of the mind to split, to divide consciousness, to separate or dissociate ideas is part of its normal capacity. He believed that pathological outcome depends on other factors (Freud, 1895b, 1926).[2]

A clinical approach to defense (and resistance) can be derived from Freud's earliest view of some cognitive modes of defending. Jaffe (1966) offered a similar approach.

Isolation

If one were planning to mount a psychological defensive operation within the metaphor of a military campaign, one could phrase the problem as, "How can we hide the presence of an unwelcome idea with minimum effort and with the least disruption of adaptation and communication?"

[2]As Holzman noted in his preface to Herzog's (1991) illuminating monograph, Freud's earliest view, that psychopathology results from the unsatisfactory, reality-flouting attempt at resolution of intrapsychic conflict, is far closer and in important ways is even more advanced than the accounts of these same issues offered by modern cognitive science, which has yet to include in its purview the role of affects and motives in perception and memory.

The way of defending that Freud (1894) called "isolation" is ideally suited for this purpose. While Freud thought it characteristic mainly of the obsessional neurotic, it is in fact essential to all of us in our daily lives. Elaborating on this method of defending when advancing his new theory of anxiety, Freud (1926) referred to it as "motor isolation."

He observed that it is not necessary to blot out an unwelcome idea by repressing it; the purpose of defense can be accomplished more easily merely by separating portions of the idea that belong together. So long as the components of a thought are not contiguous, they do not have the emotional impact they would have if the thought were properly organized. In dissected form, each of its elements can safely be allowed access to consciousness. The isolation can be accomplished in various ways; in the motor sense that Freud identified, it is accomplished by interpolating an act of some kind between the elements of the idea. The act need not be gross or conspicuous; a gesture of the hand, a lift of the eyebrow, a change of inflection—nearly anything will do. Like the critical mass of uranium in an atom bomb, the total mass of ideation remains innocuous as long as the dangerous particles are prevented from touching each other.

The passage of time can serve as well as parsing by a motor act to accomplish the defensive purpose. By pausing momentarily between elements of an idea, or separating them by other ideas, or even by a "by the way," it is possible to allow noxious ideas to be expressed without having to become aware of having voiced them. Perhaps even more important, one needn't become aware that one "owns" them or has to feel responsible for them. The method also permits expression of contradictory or incompatible ideas. Both sides of a conflict may be expressed in this way, at a considerable saving of defensive "energy," one would presume, without even having to face the fact that one is in conflict.

A common approach of young clinicians to noticing that a patient has voiced contradictory ideas only a paragraph apart is to "confront" the patient with the contradiction. This technique is effective in evoking consternation, the patient generally feeling he has been "caught off base." Occasionally, however, when the patient's need for defense is low, or when the relationship is particularly strong, the analyst's offering the patient a description of the sequence of behavior he has just observed may lead to curiosity and useful insight.

An analyst who is aware of the nature of the isolation defense and its function has, however, another avenue of approach. He can call to the patient's attention the subtle way in which the patient is attempting to deal with a potentially or actually troublesome issue, for example, his mixed feelings about an important matter. It is possible to arouse the patient's interest in how his mind works without arousing the additional defensiveness that generally follows when one feels, as it were, that one has had one's nose rubbed in a mistake. As in other contexts, showing the patient what he is doing for himself (in positive terms), rather than what he is failing to do or is doing wrongly or badly (in negative terms), can be a less jarring way of accomplishing the therapeutic purpose. This first step will be followed later by observing that such defensive behavior is at the behest of anxiety in the face of internal conflict. Here is a clinical example:

> The patient was a young woman, a high school teacher, who by dint of very hard work had made a successful career. She had been abused emotionally and physically as a child and the experience left her with a sense of "not owning her life," that it was on loan to her and could be taken back at any time. She married an older man, an insurance salesman, who was jealous of her career, which, he felt, deprived him of her full attention. Spitefully, he devalued her and her work at every opportunity.
>
> When in reporting an incident of being verbally abused, she spoke with appropriate indignation at the beginning of the story, but the indignation faded just at the point where a listener might expect her to mention taking some effective counteraction, especially since, as she reported matters, she saw so clearly what was happening. When the analyst commented on her "fading out" when she might have described having taking some action, the patient responded as if criticized. She said, in an aggrieved tone, "But I told him to stop abusing me. He just wouldn't." She switched instantly to talking about her childhood.
>
> "This is nothing," she said, "Mother was so paranoid about Father, and I was always in the middle. I wasn't the target of Mother's rage, only the messenger of bad tidings who got hit for bringing the bad news. But I wasn't really the target."
>
> The analyst commented, "It sounds as if it would be all right to be abused by Mother, since you were aware you weren't really the target." (The analyst chose to stay in the metaphor of the mother, but the implication of his comment was that in the same way she felt it was "all right" to be abused by her husband and to be criticized by the analyst.)
>
> The patient was silent for a moment and, showing that she had heard the implication for the incident with her husband, said softly, "It's not really all right, but you know if I stand up to him he attacks my mental health, and then I feel, since there's a grain of truth in what he says, I'm forced to agree."

The analyst responded, "Then if you're abused you can't really complain because you're not really the target. But, if you do complain, your complaining provides the evidence that you're really crazy and therefore deserve to be the target of abuse."

Again silent for a bit, the patient said, "It doesn't sound logical when you say it, but it seems to make sense when I'm in the middle of it."

Putting together in one sentence the two ideas that the patient had kept separated—that to be punished although innocent was preferable to complaining, which would serve to justify being abused, permitted the patient to examine the cultivated illogic that kept her powerless in that situation.

I mean here merely to illustrate the defensive use of a capacity to separate related portions of an idea, not to offer a complete dynamic account of the patient's difficulties or even of that transaction.

An Emphatic Form of Denial

Clinicians have long been aware that commonplace verbal formulae that tend to pass unnoticed in everyday conversation may have special significance when heard in the clinic. For instance, "To tell the truth," "My real feelings are," "Let me be frank with you," and such are taken as mannerisms and are not generally registered by ordinary listeners. As MacKinnon and Michels (1971) remind us, they may tell the clinician that the patient has something to hide and is denying it.

Analysts, too, will understand that a protestation of honesty may well signal that the speaker doubts that what he just said or is about to say will be, or ought to be, believed. But it seems to me more interesting to consider how peculiar, but ubiquitous, it is to hide one's intentions from another by flagging them. We may wonder if that is really the primary motive for using these formulae. I think the situation is more complicated than that. If the analyst only understood that the patient is denying and hiding something, it would seem to lead the misguided clinician to the mistaken technical obligation to "call" the patient on it, to confront him with a breach of the therapeutic contract—to demand that he tell truly, tell all, and at once! Indeed, that is what alert beginners do when they see such a "flag." Interesting, and sometimes useful, sequelae may follow.

But consider the probability that at times the formulae may not, in the first place, represent an attempt to keep something from the analyst, but may represent a difficulty the patient is having in being straight with himself. As the patient tries to speak with one voice about matters that are deeply conflicting and about which mixed feelings interfere with each other, he hears at least faint echoes of his divided self. Nevertheless, he still feels compelled to expose and at the same time disguise the conflict from himself and the listener.

The process is similar to arriving at the compromises represented by symptoms, character structure, and dreams. While hearing and, to some extent, grasping that he is trying to straddle diverging positions, he attempts to assure the analyst that he is aware that there may be more than one version of what he is saying. But he would like to convince himself and the analyst that *this* spoken version, at least for the moment, is the correct one. The analyst will understand that the larger version, the one that includes both revelation and denial, is the correct one in that it exposes the conflict the patient suffers from.

This way of understanding things leads us to consider alternative interventions. Rather than only betraying that he is hiding and denying something, the patient may be getting closer to being able to give up defending a formerly monolithic position and now may be more open to a richer and more complicated experience of himself. One might say to such a patient, who has just assured us of the truth of his most recent utterance, "I think you just had a glimpse of a quite different view of matters, one that does not fit with what you just told me." Or, "As you were telling me that, I think another feeling intruded, one that you felt compelled to put out of mind."

This illustration sketches the kind of process that often ensues when a patient's defensiveness is lessening, at which time the analyst is more likely to see such ad hoc defenses, which reveal even more than they hide. The example also illustrates how difficult it is to draw clear boundaries around categories of psychological response. Clearly, with such little formulae that "protest too much," the intellect is being used for defensive purposes and one can assign them, as do MacKinnon and Michels (1971) to the canonical category of "denial." But one could also argue that the more interesting venue is interpersonal or object relational, and the example could be presented in such a way as to underscore this aspect. But the operations involved in defending make use of the ingredients of *everyday language*. They do not require us to invoke special "mechanisms" to describe and explain them.

This last point has a semantic aspect that I would like to make explicit. As Schafer (1976) has pointed out so clearly, our tendency to reify and name processes has caused much mischief in clinical discourse and in theorizing. My last statement could be paraphrased as, "Defending does not require defense mechanisms." But, first of all, that would be a statement about usage, and it implies that it is easier to think clearly about psychological matters if one avoids making nouns out of the verbs we need to describe processes, as we have also done, for instance, in our common usage of transference, resistance and analysis.

Deleting or Replacing Conjunctions

We have seen in Chapter 6 that defending can be accomplished by separating the critical elements of an idea. Separating also can be accomplished by removing or changing the conjunctions that tell us the nature of the relationship between words and phrases. Again, it is not necessary to raise a barrier of repression to avoid feeling the power of an idea; it is enough to alter the connection between the key words so as to conceal from ourselves the meaning of our thoughts and even the thoughts themselves. It may even be enough merely to substitute a "softer" conjunction for a more specific one and blur unwelcome meaning with little obvious disturbance of the continuity of communication.

Unless the analyst is alert to how the ordinary properties of language and the conventions of polite discourse can be used effectively for defensive purposes, such instances may pass unnoticed. Thus, two ideas that *should* be connected with a "but" or an "in spite of" may be allowed to dangle unconnected or to be joined by the weaker "and." The interpretive response, of course, is to suggest what the replaced conjunction might have been. By way of example: a patient described a longed-for, but painful, visit by saying, "I went home . . . and my father was there" when the more precise sense would have been conveyed if the patient had said "in spite of the fact that my father was there, I went home" or perhaps ". . . because my father was there."

Suddenly Changing the Topic

When a patient changes the topic in the middle of a sentence, with or without the interpolation of "by the way," or "that makes me think of . . .," or "Did I forget to tell you that . . . ," he effectively breaks off one line of thought and seduces the listener to follow the new line and forget the abandoned one. Pausing and then changing the topic is another common way of isolating. Frequently, a patient will stop in the middle of an idea, pause pregnantly, and then go on either with the same idea or with another, with no mention of what went on during the pause. Again, the interpretive intervention is obvious.

Vagueness and Indefinite Reference

Lapsing into vagueness is a common and efficient means of defending without disrupting smooth communication. At ticklish moments you may hear a patient lapse into vagueness by judiciously using pronouns to replace nouns and names or by slipping into the passive voice. Just at the moment when you long for precision—Who did it? What was the "it" that was done?—the story becomes fuzzy.

The use of a pronoun in ordinary discourse assumes a mutual understanding of the referent. When the need for defense is high, however, patients will refer to understanding "it" or what to do about "it." When the pronoun is distant from the possible referent, or is equidistant from several plausible referents, sense is obscured. Using "it" in this way often is accompanied by slipping into the passive voice or an impersonal construction, and the sense of agency as well as the sense of personal responsibility are surrendered. The defensive purpose is accomplished through diffusion of meaning. For instance, a patient ended a detailed account of the violent argument that had led to the breakup with her boyfriend with a weary and resigned coda, "And that's the way it happened." Everything had been detailed up to the denouement, but left vague was who had made matters irretrievable by doing or saying what.

The Uses of "Knowing"

The term intellectualizing generally brings to mind a patient who reports his thoughts about life events in tedious detail, but without appropriate feeling. While that is certainly an example of the use of the intellect for defensive purposes, it is hardly the most common use or the clinically most important one.

More common, and also more important, are the occasions when a patient says, "I know that" or "I see that," but with the clear intention to prevent the analyst from commenting further on the matter. The analyst, in turn, is likely to feel a bit put down or disarmed, for, if the patient "sees it," what would be the point in telling him what he already knows? For example:

> The patient had been carrying on about the stupidity of his boss and his ingratitude—no matter what the patient did, it was not enough and was not appreciated. If only the boss were to recognize his good work and his loyalty, he wouldn't feel so mistreated and be so bitter. These themes mirrored closely the reproaches the patient had also made about the analyst, who was aware of the displacement. Nevertheless, he bided his time and allowed the patient to continue. Before long, and almost without breaking stride, the patient glanced toward the analyst and angrily said, "I know that what I am saying could refer to matters here as well" and continued with his tirade against the boss. The analyst sat back,

feeling deflated. The interpretation he was about to give the patient now seemed superfluous, and he felt he had nothing much to offer.

This example is representative of the broad category of intellectualizing defenses. In the first place, even though the patient was aware, or nearly aware, of the wish to hold the analyst off, his angry tone of voice as he declared "I know . . . ," suggests that he had in mind an image of the analyst about to interrupt him. We may presume that, at the moment, he was not able to accept what came to his mind and defended against that thought by insisting that he was only thinking about what the analyst was thinking and feared that he would insist on being included, an implication that the patient had noticed but, for the moment at least, did not want to face.

We might assume that one reason for his reluctance was that it is easier to denounce an absent boss than to tell off the analyst directly and easier also to denounce either one rather than perhaps, face how much he denounced and criticized himself. At the very least, we may assume that he could more easily justify carrying on about the boss, who is actually an authority figure, without offending his sense of reality. He had an important and impassioned statement to make about the transference figure and, by implication, about some figure in his genetic past; and he was able to do it safely, at the moment, by way of a convenient displacement object.

Discussing this incident under the heading of defense should not distract us from noting that the defensive operation was also an expressive operation. It enabled the patient to tell the analyst something important, provided only that he did not have to say it directly. I think it generally advisable to allow a patient to do so and to reserve until later the unveiling of the displacement figure to reveal the analyst and, ultimately, the father of childhood. As his anger expends itself and defensiveness lessens, the patient will likely have less need for this defensive operation, at which point he will be able to see through the veil himself.

That, in fact, is what happened when he said so truculently, "I know," though he was not quite ready to collaborate with the analyst about it. The patient is likely to get to it in his own time, and allowing the patient to do so both promotes his activity in analyzing and encourages his self-analytic capacity. The patient's doing so does not preclude the analyst from taking up the matter again later, if he feels a need to. Recall also that both the boss and the present-day father are also transference figures, scapegoats for enacted messages that could not have been delivered directly to the objects of ancient times. In this instance, too, the patient, suspecting rightly that the analyst was about to intrude on his tirade, was able to act, safely, on his wish to thwart the transference object.

That example of intellectualizing defense makes use of the capacity to listen to oneself while speaking, an ability vital to our self-monitoring to be certain we are saying precisely what we intend. This capacity indeed serves clarity of expression, but it does not always serve it perfectly. We tend to listen to ourselves selectively and with considerable tolerance for our habitual style of speaking. If you have ever listened to a recording of yourself speaking extemporaneously, you will recall the shock of hearing how many false starts you made, how often you began a sentence with one idea and ended it with another.

The defensive self-monitoring in the example is different in some respects from the supervision by the grammarian resident in our head who tries to keep our syntax from scrambling. Self-monitoring seems to entail the patient's awareness of a parallel process of silent, perhaps nonverbal conversation with the analyst, one that threatens to become salient and interrupt the consciously "intended" speech. The analyst who is fantasized as about to intrude must be fended off and kept from interrupting. Like the boss, he does not appreciate how hard the patient is working. Yet the patient knows that the impatient analyst does have a point, if only he would wait until a more opportune time to make it! It is common knowledge that the self-monitoring capacity that is so forgiving of our own slovenly speech, peculiar accent, and shaky logic is acutely attuned to the intentions of the object assigned the role of the "other" in our conflict of the moment. Thus we have another instance suggesting that a theory of defense requires a theory of object relationships as well as a theory of cognition.

Shifting Emphasis

One of the most common and also most subtle forms of defending consists in shifting emphasis from one idea to another or shifting emphasis from one element in a sentence to another. The shift generally is from an important element to a seemingly less important or trivial one. For instance, the emphasis might be shifted from the major clause to the minor or preparatory clause, as commonly occurs in jokes. Recall the long story about welcoming a friend home from a voyage with condolences on the death of his dog. And when was that? When the house burned down. And how did the house burn down? When your mother had her stroke and left the stove unattended! Another joke that shows the process more succinctly tells about the man who went to his ophthalmologist to complain, "Every morning, just before I vomit, my eyes begin to water."

This form of defending is particularly efficient in that it does not require the "brute force" of repressing or even suppressing. Everything is laid out in the open; what is concealed is, like the "purloined letter," under one's nose, in plain sight.

Generalizing

A particularly effective form of intellectualizing defense is accomplished through the timely use of generalization; timely in that it is used when concreteness, personalizing, and specificity would be expected. Generalizing, or conceptualizing, is so commonly used in everyday conversation that a clinician may not be attentive to its subtle, defensive potentialities during sessions. Consider the following example:

> The patient had been describing a particularly acerbic family exchange in which her daughter blew up at her. The patient presented the story as if she were blameless. When the analyst pointed out correctly that she had "lighted the match" that started the explosion, the patient, after a moment's reflection, agreed, saying, "Yes, I do that," and went on with her story.

The simple shift from the expected, "I did that," to "I do that," is all it took to accomplish the defending. The generalization carried no emotional impact other than, one might suspect, satisfaction at having her power recognized, and some smugness at having gotten away with it. But her response implied that no tension had been generated within her; no problem with her behavior was recognized and, hence, no impetus to change. Statements with an appropriate feeling of regret or ruefulness, such as, "Yes, I'm afraid I did do that," or the shocked query, "Did I do that?" could have implied some desire for a different role in the story, and readiness to take responsibility for what she had done.

"Private Language"

We are all familiar with the way that two persons in a continuing relationship, whether a marriage or a psychoanalysis, tend to develop a "private language"; their private language develops as a function of the length of time they have been together and the degree of personal familiarity and shared interests or communality between them. Allusions, cryptic references, meaningful sighs, and gestures are prominent in a private vocabulary, and their meaning in that special context is not easily understood by outsiders, whether nosy neighbors, in the case of the marriage, or analytic supervisors, in the case of the analysis.

In supervision, when a candidate does not comment on the patient's idiom or translate it spontaneously and the supervisor feels impelled to ask, "What did the patient mean?" it may be an indicator that the analyst and patient have developed a common understanding of unsaid things that may amount to a private language. More important, the candidate's failure to translate unasked, for the benefit of the supervisor, may reveal that the candidate is less than optimally aware of the nature and degree of his involvement with the patient and therefore does not realize that the supervisor, an "outsider," could not be expected to understand. I have found that this phenomenon is a fairly dependable indicator that the analytic relationship may be drifting from serving the analytic purpose toward becoming an end in itself.

When the analytic relationship has developed in this way, certain themes tend to recur frequently. They generally are recounted in the same way and most often are offered to be understood in the same way, usually as paradigmatic of "that's the way life is." Only a "precious few" perhaps can understand and comfort each other, but there is really nothing to be done about it, and it is pointless to try. It would be illusory and cruel to expect me to change. "That's just the way things are." If the analyst has bought into this view of the patient, he is likely to present it to the supervisor in the same way, an example of parallel process.

Private language, which is well suited to composing messages of calm or resentful resignation, is less well suited to composing "get well" messages. It is not a language for greeting cards, other than perhaps the "modern," cynical ones. Definitely thorny issues in a patient's life are seldom referred to in this language. Or they are alluded to only in the elliptical mode I referred to earlier, using use of pronouns and vague references to signal tacit agreement that, since we have no better way of dealing with it, it is best left unmentioned.

Clearly, the appearance of a private language is a sign of mutual adaptation. It can be useful in cementing a marriage. But, while it is also a natural and "normal" development in an analysis, if unrecognized and unexamined it can grow into a shared defensive posture and eventually lead to a stalemate. This outcome is especially likely if the analyst either does not recognize that a private language has developed or values it for its own sake; and if he is not aware of its capacity to serve adaptation rather than analysis and allows it to smooth out the essential degree of mild tension (Schafer, 1982; Schlesinger, 1989) that marks the progressing analysis. In the interest of "not making waves," important issues are left unexplored ("it might hurt the alliance") and the unmentionable is not mentioned.

A common motive for such collusion is a form of analyst transference in which the listening analyst drifts into becoming a projection of the patient, as it were, by identifying with the patient as he tries to explain himself to a possibly unfriendly outsider. Filling in for the patient, "knowing" what must have been meant and therefore "understanding" what was not actually said, and sympathizing with the patient's difficulty in making himself understood to the transference object can amount to joining the patient in resisting (Schlesinger, 1994b). Here is a clinical example:

> The patient was a successful attorney in a large law firm who, while deft and direct at work, had developed in his personal life a practice of getting what he wanted deviously and uncertainly. The most difficult question for him to answer was what he "really wants to do." He sought cues to what he ought to want to do, that is, what he thought nameless others thought would be the correct thing for him to want to do. He was afraid that any choice he made would be criticized, since it would inevitably turn out that, despite agonizing effort, he had "once again" made the wrong choice. He would temporize and not choose, but, rather, would wait until someone decided for him or until the opportunity to choose had passed. Despite this self-defeating stance, he has had a long and prosperous career, which, he explained, came about simply because he arranged to hang out in the places where people were selected for various educational and vocational openings. Thus he had never had to choose a course and push himself forward directly.
>
> Investigation of this behavior pattern revealed a number of deeply held convictions that were not part of the patient's conscious belief system. For instance, though he was highly intellectual, reasonably informed in many areas and well read in some, he had come to see that in his personal life his guiding principle was that it is best not to know. Not knowing, or at least not being convinced that he knew, protected him from an unknown danger. If he knew what he wanted, he would have to act on that knowledge; and, since he was certain that his choice would be wrong, to contemplate acting stimulated great anxiety. He would rather forgo the uncertain pleasure of getting his way in favor of the drab safety of drifting without choosing.
>
> He reluctantly acknowledged that this belief system was at odds with his more general stance that the more you know, the more freedom you have. In his personal life, he actually was guided by the certainty that the more he knew, the less freedom he would have. He developed a pattern of thought avoidance marked by an anxious, wincing expression when he came too close to uncomfortable insight. If he were to know, he would have to act;

and the very next thing he might come to know might be the critical idea that would push him over the edge into a cascade of irretrievable actions.

A similar mechanism kept him from directly going after pleasure. He, in fact, had a good capacity for enjoyment and took pleasure in a wide variety of experiences, but only if they occurred as a "side effect." He was afraid to go after pleasure directly; anything he decided in the interest of promoting enjoyment would magically be converted into an obligation to continue to do it indefinitely. Like "The Sorcerer's Apprentice," he would not be able to stop. To prevent this dire outcome, he had to defy and oppose the "invoked obligation" to enjoy himself just as he would oppose any other onerous imposition. Then he would submit resentfully, grumbling all the way and with no memory of having started out to have fun.

This pattern of defense also kept him from becoming fully aware that he enjoyed working at his profession. Although he would report dragging himself reluctantly to work, he often enough mentioned, "by the way," that he had been praised for what he did. If the analyst commented that it sounded as if he had enjoyed an encounter at work, though his account had begun as usual with a sigh of exasperation, he would react with guilty surprise. Only slowly was he able to recapture the glimmering awareness of pleasure in sensing his mastery of the situation and his enjoyment when others recognized his competence.

Just as slowly did he come to note spontaneously, and with some surprise, that he had always thought it a terrible burden to have to read law journals. He had caught himself reading a law journal with enjoyment and instantly thought there was something wrong. He interrupted himself with the thought, "Do you really want to read this now?" This challenging query had the outward form of an invitation to consider even more enjoyable alternatives. But, in effect, it was not an "opener" but a "closer." It was a "nag," spoken in the weary intonations of his mother's voice. Designed to spoil his nascent pleasure, it reminded him that, since he had chosen to do it, it would turn out to be wrong and potentially humiliating. The query was intended not to open the gates to more pleasure but, rather, to divert him from the pleasure he was now enjoying lest he fall into some unnamed danger. Better to restore the bland safety of the desireless status quo ante.

You have probably been struck by the similarity between these convoluted ways of defending against anxiety and the symptomatic patterns of thought and action in an obsessive-compulsive neurosis. They are indeed designed along the same plan, and yet this patient had none of the other stigmata of that disorder. He was not plagued by obsessional thoughts or driven to compulsive practices. Indeed, he had a quite practical turn of mind and quickly saw to the heart of problems in the application of law that had baffled his colleagues. He was not a worrier and could act swiftly, correctly, compassionately, and decisively on behalf of others, if not on his own behalf.

One's personality uses for defensive purposes the same intellectual and moral capacities that establish and maintain a highly effective level of adaptation. I allude, in particular, to the early developmental achievement to be able to hold more than one idea in mind at a time. A later development, essential to most higher order functioning, is the ability to entertain antithetical and contradictory ideas without pain and without acting on any of them. We recognize the lack of this capacity in young children, who cannot tell a lie, who cannot know one thing and say another, and in even younger children, who cannot hear the word "candy" spoken without instantly looking for it and demanding some. We sense that the capacity is not sufficiently developed in somewhat older children, or even in literal-minded adults, who cannot appreciate certain subtle forms of humor, such as humor that requires the ability to relish a story told with a straight face, since, to enjoy the humor, listeners must envision the inevitably comical consequences that logically follow from the absurd premises.

When used defensively, the capacity to entertain antithetical ideas is employed straightforwardly. The defensive ends are accomplished by deviously assuming the truth of a false, or at least untested, premise. In the last example, the patient believed, "If I choose, I will choose wrong, or if I want it, I will have to keep wanting it forever." An intellectually sophisticated patient will be able recount daily efforts to avoid mythic disaster so persuasively that the listener will be dissuaded from questioning the premises that require such complicated maneuvering. An interesting sidelight is the way such extravagant efforts at defending acquire the sanction of moral necessity.

Here is another variety of defensive use of the capacity to explore alternatives logically. Occasionally, a patient will respond to an interpretation that has had some emotional impact by dealing first with its logical consequences. Rather than allowing the interpretation to "work" on him, and possibly letting it evoke associations that might establish its relevance to him personally, the patient typically takes a pseudoactive stance of reasonableness. He assumes the truth of the analyst's remarks rather than envisioning what the consequences might be if, indeed, they happen to be true. The patient is more willing to assume the truth of the interpretation than to test it to discover whether or not it is true for him. The defensive maneuvers in these last several examples are much the same. They could be thought of as reflecting character resistances since they were embedded deeply and were made objects of scrutiny only with great difficulty.

10

On Therapeutic Activity

Activity and Passivity

Let us reconsider the term activity in connection with its seeming alternative, passivity. I hope the discussions in Chapters 1 and 3 have convinced you that the surgeon, who certainly is active as he operates on an oblivious patient, is a poor analogue for the analyst interacting with his patient. I suggested that the midwife offers a more useful one. Both the midwife and the analyst participate actively in their respective helping processes. The midwife, who during a delivery stands by, expectantly observing events, is not at all passive.

During most of childbirth or analysis, we could better describe the midwife or analyst as having a diagnostic and expectant attitude about what is going on. Each judiciously refrains from interfering unnecessarily and in this way allows the patient to do what only she can do. It is an active stance, even though the activity for the moment is mostly in the clinician's head and is expressed physically in restraint.

The analogy is much clearer if we imagine an emergency arising during a delivery while the midwife continues in the same noninterfering stance. Then we certainly would consider her to be actively mishandling the case. If she failed to do what was indicated, she would be considered an active participant in, and partly responsible for, any mischief that might result. In principle, it is the same for an analyst who fails to interpret when interpretation is indicated.

Incidentally, the proper antonym of activity is not passivity, but, rather, inactivity. There is little analytic use for the terms inactive or passive with reference to the analyst, for the analyst is always an active participant in the analytic process. Of course, the patient is always free to complain that the transference figure is frustratingly inactive or passive. That is another matter altogether.

In comparing the position of the analyst to that of the midwife, I implicitly approve the way the midwife stands by encouragingly. Is there any place in our technique for the analyst to hold such an encouraging attitude or even to encourage the patient more actively? Is encouragement ever necessary? Could it interfere with or be harmful to the analysis? Freud (1912a, 1915, 1919) recommended that the analyst be neutral, anonymous, and abstinent; and the last admonition seems to exclude encouragement. How do we understand these time-honored terms today? Consider the following illustration:

> Not long after the beginning of a session, when the patient paused after saying there were several things on her mind about what had occurred at the office the day before, the analyst took the pause as the occasion to tell the patient that he would like to change the time of her appointment next week. The patient agreed with a shrug and an OK.
>
> Resuming about events of the previous day, she commented ruefully but with lively interest that, once again she had allowed a colleague to take advantage of her "goodness." As she detailed the circumstances, the analyst could hear a possible resonance with her quiet acceptance of his announcement of a change in a session time. He did not comment about his inference directly but noted, in a tone of mild approval that she seemed to have become more aware of when she was imposed on and seemed to be clearer about how she felt about it. The patient nodded. After a moment of silence, she added, in a more aggrieved tone, that her colleague seemed to have no idea of how her demands inconvenienced her and seemed not to care how much trouble it took to accommodate her wishes.
>
> The analyst noted that she felt conflicted, wanting to please her colleague but also feeling some resentment that her compliance seemed to be taken for granted. Again the patient grunted her agreement and went over the same details, working through the sense of injustice she felt and what she might have done about it at the time. The analyst waited as the patient continued her mild tirade against her colleague. He observed that she was slowing down, becoming more vague.
>
> Then she broke off the topic altogether, seemed to shrink, and then pulled her arms in. The analyst guessed that the patient had had the bitter thought that neither did he give any thought to how inconvenient it might be for her to accommodate to his changing the time of her appointment. After an initial half-hearted protest about how good the analyst had been in accommodating to her needs and how she could not possibly justify being ungracious, she

was able to look at this darker side of the transference. In the same encouraging tone of voice, the analyst repeated his earlier comment about her growing awareness of how she had allowed herself to be imposed on. He added that she now could see that she could do something about it while it was happening rather than bemoaning it after the fact.

Coming to life, as it were, with increasing enthusiasm, she was able to draw together the events at work and what had just happened in the session and began to see that the analysis had gradually become a way for her to serve the analyst, rather than a way for her to be helped out of the character trap. From there, her associations led to the efforts she felt she had had to make to maintain her shaky position in her childhood family by becoming the reluctant Cinderella.

The analyst in that example listened for his implied presence as the transference figure in the patient's thoughts and tried to facilitate the fuller expression of her conflicted feelings within the metaphor of her office setting. The way the analyst first intervened implied approval that she was allowing herself to be aware of feeling imposed on *now*, even though "now" referred only to the storied events in her office. The sense of encouragement was conveyed mainly by the analyst's tone of voice when he commented on the way the patient was feeling at the moment, and it was incidental to the message of his intervention. Encouragement was also implicit in his comment about the patient's nascent awareness that she did not have to feel imposed on nor did she have to put up with it. And it was also present in the way he spoke acceptingly about the patient's uncomfortable discovery that she had been alluding unwittingly to the recent feeling of being imposed on by the analyst.

Such forms of implicit encouragement have a valuable function in analysis; the patient's tasks are difficult enough. After all, simply listening quietly (usually) implies acceptance of what the patient is doing. Seeing, or being helped to see, that the "analytic work" bears fruit, often immediate fruit, is one of the intrinsic rewards of engaging in the process. I do not think that these forms of implicit encouragement threaten a return to the era of "suggestion." On the other hand, I do believe that, if the analyst strains for an abstemious technique by trying to filter out any indication that he appreciates what the patient is trying to do, he may well signal to the patient that the analyst is uncomfortable about being seen as warmly human or that he considers the efforts unworthy of recognition, not good enough. The patient may regularly experience both encouragement and gratitude, but, if she feels the process is supposed to be "sterile," or if she has inferred that it might make the analyst uncomfortable to acknowledge those feelings, she may not voice them. Let us consider how these observations square with the few principles of technique left to us by Freud.

Neutrality

Does that case example meet the test of neutrality? Neutrality is misunderstood by some even today as requiring an analyst to strive for the emotional equivalent of the surgeon's sterile operative field. No matter how often it has been pointed out that the ideal of the objectively impersonal and masked surgeon in the operating room that Freud (1912a) once proposed is literally unattainable in the analytic situation, and is not even desirable, the ideal persists. Granted, a high degree of objectivity is essential for analyzing, but the objectivity must be in the context of deep concern for the patient.

A closer analogy for the desired neutrality would be the position of the judge in a courtroom. The judge presides over a trial, and her main function is to assure that the parties in conflict are treated equally under the law (Menninger and Holzman, 1973).

The systems point of view recognizes the inevitability of conflict in human life and that, for our patients, much of the time, conflict is the central fact of life. Respect for both sides implies, as it does for the judge, that we do not try to take over the conflict from the patient. Also, like the judge, the analyst does not permanently take the side of either contestant but is quick to take the side of either party when the other party fails to follow the "rules." For the analyst, who cannot rely on the opposing attorneys to object, this proviso means that he may speak for the legitimacy, or against the illegitimacy, of the outrageous or excessive claim of either party as the occasion requires. He does not allow one agency within the personality to beat up another but makes it clear through interpretation what the patient is doing to himself. The analyst makes the presence of conflict more obvious to the patient.

Was the analyst in that example neutral in this sense? He was by helping the patient to "own" the conflict instead of projecting one side of it to others and then accommodating to that constructed situation. But in all of his conduct, as far as the brief example permits the inference, he was *for* the patient. The general issue of neutrality must be considered in connection with the analyst's maintaining the therapeutic split (Sterba, 1934).

Anonymity

Many writers (e.g., Hoffman, 1983) have noted that the "blank screen" model of anonymity once put forth by Freud (1912a) is in practice unattainable; by striving for anonymity, the analyst may manage only to signal to the patient that there are aspects of himself he would prefer the patient not to see or know about and that the patient certainly should not inquire about—hardly an atmosphere conducive to discovering truth. Every analyst has known a patient who, having begun to evince curiosity about the analyst, stops himself, embarrassed, and says, "Excuse me, I forgot I am not supposed to ask questions." Patients generally do not need much encouragement to assume that their analysts would prefer not to be known; it is an easy transference from the earlier parental situation.

Still, analysts would do well to wonder how they might have contributed to such transference attributions. Unfortunately, like some parents of childhood, some analysts do indeed prefer that patients stay in their place, that they pretend not to notice what obviously is occurring or that they not be openly curious. They are supposed to be "good patients." If I may paraphrase an aphorism, just as "nice guys" don't win ball games, "good patients" don't get analyzed.

What can we say about the conduct of the analyst in the example with regard to anonymity? (Freud, 1912a). Clearly, he made no effort to hide his position in favor of the patient and her efforts to come to terms with her conflicts. But the example is too brief to inform us about his attitude toward more personal and less useful disclosure.

Abstinence

An offense against the principle of abstinence so stressed by Freud (1919), seems most likely to be raised by suggesting there might be a place for encouragement in the analytic situation. Supervisors often caution beginners about being overly friendly; they admonish them not to "feed the transference." If this advice were construed "as one should refrain from acting out in the countertransference," it would seem unexceptionable. But the devil is in the details. We need examples to help us distinguish a usefully encouraging attitude, with encouraging actions offered only as needed for analytic purposes, from acting out that serves the analyst's conscious or unconscious purposes rather than the patient's actual needs. A deliberately abstemious attitude would "feed the transference" at least as much as would an indulgent one (Schlesinger and Appelbaum, 2000).

The advice to abstain from feeding the transference is generally extended to exclude supporting the patient and merits the same criticism. Consider, how in an analysis can one avoid supporting the patient? The analytic situation itself, with its regular, closely spaced appointments and consistent atmosphere, is designed to support the patient so that he feels safe enough to regress.

For most analysands, the support intrinsic to the analytic situation is sufficient, and no special measures are needed. But for some patients, the need for additional support may arise occasionally, and for a few patients the need may extend for significant stretches of the analysis. (The measures intended for support consistent with analyzing are discussed further in Chapter 14; see also Schlesinger and Appelbaum, 2000).

Beyond the support built into the analytic situation, the major support an analyst provides is by interpreting accurately and in timely fashion what is going on with the patient. Every interpretation disturbs the status quo; it interrupts what is going on and reframes the patient's experience about it. If the patient is becoming increasingly anxious about what is coming up, the interpretation is likely to provide the cognitive and affective input necessary to deal with it. Old timers will remember that before neuroleptic agents were invented, we had to learn how to abort acute and dangerous regressions by interpreting the patient's rising panic.

There are times in analysis when it is necessary for the analyst to intercede on behalf of one agency of the personality when another agency is mistreating it. To use the language of the structural model, the analyst may have to support the ego against temptation from the id and subsequent punishment by the superego, or he may have to prevent tiny stirrings of desire in the id from being squashed. The proper question is not whether or not to support, but how. If the analyst keeps in mind that every interpretation has a general supportive effect in addition to any specific analytic effect, this question becomes moot (Schlesinger, 1969).

Because every interpretation also amounts to an intrusion into the patient's conflict, it is also not possible for the analyst to avoid disappointing one of the conflicting parties even as he accepts that his interpretation will incidentally offer support to the other. An old joke is apposite: The masochist begs, "Beat me." The sadist says, "No."

Silence Is Not Abstinence: The Loud Sound of Silence

Many candidates seem to come to their first case with a literal, not to say a fundamentalist, view of Freud's triad of anonymity, neutrality, and abstinence. For those candidates, these basic principles have been degraded into a single governing idea that could be expressed as: "Sound classical psychoanalytic technique is defined by what the analyst does *not* do." It follows, they seem to believe, that to keep quiet is always safest. Probably this last belief also draws support from the admonition to medical students, "If you don't know what to do, don't do anything," a version of the Hippocratic admonition, "In the first place, do no harm."

That sound medical advice does not fit the analytic situation without considerable adjustment. There certainly are times in analysis, as there are in life in general, when it is wiser to keep one's mouth shut. But in principle, and most of the time in practice, it is not possible for an analyst to avoid doing harm simply by keeping quiet. The analyst is an active participant in the process, silent or noisy, and he must therefore remain aware at all times of the part he is playing in the patient's dramatized recital. He is cast as an actor in the patient's drama whether or not he auditioned for the part and whether or not he enjoys playing it.

Most of the time, the transference role assigned to the analyst is distasteful to him, alien to his benign view of his character, and repugnant to his self-esteem. When one stops to think about it, it makes sense that this should be so; the fantasies about ancient relationships that generate most transference attributions are not populated by the kindly, benign, and nurturing figures we feel most comfortable being. A common reason for young analysts to prefer silence to the more effective participation the situation calls for is distaste for the role in which they have been cast in the reenactment of the patients' unconscious fantasy, and their more or less unconscious and silent repudiation of that role.

A more appropriate target as a violation of the principle of abstinence is the action (or inaction) an analyst might take to reject being cast as the "heavy." One such action occurs when an analyst "points out," ostensibly in an effort to aid the patient's reality testing, that he is "not really like that." The principle of abstinence should be understood as requiring that we neither attempt to modify the transference by indulging the patient nor mitigate unwelcome attributions either by changing one's behavior or by insisting on one's own view of self-presentation. The situation calls for interpreting. Expressed displeasure with one's assigned role by unwarranted silence could be understood as (counter)acting out.

In any event, undiscriminating silence is a poor proxy for sound technique; it is not a dependable expression of the principle of abstinence. Analyst's silences, when they are responses to patient's behavior rather than facilitative of the patient's associating, must be understood as actions, highly expressive but relatively inarticulate actions. One can easily imagine a circumstance when a patient is likely to experience an analyst's silence not as a neutral abstention but, rather, as an action taken against him by the transference figure. The analyst's silence might possibly signify rejection, humiliation, turning a deaf ear, or giving the cold shoulder. Or it might be construed as silent assent, covert approval; or it might imply the dismissive, "Do what you want. Just don't bother me." Again, the analyst-as-transference-figure participates whether he wants to or not, and he does not have a vote about the role the patient casts him in. The technical implication is that the analyst must listen for the patient's response to his silence, as well as to his speech, and consider when and how to interpret it.

The patient is especially likely to hear the analyst's silence as an action—perhaps deliberately and unjustifiably ignoring the patient—if he feels legitimately entitled to a vocal response, such as after asking a question or after making a deliberately outlandish or provocative statement. Then the patient is likely to take the analyst's silence as a deliberate intervention, a put-down. I do not advocate that to preclude the patient's jumping to that conclusion, an analyst necessarily answer questions in the same terms the patient posed them. But, the analyst should be prepared to take account of any explicit or implicit meaning a patient assigns to his behavior. Most of the time, the fact that a patient has suddenly turned to querying the analyst is more important, analytically, than what the query ostensibly is about. Thus, I do advocate distinguishing betweeen analysts' answering questions and responding to the act of questioning. The next chapter makes the necessity of this distinction clear.

11

Questioning, Con and Pro

How We Use Questions in Everyday Life

Those last thoughts may suggest that, for technical reasons, questioning may be risky for the therapist. Indeed, the thoughtless use of the questioning form can cause much misery. To lead into a discussion of how and why therapists use questioning as a technical tool and how to understand the meanings of patients' questions, it is useful to consider how we use questions in everyday life.

In daily life, we ask questions and use the questioning form (which often are not the same thing) for a variety of purposes in addition to obtaining information. Using the questioning form is so ingrained that we shift automatically from one usage to another without noticing that we are doing so and without taking account of the effect on the person addressed. In particular, we do not consider that the act of asking a question is inherently coercive in at least two senses.

First, the person asked a question will feel some obligation to respond. Of course, he may turn away from the questioner or openly refuse to answer. But in polite society, a question demands a response, an action, positive or negative. The person queried must take a stand if only, as when confronted by a panhandler, to pretend not to notice. Second, the questioner, by framing the question has also framed the answer, that is, has determined what sort of utterance will be responsive to the question. For instance, if one asks a stranger on the street, "What time is it?" one will generally get a polite and useful answer about the hour, not a comment about the weather. Even persons who guard their personal space and avoid eye contact in public will feel impelled to glance at their watches and give the information requested. Not to do so would seem a breach of expected social behavior and would be regarded as offensive.

While the so-called neutral question generally yields the ostensible desired response, a more personal question might not elicit one. To ask that same stranger his or her name, or any other personal information, would seem intrusive and would, under most circumstances, be ignored or rejected; these too are responsive actions. There are times, of course, when such personal questions will be answered, promptly and accurately, such as when one recognizes that the questioner has the power to require compliance: the traffic officer who stops one on the highway, the IRS, the judge in the courtroom, the parent of a young child. The point is that, beyond obtaining the information requested, the demand for information establishes the nature and degree of the power disparity between the parties.

In politically repressive societies, the most minor functionary has the right to demand immediate and truthful answers of the citizenry, and anyone who answers evasively, lies, or refuses to answer commits a serious offense. The right to question and the obligation to answer are emblematic of the tilted relationships between the "authorities" and the rest of society. Kafka (1925) in *The Trial* captured the terror of an ordinary man required to answer imponderable questions by questioners who do not listen to the answers; the questions were not intended to elicit information but only to intimidate K and make him feel in the wrong, guilty, and helpless.

Ordinary conversation is peppered with utterances that have the outward form of a question but that are not intended to be understood as a request for information or an action. Even the common and seemingly unexceptionable questions, "What time is it?" or "Do you have change for a dollar?" may also serve other, covert purposes. For instance, a man on the street has suddenly noticed that the woman beside him also waiting for the bus is uncommonly comely. After looking her up and down, he hesitates and then asks, "Excuse me, could you tell me what time it is?" We would understand that a likely purpose for the "innocent" question was a desire to strike up a conversation that might lead to more. It is likely too that the woman would quickly understand from the man's tone and manner that he is coming on to her and would be prepared either to accept the gambit or simply to tell him the time in a way that indicates he should get lost.

While all forms of verbal interaction may contain ambiguities or multiple senses, the questioning form is particularly liable to being burdened with multiple meanings that may not consciously be intended by the speaker. This ambiguity makes questioning in the clinic particularly problematic; the unintended meaning may predominate in the patient's mind and lead to undesired and unproductive behavior. It is incumbent on the clinician to be as clear as possible in his communications to patients, unless he intends, for good reasons, to be vague or ambiguous.

The following list is hardly comprehensive but will underscore the multipotentiality of the questioning form:

A Request for Information

The simple question, "Could you please tell me what time it is?" or "How do I get to Carnegie Hall?" seems straightforward enough, but it is governed by a deeply engrained social code that defines who is privileged to ask questions of what kind and of whom and under what circumstances. We are trained from childhood to answer polite questions politely. If a question is asked appropriately in an appropriate setting, we will tend to respond in the terms we suppose the questioner had in mind. We are not likely to object, though we may feel irritated if, in order to answer, we had to break off our own train of thought and enter the mind of the questioner. But we are not likely to complain. It is, after all, more efficient to answer the question and thus get rid of the questioner than to take up the issue of the imposition.

But sometimes getting an answer to this opening question emboldens the questioner to persist with more intrusive questions, and one finds that one has invited a sales pitch. To repeat, implicit in all questioning is an imposition of constraint over the listener; the question both makes a demand on the "time" of the other and establishes the terms of what will be acceptable as an answer. To comply, one must adopt the frame of reference of the questioner and organize one's response to fit what one infers to be the questioner's intention in asking. It is worth noting that in the clinic, we tend to judge the degree of disturbance of a patient, his level of socialization, and his social "appropriateness" by his ability and willingness to enter into the framework of our questions and to anticipate correctly our response to his answer.

As a Signal of Reassurance

Almost invariably, when introduced to another, we respond reflexively with the conventional formula, "How do you do?" to which the expected ritual response is, "Fine, thank you." The questioning form at the opening of acquaintanceship is intended not so much to gain information about the other's health or state of mind as, like a handshake, to assure the "stranger" that we are familiar with the customs of polite discourse and are prepared to abide by them, that we can be trusted not to offend without cause. The ritual response serves the same reassuring purpose. This use of the formulaic question–response mode is likely to persist as the two strangers probe to find out at minimal personal risk if they wish to engage further with each other. As each responds safely to the other and as mutual interest deepens and risks seem to diminish, they will proceed to self-initiated disclosures intended to deepen the relationship while inviting reciprocal disclosure. Alternatively, as interest flags in one or the other, the interaction can be broken off with minimum offense and pain. This scenario assumes that the two parties are of approximately the same age and status, though not necessarily the same sex, and hence initially are equally empowered in the prospective engagement.

From the way the clinician initiates or responds to the formulaic opening greeting, a new patient will instantly decide if it is safe to go ahead.

To Establish and Maintain a Stratified Relationship

The questioning form is commonly used to establish or confirm which of the parties has the right to ask questions and which has the obligation to answer but does not have the right to ask questions in return. In a formally stratified relationship, such as an employment interview, the applicant will expect to have to answer questions and will be diffident about querying the interviewer in return. The way the interview proceeds will depend on how interested the employer is in hiring and how eager the applicant is for a job. If the employer is eager to hire, he is likely to invite the applicant to ask questions as a way to award him status and to make the prospects at this company seem more attractive.

A more typical example of the use of questions to establish a status hierarchy occurs when one is stopped for a possible traffic offense. However polite and respectful the officer may be, the sense of constraint to answer pleasingly can be overpowering. When a relationship is just opening, in which the power relationship of the parties is not yet established, one party may attempt to achieve dominance by opening with questions in a voice that indicates the expectation to be answered as a matter of right. The other party may acquiesce to the arrogation of power by answering agreeably or even meekly. But if the prospective imbalance of power is unwelcome, the other party may challenge it directly or, more subtly, may answer matter-of-factly and, especially by answering slightly off the point, may signal nonacceptance of the arrogation of power, but not yet a wish to contend against it openly. The imposing form of questioning will be understood, in the first place, not as a request for information, but as a signal of the kind of relationship demanded by the questioner.

An interesting inversion of this usage occurs when a person, typically male and quite used to using the questioning form to establish his authority, refuses to ask for directions when traveling, although he badly needs the information. To ask a question under those circumstances would be a humiliating, unmanly confession of need.

The Rhetorical Question

The rhetorical question, of course, is one the speaker intends to answer himself. Such questions hold the listener's attention while the speaker pauses for effect; they are intended to lend weight to the about to be self-supplied answer. Verbal tics, such as "Do you know what I mean?" "You hear what I'm saying?" which so frequently punctuate the speech of some speakers, are mutually understood as not requiring a specific answer by either party. They may simply imply a wish to prevent interruption, to keep holding the floor while collecting one's thoughts, or they may express anxiety about whether or not one is getting across, or they may be a way of emphasizing the importance of what is being said to another who might not appreciate its high personal value. Note that in all these examples the questioning has imposed a degree of control over the thinking and behavior of the other. It may not seem a large extrapolation to propose that, wittingly or not, all utterances that use the form of the question involve an imposition of power over the other. Canetti (1962) has discussed this issue in general terms.

Expressing Deference

When presenting yourself as a supplicant or when addressing someone you assume to be a superior, you may put your ideas tentatively as questions, rather than as assertions, thus indicating your willingness to defer to the other. By questioning, rather than asserting, you can also express adherence to the code of "manners" that regards direct, affirmative speech as rude. Many families have an elderly "Aunt Minnie" who at table asks, "Would you like some gravy," when she would like you to pass it to her. To be sure, Aunt Minnie is accustomed by now to being out of step with the younger generation and only smiles politely at their amusement, which she still does not understand. She is only behaving according to the table manners she was taught—it isn't polite to ask directly for what you want; that would seem too crude, too direct, too grabby, too selfish. But, then, how to get more gravy? She must conceal the wish behind a seeming concern for the welfare of others, a harmless pretense, one even endearing in its transparency. Besides, it isn't altogether insincere, for when passed the gravy, Aunt Minnie invariably does offer it first to her neighbors before graciously accepting some from one of the incidental beneficiaries of her little subterfuge.

Showing Interest

In some circles, it is a customary expression of good manners to show or feign interest in the others in whose company one has been thrust by asking questions about what they "do," where they live, or whom they know. If the questioner is exceedingly well mannered, it may be difficult at first to discern whether the interest expressed is sincere or merely polite and whether it reflects a wish to know one better or merely to find out if one is worth knowing. This use of questioning, which may or may not be accompanied by parallel disclosures, may be seen as a continuation of the handshake, a way of testing out, in a controlled fashion and at minimum personal cost, if one would like to deepen the relationship. The answers are instantly evaluated toward that end, and the parallel disclosures may give away the results of the evaluation, for instance, "Where did you go to school?" "City College?" "Oh, my brother went to Harvard." On the other hand, such questioning may come to be expected as a sign of deserved interest; one can imagine having to comfort a teenager returning from a date distraught because, "He didn't even ask me any questions."

How We Use Questions in the Clinic

Each of these uses of questioning in social situations has its counterpart in the clinic, and it is useful to illustrate only a couple of them. When an analyst asks a question, he should be aware that the patient may respond to the form rather than the content and may experience the analyst as acting on him or against him, as defining or redefining the relationship between them. If the analyst is insensitive to these possibilities, mischief is likely to result.[1]

Beginning psychotherapists are especially likely to carry over into the clinic the social skills that have stood them well in daily life. Mostly these skills foster good manners and social ease and transfer very well. But some imports, in particular the uncritical use of the questioning form, may work against one's explicit intentions. Good therapeutic technique requires that the form and content of interventions reinforce each other, and especially that they not conflict. The various uses of questioning in social situations may also appear in the clinic.

The Defensive Use of Questioning

Much casual use of questioning by clinicians does not serve a technical aim but is intended unwittingly, like the deferential use of questioning in

[1] The problems of handling patients' questions and the use of questioning by the analyst are dealt with more fully by Olinick (1954, 1957). See also Dorpat (1996).

social situations, to serve one of the clinician's needs. For a young clinician, the typical auxiliary intention of shifting to is to provide "cover," to disguise that the therapist is uncertain about his clinical skills or his right to hold himself forth as a healer and that he is intimidated by the patient. He is fearful that the patient might see through his pretense and walk out. If the therapist shifts to asking a nonessential question, it could signal that he is at a loss about what to do next, or that he fears he might lose control of the therapeutic situation, or that he fears that the patient might object to the idea he is about to voice. For example:

> The therapist reported to the supervisor that he had interpreted the patient's behavior toward him as transference. The patient had been expressing her disdain for weak men by cataloging the frailties of all her acquaintances and intimates. The therapist could hear the metaphoric reference to him but was reluctant to address it. After a while, the patient paused, shrugged, and wearily changed the subject. The therapist thought he ought to make the link explicit; but, recalling how scornful the patient had been when he once attempted to interpret along this line, he tried to soften her likely objection by putting his observation as a question, "What do you think about me in that connection? Do you think I might belong on that list?" The patient straightened up, looked him up and down, shrugged, and then continued on her new line of thought, though without showing much interest in it. The therapist felt he had failed to make his point and desisted.
>
> The therapist wondered why his "interpretation" did not work. The supervisor helped him to see that his idea was correct. Indeed, as he had described the patient slowing down, slumping, and changing the subject, she probably had come uncomfortably close to the idea herself. But, by putting forward his idea as a question, in the hope of not arousing strong objection, he had actually demonstrated the very weakness she had been complaining about. Her reaction suggested that she was perhaps reluctant to take up the invitation in his "interpretation," perhaps because his behavior suggested he might be too weak to stand up to her and she was unwilling to chance a retort that might lead to a breach.
>
> The therapist conceded that he had worked on his formulation so as not to offend the patient and that he felt "one down" and unready to follow up her reaction lest it lead to a blow-up. He could also see that by doing so he had enacted his acceptance of the transference attribution of weakness.

What else might he have done? Clearly, feeling as he did, he could not have done differently at the time. But, if he had not felt intimidated by the patient, he might have been able to comment, when the patient suddenly lost interest in her tirade, that perhaps it had occurred to her that he also could be included on the list of weaklings. Depending on her response, he then might add that she did not feel ready to deal with that idea. The precise wording is unimportant. The main idea is that the therapist would do better to address the patient's attribution of weakness in the transference without enacting his acceptance of it, that is, without demonstrating that he had bought into the transference by putting forth his idea timidly as a question. The enacting of weakness in the form of the intervention made the content unusable.

Questioning to Establish Dominance

The clinical situation embodies an inherently stratified relationship. A new patient, while in actuality a "customer" who should be able to choose freely where to purchase the service he desires, actually feels like a supplicant coming to an authority who may be able to do for him or withhold from him something he needs badly. Feeling "one-down," perhaps even morally tainted for being troubled, he both fears rejection by the therapist and is unsure about trusting him. This ready-made transference fits well with cultural role assignments of doctors and patients and is socially sanctioned; the new therapist (more or less secretly) welcomes the deference, since he too feels unsure of his actual competence and is grateful that the patient is not challenging him. In this circumstance, most new therapists tend to accept the patient's attribution of authority and will confirm it by asking questions. The patient's willingness to answer confirms that he is a "good patient" who will not resolve his doubts by challenging the competence of the therapist directly.

If you have a chance to observe such an interview, you may suspect that the therapist already knows the answers. Gaining information is not the point of asking. We can see examples of such usage when a clinician asks a new patient his or her name, "What brought you here?" and other such questions even though the information is on the referral form that preceded or accompanied the patient. Seldom does a patient challenge these ponderous redundancies with, "Don't any of you ever read the chart?" Not infrequently, in a clinic or hospital, the patient will be asked the same demographic questions by each new functionary who ostensibly is there to serve him. Each helper may have the same covert purpose—to establish who is in charge as well as the more easily acknowledged purpose to assess quickly the mental status and cooperativeness of the patient. In many clinics and hospitals a new patient is expected to adapt to the routines that mostly serve the convenience of the staff and to accept the implicit message that meeting their needs comes first. Only when the patient has accepted being "processed" will his needs be considered. The young therapist who finally meets this patient for his "first" session may not realize that he has inherited the burden of resentment (in the healthier patient) or the reinforced passivity (of the sicker patient) built up by the experience of repeatedly having been "processed."

Occasionally, a new therapist may ask a patient a question the general nature of whose answer could be inferred from the context of the interaction. A common example occurs when the patient tells about an event in a way that carries clear emotional overtones, yet the therapist, after perhaps a moment's hesitation, asks, "How did that make you feel?" Rather than a wish to exert power at that moment, I suspect such questions arise from a sense of induced helplessness, the therapist perhaps feeling identified with the patient, overwhelmed by the emotional weight of the patient's story and the implied demand to "do something" to relieve him. The therapist also might fear becoming too quickly involved with the patient or possibly that he might say the wrong thing. At such times, asking a question, even one that has an obvious answer, seems a safer, less committing move than offering an empathic comment. The patient may sense what the therapist would prefer to conceal—that he felt forced to withdraw from emotional involvement with the patient at that point.

Anxiety is perhaps the commonest reason for therapists to slip into unnecessarily questioning the patient. The therapist who already has more "material" than he knows how to use may ask a question that sounds as if he needs more information. At that point, the question might be intended to forestall the patient's expectation that he do something for him, such as answer the as yet unasked question, "What should I do about that?" or, "Can you stop the pain?" An analogous phenomenon can be seen in the case conference. If a lull develops and the conference leader does not break it, anxiety will mount among the participants and someone is certain to break the silence by asking a question. One can easily discover that the question was intended to relieve anxiety rather than to elicit needed information; one merely has to ask the questioner what he would understand differently or do differently if he knew the answer to that question.

If the new therapist is of an egalitarian temperament, he may feel too uneasy to accept the unearned attribution of expertise implicit in assuming the role of therapist. He might well express his discomfort by attempting to level the field to make the therapeutic situation more "democratic," by becoming familiar rather than formal, perhaps encouraging mutual use of first names. He is likely also to use questions rather than assertions to express his antiauthoritarian bias and to relieve the discomfort at finding himself in a stratified relationship, elevated additionally by the patient's idealizing transference. Consider this example of a first session by a beginning therapist:

> Looking sheepish and uncertain, the patient entered for this first interview. The therapist rose from his seat, came to the door, and offered his hand, which the patient shook uncertainly. Motioning the patient to a chair, the therapist asked if he thought it would be comfortable or if he would prefer the other one. Looking even more uncomfortable, the patient sat on the edge of the seat of the first chair offered and waiting expectantly, looked anxiously toward the therapist. After an awkward silence, the therapist asked in a hearty voice, "Well, how are things?" After several seconds, the patient responded, in a weak voice and with a rising inflection, "OK, I guess."

The rest of the interview went the same way. This brief account of the opening may be enough to illustrate that the therapist had his own anxiety-driven agenda that kept him from noticing and making clinical use of the ample behavioral evidence of the patient's distress. Neither could he see that his overly hospitable manner was unresponsive to the patient's emotional state. Indeed, the therapist's hearty welcome and instant focus on the patient's seating comfort obligated the patient to conform with social niceties at the expense of expressing his discomfort both with the issues that had brought him to the clinic and with the prospect of unburdening himself to a stranger.

We do not have enough information to decide whether the therapist's attitude expressed a general reluctance to be seen as an authority figure, transference toward this patient in particular, or perhaps resentment toward the clinic for forcing him to occupy an authoritarian role. It is even possible that his attitude was triggered by a glance at the patient's hangdog mien as he entered and that he feared it might portend a plea for help that he felt unable to give. If so, we could consider his attitude as expressing countertransference.

As when a therapist feels intimidated, it is not the discomfort with being invested with unearned authority that is the problem but rather what the therapist does about it, usually unwittingly. If the therapist recognizes his more or less unconscious investment in one or the other characterological position, he might be able to deal with his own and the patient's issues independently and, possibly with the help of his own therapy, will be less likely to misuse the therapeutic situation to treat himself.

Whenever a therapist interrupts the patient to ask a question he should be aware that he has "changed the rules" and has assigned new status to himself and to the patient. In effect, he is saying, "I know that I asked you to say whatever might come into your mind, but I want to interrupt you now because I'm more interested in what came into my mind and I can't wait to find out what your response to that might be." The analyst's metacommunication behind the question is, "Please understand that you are free to voice your associations until I think of something better to talk about."

The analyst's question also signals to the patient that he expects something new of him. The "new" may range from merely heightened attentiveness, to the rhetorical question, to a more active and specific response to a direct question with such implications as, "Be clear," or "Justify that last opinion." For the latter, the analyst has reserved the right to judge the adequacy of the response. The questioning form itself can thus be seen as coercive, at least in the formal sense, in that the question prescribes the nature of the response required. In that sense, the question is intended to, and frequently does, control the behavior of the patient, an ironic violation of the principle of abstinence.

If the patient has been associating freely or has been speaking relatively unselfconsciously, the therapist's question will interrupt that state. A question demands that the patient pay attention to what the therapist has in mind. Of course, it matters very much how the question is put, the tone of voice, and inflection. But regardless of how elegantly it is formed, the questioning form pulls for a cognitive shift. Every therapist has noticed the effect. Suddenly, the patient looks up or away, his mind apparently racing to figure out what the therapist wants him to say. The therapist who is alert to that change of state may possibly have a chance to undo it, perhaps by saying, "I guess I'm asking you to read my mind," and then stating as an assertion the idea he wanted to bring to the patient's attention.

Again, it is worth distinguishing questioning that comes about as a result of transference from that engendered by countertransference. For example, when the patient has been associating freely for some time but the analyst has not yet caught the drift of the associations, the analyst is likely to feel bored or anxious because he does not understand and thinks he ought to. Interrupting the patient with a question to reestablish a sense of being in control can be viewed as transference.

On the other hand, if the therapist feels impelled to interrupt, a sharply put question may express his irritation at being left out and demand that the patient be more considerate of his need to understand. This action, too, may be regarded as transference. But if the patient's vagueness amounts to a more or less unconscious invitation to the analyst to find fault and interrupt, the behavior might be better considered as countertransference. The effect on the patient when the analyst is driven by transference or by countertransference is likely to be different in the long run and in a way not easily captured in a single illustration. For instance, a patient who is interrupted by the analyst might well feel misunderstood and resentful, but he would likely absorb the implied scolding and supply the withheld information. In addition to whatever else might ensue, this development might belie the permission-instruction given the patient to pay attention to the way his mind works without having to keep one eye on the analyst.

It might be raised in objection that most patients expect to be asked questions, even searching and penetrating ones when they come to see the doctor. Indeed, they do; that is just the point. The confluence of transference with acceptance of the social role of patient makes it incumbent on the analyst or psychodynamic therapist to help the patient differentiate the role of psychotherapy patient from that of medical patient. The patient who is ready to submit to medical authority will also expect that the doctor knows the solution to his problem, has the authority to prescribe it, and shortly will do so if he is satisfied with the patient's answers to his questions.

Technical Implications of Questioning

Perhaps the best way to spell out the case against questioning as a technical tool is to remind ourselves that the aim of technique is to maintain the analytic situation, that is, to maintain the conditions under which the patient feels safe enough to say what comes to mind and to remain an active listener to what he says. What the patient does not feel safe enough to say may be even more interesting, analytically, than what he does feel safe to say. By listening to the pattern of disclosure and withholding, the analyst may advance the analytic purpose more than he would by relieving his mind of a temporary ambiguity.

Empathic, facilitating comments tend to keep the patient engaged in telling his story and perhaps may clear up an ambiguity. The analyst should deal with any persisting ambiguity or repeated omission as a positive act, not a negative one, not as an error. Take for example, a patient who persistently omits from his account of his childhood any mention of his father's absence, which certainly figured importantly in his childhood. Rather than interrupting the patient to clear up that nagging omission by asking, "Why did your father leave home?" the analyst would best wait until a more suitable time to pursue the question. After the patient has finished telling his story, the analyst might observe, "You told me all about your father going away except why you thought he left," or "You told me about it as if you had no idea about why he left." Either observation, even without the rising inflection that signals inquiry, would lead the patient to reflect, and the analyst might discover whether the patient was even aware of the omission. It would also imply that the analyst is ready to hear the rest of the story or to have the patient address the incompleteness in some other way.

That way of calling the patient's attention to an omission respects the possible dynamics of an omission. It also respects the possibility, for instance, that the patient may be too embarrassed to tell about that just now. Recognizing that the patient might prefer to go into it when he feels more comfortable both respects the patient's feelings and promotes the development of the analytic situation. Questions of any kind require the patient to shift focus from what is going on in his own mind to guessing what the analyst is interested in. The alternative interventions would not interrupt the patient's story telling and would invite the patient to reflect on the fact of the omission itself.

I noted earlier that the questioning form is inherently coercive, and it is also inherently ambiguous. To pose a question, the speaker must convert an idea that occurred to him as a statement but about which he also feels anxious, an anxiety that might appear as a doubt. The doubt might be about the truth or source of the idea or about how the patient might take it. The analyst accommodates to the anxiety/doubt about whether to say it or not by compromising. He converts the statement to a question and in this way disowns the idea while stating it. English is rich in semantic formulas to indicate precisely one's relationship to an idea; there is thus little reason to use the questioning form with all its ambiguities. It would be useful, of course, for the analyst to be aware that putting his idea forth as a question might be driven partly by anxiety. If so aware, the analyst would have the opportunity to resolve his doubt and voice the idea, or not, as he judges appropriate.

The general goal of analysis is to help the patient to live in the world rather than in fantasy and to free the patient from the power of compulsion. The analyst ought to interact with the patient in a way that does not reinforce the transference-based perception of the analyst as the revenant of the authorities of infantile life. Asking the patient a question says, first of all, that the analyst has the right both to ask that question and to impose on the patient an obligation to answer. By acting in this way, the analyst exercises the power of authority and thus stratifies the relationship unnecessarily. That the patient probably would gladly offer the analyst the privilege of questioning him is beside the point. That willingness is a matter to be analyzed rather then indulged.

This caveat has to do with the use of the questioning form, irrespective of content. But the caveat has particular force when the analyst asks a "why" question. The "Why did you . . . ?" type of question implies that somehow the patient did something wrong. It asks the patient to justify himself to the analyst, who will then weigh the quality of the justification. While the analyst ought not to counteract transference attributions, neither should he reinforce them. The principles of abstinence and perhaps of neutrality apply here.

Keep in mind, too, that the analyst should interact with the patient in a way that promotes the patient's activity in the analysis. The analyst should allow the patient to do what he can do and not take over functions the patient could perform well enough by himself. When he uses the questioning form, the analyst seizes the initiative and makes the patient a respondent. The patient must enter the analyst's frame of reference in order to deal with the question. It hardly seems to be a way to encourage the patient's initiative or free association.

If we assume that the patient is doing the best he can, we might suppose that the omission or ambiguity that troubles the analyst is not a lapse that must be cleared up immediately, but is part of the story. More precisely, the ambiguity probably reflects conflict in telling the story; it is part of the "metastory," the story about the story. It implies that the patient is reluctant to tell the full story voluntarily to the transference figure. The ambiguity thus should be thought of as intended to draw the analyst into participating in playing out the patient's unconscious fantasy by "demanding" to be told "the truth." In this instance, the analyst's seemingly innocent request for clarification might be viewed as countertransference.

When and How Questioning May Be Used Appropriately in the Clinic

These caveats about the calamities that might follow injudicious questioning may leave the impression that it is never proper to direct a question to a patient. On the contrary, questioning is a legitimate way of obtaining information in the clinic as elsewhere. The problem is how to use questions, when they seem needed, without invoking the undesired "side effects."

When the Patient Omits Obviously Important Details

Occasionally, while conducting an initial (or subsequent) interview by allowing the patient to tell his story in his own way, the analyst may notice that an aspect has been omitted or glossed over. He may have some idea about the dynamic significance of the elision but may choose to wait to see if subsequent associations confirm his surmise. He may also choose, at some point—perhaps because his anxiety about not knowing has become intrusive, and he wants to "save time"—to ask the patient to fill in the gap. How to do this without offending the principles of technique?

It is tactful, and lessens the possibility of adverse effects, to inform the patient that you would like, as it were, to "change the rules" for a while to obtain some additional information that will help you understand the patient's situation better. Depending on context, signaling a change in the way the interview will be conducted can be accomplished in various ways. You might ask the patient's permission to raise a question, or announce, "I would like to ask you something about that." Or you could follow up an observation about what the patient has said with a note of uncertainty about which of two possible meanings was consciously intended. If the content of the questions are at some remove from what the patient has been saying, a more or less formal explanation of what you plan to do, and why, would be called for.

When the Patient Interrupts Himself

When the patient has interrupted himself, the analyst may be able to facilitate a return to associating with a question, but I do not recommend it as a general approach. (I discussed the issue from the point of view of defense in Chapter 9.) Patients of an obsessive cast will often interrupt a line of association when a twinge of anxiety warns that they are approaching a dangerous area. They typically interrupt themselves with a shrug and say in a resigned or irritated voice, "What's the use of this?" or "What should I do about it?" or "What does that mean?" Suddenly switching to this sort of seemingly utilitarian mode should be understood as defensive. While, taken alone, the words sound as if the patient wants to know the answer to those questions, the tone of voice says that the intention is to cut off a line of associations that might prove frightening. The analyst would be well advised to point out that the patient had stopped himself, presumably when things were getting too hot, and only then complained that he was not getting anywhere. If the analyst asks the patient about the thought that was forming when he interrupted himself, the patient typically will not be able to remember—an interesting finding in itself. Occasionally, a patient who has been alerted to that defensive maneuver will be able to report a thought that, with encouragement, he will be able to follow up.

When a Patient Insists on Being Questioned

Occasionally you may be referred a patient who seems so frozen by anxiety as to find it impossible to enter spontaneously into the therapeutic situation. The patient begs you to ask questions that he will be glad to answer if he can. A dynamic reason for the inhibition might be that "telling on" or snitching is a forbidden or disloyal act unless coerced by superior authority. If the interview continues, the patient may find it possible to engage more actively and the reasons for the initial inhibition may emerge. But how to begin in order to get to that eventual point? The overriding principle is that the patient is doing the best he can and that you should meet him where he is. To insist from the outset on "the basic rule" might make it impossible for the patient to engage at all. You could agree to go along with the patient's request while observing that you would hardly know the right questions to ask without the patient's help. If the patient accepts this reasonable stance, you could then feed back bits of the story to the patient as they emerge. How does the patient react to the story you are constructing from the bits and pieces? Perhaps the patient can be helped first to become an editor, if not yet an admitted author, of his story.

When the "Side Effects" Are Intended

Some of the inevitable "side effects" of questioning may, under certain circumstances, be the very effect desired. In the days before patients with severe mental illnesses were routinely medicated, it was common to encounter episodes of unwanted regression during therapeutic interviews. Many a therapist then discovered that, by sharply asking a question, he could help a patient who seemed to be slipping away into regression. The content of the question would have something to do with current reality, but its content mattered less than the inherently demanding quality of the question—"Listen to me!"—that had the effect of intruding helpfully on the patient's withdrawal, reorienting him to reality, and insisting that he not exclude the therapist.

12

Responding to Patients' Questions

So much for therapist's questions. But how do we "handle" patients' questions? Young therapists become edgy if asked what they do about patients' questions. Supervisors have told them that such questions are best thought of as resistance (that is, misbehavior) and should not be answered. Some have even advised that they include in the initial instructions to the patient that the analyst will not answer questions, thus establishing that fiat as a matter of analytic policy. In this way, they say, we encourage the patient to look into the meaning of the question; not answering questions is essential to the success of the treatment and, the implication goes, is neither impersonal nor unmannerly.

This policy seems designed more to discourage patients from asking questions than to encourage them to discover the answers themselves, and most young analysts do not find the advice liberating when, inevitably, a patient does ask a question. They feel under some social compulsion to answer and at the same time are enjoined to withhold responding. They tend to freeze, to remain silent until the patient gives up. Occasionally, a patient will catch on and say, "Oh, sorry, I forgot that I am not supposed to ask questions." Other patients, of course, will be offended, even incensed, at being ignored when they feel they have a legitimate expectation to be taken at face value, not as simply offering "material" for analysis.

Why are patients' questions such a problem? Let us look at a patient in analysis. He is gingerly exploring unaccustomed states of mind and cautiously permitting new experiences: should we not expect that he would have many questions? Indeed, it is surprising that patients ask so few. If, indeed, the analyst did lay down a rule, that rule would, of course, tend to discourage questions, but it would hardly keep them out of the patient's mind. Obviously a rule about not answering questions tends to contradict the "basic rule"[1] to voice all thoughts that come to mind, regardless of their form.

[1] Whether stated as a rule or as a permission, or left unstated, our basic expectation is that the patient wants the analyst to understand him fully and therefore intends to speak

Suppose a patient confronted the analyst who had just given this instruction: "I thought you wanted me to say everything that comes to mind. Are you now saying, everything except for questions?" The analyst might reply, quite properly, " I didn't say you shouldn't ask questions, but that I would not answer them." "But what's the sense in my asking questions that you won't answer?" To which the analyst might well respond, "For the same reason that you say everything else, so that we may examine it and come to learn what is behind it." "But suppose I need to ask if I can change a session. I'll be happy to tell you what's behind it, but I will need to have your answer?" You can see that, were we to continue, the example would become niggling, legalistically defining conditional exceptions to the "rule." The grounds on which the analyst tries to base his case have become uncomfortably narrow. If you put yourself in the analyst's shoes, you might agree that he has no good moves at that point and might well wish he had never proposed such a rule. The example should serve as a reminder that any effort to remove issues from the analysis, either with explicit rules or with subtle hints, such as tacitly acquiescing in the patient's avoidances, will invite the same outcome.

A uniform policy about not answering questions is untenable. If you announce one firmly, you may cow the patient into submission or invite a discussion most analysts would rather avoid. Of course, only a few patients would push the analyst to the wall at this early point, but even those who refrain from challenging will be left with an ambiguous message about the "unwritten rules" of analytic procedure. It is now folklore that analysts, unlike many other therapists, do not answer questions. A patient may even take perverse pride in the fact that his analyst never answers questions or gives advice. These stern abstentions seem to be negative proofs that the patient is *really* in analysis with a *real* analyst, a tough one. The patient is flattered at the implication that "he can take it."

As patients catch on to how analysis proceeds and how it gives them an unparalleled opportunity to discover how their minds work, they come to accept that ideas put as questions are best treated—like ideas in any other grammatical form or with any emotional coloring—as stimuli for associating. But even such paragons will, from time to time, let slip a question that they will want to have answered; they feel both entitled to an answer and perhaps defensive about having "broken a rule." Voicing

without reservation. Whenever an analyst notices that the patient is holding back, consciously or unconsciously, rather than insisting that the patient adhere strictly to the basic rule, as we were once advised to do (Ferenzci, 1919, pp. 177–183), he will consider it an expression of conflict and hence a matter for psychoanalytic investigation.

a thought as a question is an analytically interesting event. Why should it be such an embarrassment to the analyst?

Earlier I briefly discussed the coercive power of the questioning form and how it affects the person queried. But the effect of being questioned on the analyst is much greater than on the man in the street. After all, the analyst has accepted the responsibility to listen, understand, and help, and he has invited the patient to say whatever occurs to him in order to study how his mind works. The trouble, of course, is that, like the man on the street, the analyst feels acted on, pinioned by the questioning form, which demands an action in return—an answer.

When a patient suddenly asks a question, the analyst feels as if the patient has "turned the tables," seized the initiative, and put him on the defensive. It feels unnatural not to answer a question, even if he may sense there is more to understand. But how to get at that "more"? Most young analysts feel uncomfortable with the first tactic likely to be proposed to them—to ask the patient a question in return, such as, "What do you think?" It sounds "shrinky," especially if one regularly turns the question back to the patient. And it clearly appears to be an evasion. Moreover, patients soon understand that being questioned makes the analyst uncomfortable. Depending on his character and disposition, the patient can use that information either to desist and "be good" or to continue and bedevil the analyst. We must consider also that any stereotypical way of responding informs the patient about our unspoken rules and thus potentially violates the principle of anonymity.

Responding to Questions versus Answering Them

I suggested earlier that it is useful to distinguish between answering a patient's question and responding to the patient's act of questioning. There indeed are better ways to deal with patients' questions, a way that will promote understanding, than to outlaw them with a rule or to evade them with a tactic. To develop the argument, let us look first at a more important issue: what makes patients' questions an especially interesting class of communication?

We can safely infer that, when a patient interrupts himself to ask a question, he believes he has, at least temporarily, stopped associating freely. Of course, the analyst still ought to listen to the question, both its content and its form, as an association. The asking, especially, is also a phenomenon important in its own right.

Consider again how a question is constructed. The idea contained in a patient's question is one about which he has changed his attitude. He has some doubts about the idea and works it over. Expressing his uncertainty and mixed feelings about it, he converts it to a question from the declarative form in which the idea previously occurred to him. Simply by inverting the word order and voicing the idea with a rising inflection, he distances himself from it. Importantly, he also has stopped himself from associating or from voicing his associations as he waits for the analyst's answer. He has appointed the analyst as the source of needed information and requires that the analyst deliver immediately. He has "changed the rules," has tossed the ball to the analyst. Now the analyst must do something, and for the moment, the patient is off the hook. If he recognizes this switch to quizzing him as a defensive maneuver, the analyst may be able to infer from the context what the patient's effort to hide also reveals.

Let us return to the moment when the patient interrupted himself to formulate his question. I propose that that process began with some anxiety about an incipient errant association, presumably transference. The spike of anxiety, implying a potential loss of control, led immediately to a defensive reaction, a turning away from what was about to come to mind and toward the analyst. Turning the idea into a question is a way to exert power over the analyst and, incidentally, reduce the threat from the emerging transference. In effect, the patient is saying, "I don't care to perform for you any more. It's your turn to perform for me." But the underlying presumption is that turning the tables on the analyst was intended, first of all, to dispel a spike of anxiety in the patient. This process, of course, could also be described as solving a conflict by compromise formation.

I trust that proposing a theory about the process that led to the question is enough to establish the act of questioning as analytically interesting. It is likely that the context will tell the analyst something about what the question means, and perhaps also why the patient's attitude toward that meaning changed, why the authority of the analyst had to be invoked just at that point, and why the analyst had to be directed to participate. My main point is that the analyst should consider separately the form and the content of what the patient says.

Responding to General Questions

What to do about the patient's question? If the analyst was made defensive by the patient's questioning, he likely will have lost his therapeutic split and feel trapped, as the transference object, between the impulse to answer and the prohibition against it. If he could recover the stance of the therapeutic ally, he would find it possible to respond to the *act of questioning*, to the verb rather than to the content, the noun—the question—for instance, with a comment having the general form, "I think something occurred to you (or disturbed you) just before you asked my opinion about. . . ." Note that the analyst has begun to address the presumed function of the question by suggesting that the patient look at the context for asking; he has neither answered nor refused to answer the question.[2]

My focus is on the patient's *act of questioning*. The governing principle is the logic of the interpretive process. Our first concern is for the *function* of the question: what is it doing here now? We could adopt as a new analytic aphorism, "A quick answer can ruin a good question." It captures the point precisely: there is much more to understand about a question than its content, and a quick answer might preclude further inquiry. But that would be the case only if the analyst (as well as the patient) were satisfied that the quick answer had eliminated all further interest either in the question or why it had been asked just then.

There is no reason, in principle, why an inquiry into the act of questioning, and into the circumstances in the stream of associations that forced the interruption and substituted the question, could not continue after the analyst offered some information by way of an answer. The analyst might try the experiment of briefly answering a question and then observing the effect, although I do not recommend doing this as a regular practice. I believe he will find most often that a pause follows and that the patient seems let down. The analyst then can pursue *both* the sense of anticlimax and the events immediately preceding the asking. Again, there is no need for a rule of procedure about this issue.

To continue how one might respond to being questioned, depending on how the question was asked and what the analyst understood about it, the analyst might observe that the question seems to be one the patient has had in mind for some time. Or he might comment that the question was asked in a hesitant way or was voiced in a way that sounded as if the patient did not really expect an answer. Or he might observe that the patient seemed to have difficulty in framing the question. In short, there are many aspects of the patient's asking that the analyst could address to bring the act into the immediacy of the analytic situation. I reemphasize that the point is not to discover ways to avoid answering the patient's

[2] I have no objection in principle to the patient's getting the information he asks from the analyst—provided it is germane, provided the analyst is sure the patient does not already know the answer, and provided the analyst can reasonably be expected to know the answer and would be the best, if not the only source for it. Analytic inquiry into the question as an interruption can proceed as well afterward. Clinical and social judgment should prevail here as elsewhere.

questions without seeming to do so, but rather to respond to the patient's asking in precisely the same way one would respond to any other association, not to be imprisoned by the fact that the association was framed as a question.

Again, nothing in these suggestions should be taken as prohibiting the analyst from answering a question at some point if indeed it is one that needs answering. I am not advocating, as some supervisors do, that the analyst should say he will put off answering the question until after it has been thoroughly understood. Answering should not be a reward for good work. Rather, answering the question, dealing with its content, is a different matter from addressing its form and the analyst may answer any time he believes it would advance the analytic purpose, or at least not interfere with it. It is entirely within the spirit of my proposal that the analyst might regard the content of the question as trivial, perhaps intended to provoke him to become silent. The analyst might choose to regard the answer as a "throwaway," give it matter-of-factly, and then comment on the patient's likely purpose in asking it. Or he might observe that the patient did not wait for an answer and probably did not expect one.

We can observe that the content of a question may be far less important than the act of asking it. Often, when the asking has been addressed and worked through, the patient will have forgotten the subject matter of his query. If the analyst reminds the patient that he asked a question, the patient may well express surprise that the analyst remembered it, as the patient had quite forgotten it; the patient may then go on without waiting for the answer that the analyst might give—the matter is no longer of any importance.

Responding to Personal Questions

The questions that trouble analysts most are the personal ones. These usually reflect a persisting interest in the person of the analyst and are driven by transference. The patient asks if you are married, where you are going on vacation, if you are ill. Would we not agree that you should not answer such questions, for to do so would violate the principle of anonymity?

Recall the earlier discussions of the implications of the questioning form. To ask any question, the patient must have some reason for asking, and for asking now. He will have considered what the answer might be and what he wishes the answer would or would not be. He has a context into which he will plug the answer. Recall, that the person who asks you for the time does so because he fears he might be late and either has no watch or does not trust the one he has. He expects an answer within a very small range of time since he already knows, for instance, that it is too close to 3:00 P.M. for comfort.

By analogy, a patient who asks if you are married already has some information about your marital status. He may just have noticed that you either do or do not wear a wedding ring, or he has heard some gossip, or he has had a dream or fantasy about you. Rather than disclosing that he has some information that makes it urgent to know more, the patient takes what seems to him to be the safer course, to get you to relieve his painful uncertainty with information that will check the "facts" he already "knows." If you let yourself be aware of these possibilities, rather than feeling confined by the questioning form, you will be able to address any of them. At the very least, you could suggest that something must just have brought to the patient's mind the matter of your matrimonial status. It is common for a candidate given this advice to retort, "But suppose the patient insists?" My experience is that the candidate will not be satisfied by, "Usually they do not," as noted by Ferenczi (1919, p. 183). Here is an example:

> The patient, an unmarried but hopeful woman in her early 30s, came with the conviction, which she knew had been drummed into her by her mother, that she would never be able to please a man. Working diligently in the analysis, she occasionally voiced the fear that she might not be doing it well enough to suit the analyst, but there were only hints of erotic interest in him. When the analyst tried to explore one of the hints, the patient apologized, saying she knew patients were supposed to fall in love with their analyst but, as yet, she hadn't been able to. The analyst desisted.
>
> One day, the patient came in and breathlessly announced that she had to know if the analyst was married. Surprised, the analyst remained silent for a few moments, and the patient, presumably taking his silence to mean he would not answer, again insisted that she had to know. Recovering his composure, the analyst noted that, indeed, she seemed to have an urgent need for the information. She agreed and again pleaded for the answer. The analyst again noted the urgency of her request and added that clearly a great deal must hang on the answer. She agreed again and added plaintively that she just couldn't say what was behind her request until she knew if he was married.
>
> Taking courage in hand, the analyst reminded her of the time when he had suggested, in connection with a dream with sexual content, that she might be having such feelings toward him. He

recalled that she had responded that, although she knew she was supposed to, she didn't feel that way. Now, he suggested, rather than feeling obligated to have them, she feared that she was having them and feared further that the analyst would take them away from her, that he would tell her that once again—"stupidly again" (he quoted from her past self-accusations)—she had fallen in love with an unavailable man.

In a few moments, the patient started to cry, "I was so afraid you wouldn't believe me and that you'd say something to spoil it, just the way my mother would, but this is different. I know that you are my analyst and it wouldn't make any difference whether you are married or not. But I had this dream, and it felt so good. I felt normal and happy, just the way I always wanted to feel and I didn't want to give it up."

The analyst echoed her fear that to talk about the dream and associate to it would force her to give up the good feeling. Sensing that this was not the analyst's agenda, the patient started to talk about her dream and the events of the previous weekend that had led up to it.

Rather than being the most difficult ones to deal with, it is precisely the imperative, peremptory, personal, most obviously transference-driven questions that are the most amenable to analysis in this way.

13

The Process Point of View

Can We Define a Specifically Psychoanalytic Process?

In earlier chapters, I showed that some key analytic concepts, for instance, defense, resistance, and interpretation, are best understood as processes rather than as events. Indeed, the concept of a biological or social system, a dynamic arrangement, implies the point of view of process, as does the term texture. One appreciates the texture of a fabric through a process of passing the hand over it or feeling it between the fingers. We have seen also that neurosis is best viewed as a process, as something the patient does rather than something he has.

But frequently psychoanalysts use process when referring to an essential aspect of psychoanalysis itself, as in The Psychoanalytic Process. For some analysts, this usage is just a fancy way of referring to what goes on when they sit with their patients, and as such it is harmless. But, for others, the term has acquired connotations they believe are essential in making clinical and educational decisions, and this usage may be quite harmful.

Consider a committee of psychoanalytic educators, sitting with furrowed brows, worrying whether the candidate under discussion has "really engaged his patient in a psychoanalytic process." They seem to have something much more serious and specific in mind. Their concern raises the interesting possibility that an analyst could have been meeting several times a week over an extended period with a recumbent patient who had presented himself for analysis; yet, in the opinion of at least some knowledgeable observers, the two are still not engaged in a "psychoanalytic process." What could this "process" be?

If you have been reading sequentially, you may have an idea about why I have put off discussing this issue until so far into this book. For if one accepts the idea that analysis is what patients do, not what analysts do, perhaps there is no reason to hold the analyst responsible for the absence of the desired "process." But I can hardly dodge the issue that easily, for surely we all agree that the analyst has at least some responsibility to discern whether the recumbent patient is using the opportunity for psychoanalysis; and, if he senses that the patient is not doing so, it is incumbent on the analyst to do something about it, if only to raise the issue with the patient.

With these considerations, we may ask if it makes sense, given the combination of willing patient and analyst meeting regularly—the one mostly talking, the other mostly listening—to judge that what is going on does not meet the criteria for "psychoanalytic process." If we have as willing participants a sufficiently "neurotic" (that is, hurting) patient and a reasonably skilled analyst, both of whom intend to conduct an analysis, and if the conventional postural and procedural arrangements obtain and a mostly one-sided conversation ensues, what could the additional criteria be? Could the presence of "process" be judged as what the patient talks about, the content of the "conversation?" Clearly no. After all, the patient was enjoined, instructed, or permitted to say whatever came to his mind, in short, to facilitate "free association." So the patient could fulfill his part by saying anything, even nothing. As we all know, patients occasionally do say, "Nothing comes to mind." We may not take this statement only at face value, but neither do we jump to the dire conclusion when we hear it that no analytic process is present.

Could it be that something the analyst should be doing in response to whatever the patient says that would determine if an analytic "process" is present? This question is not easy to deal with out of hand. Even if we agree that, in general, analysis is what patients do, we would certainly concede that by his actions (including inaction), the analyst can impede as well as foster the patient's efforts. But let me put this question aside until I have disposed of some more basic issues.

Some General Thoughts About the Concept of Process

Let us reconsider the question of "process" from a more general point of view. First, the concept of process implies that what is being observed takes place over time. Processes may move rapidly or slowly, continuously or intermittently, so that, depending on circumstances, the matter under observation may display a varying pace and rhythm. Thus, for "psychoanalytic process," the time-window of observation would have to be wide enough to permit an accurate determination. But more important than assuring adequate conditions for observation is to be clear about what we mean by process. Consider, when viewing any biological or social phenomenon, one necessarily observes process, that is, one views events unfolding over time.

Here I am considering process only as it relates to social systems, of which the analytic situation is an example. This particular social system consists of the interaction of two biological/psychological systems, each with a history, who get together voluntarily at a fixed place at fixed times for a fixed procedure to bring about a change in the system desired by one of the parties. Toward this end, the patient enlists the aid of the other party, the analyst, for a fee. The fixed arrangements are designed to minimize the possibility that external forces will disturb the system. Any disturbance of the system, then, as well as changes in the parties, could reasonably be attributed to forces generated within the system. What could those potentially disturbing, internally generated forces be?

In earlier chapters we encountered these forces under such headings as interpretation, transference, and defense, all of which could be gathered under the broader concept of "intentions," as expressed in various ways by one or the other party. Since intentions are being expressed continually by both parties, we may assume that the analytic system constantly is being disturbed. Does that disturbance amount to analytic process? Perhaps the answer to that question rests on another question. Is there a direction to the disturbance, or is it merely random? Is movement or change to be discerned in the system or in either party?

Like all systems, the analytic situation reacts to all pressures from outside and from within, and like all other systems it is self-restoring and tends to stabilize in its previous condition once the disturbing pressure ceases. The same is true for the two subsystems that make up the analytic situation: the patient and analyst. This conservative property of systems—which, when referring to personality, might be called conservatism, resilience, stubbornness, backwardness, or resistance—accounts in part for why therapeutic change is difficult to achieve and for the core technical position advocated in this book. Sudden pressures, quickly removed, cannot be depended on to create lasting change in a system. Critics will be quick to point out a possible exception—that the pressures we call traumatic do just that. And, in large social systems, assassination attempts do just that. But such influences are difficult, if not illegal, to arrange on therapeutic demand today, although in our history, the snake pit and the Scotch douche tested the idea.

It could also be objected that a single, illuminating interpretation can produce lasting change. Indeed, Freud's (1895) earliest cases employed just this kind of brief treatment, and the folklore of psychoanalysis, if not its literature, suggests that it is still possible. But the subsequent history of clinical psychoanalysis (Schlesinger, 1988) tells of the discovery of transference, resistance, and character, factors that seem to justify an ever-increasing length of treatment. They suggest that it would be unwise to count on the efficacy of the single "blinding interpretation." The earlier chapters in this book dealing with resistance and interpretation as processes, and the necessity to follow up interpretations, are consonant with this view. The point is that to change a system, pressure that is accurately aimed must be sustained.

Is There a Peculiarly Psychoanalytic Process?

Let us return to the question about the nature of psychoanalytic process and consider if it makes sense to speak of an analyst and analysand who have gotten together yet still are judged not to be in an analytic process. Has the foregoing discussion helped to clarify matters? It should at least have warned us that, if the existence of psychoanalytic process depends on whether change is occurring, whether therapeutic movement is occurring, we will have to look at a sufficiently long time-sample. And, we will want to examine the nature of the influence being applied: is it interpretive, and is it accurate, well-dosed, well-timed, and followed up—that is, has the patient's defensiveness been taken into account and addressed?

These criteria are not so much psychoanalytic as educational; that is to say, they are the criteria a supervisor or a progression committee might ask to determine if a candidate knows what he is doing, if he is able to establish an analytic situation and facilitate the development of psychoanalytic process. This reminder is especially necessary if we continue to maintain that analysis is what patients and analysts do together, not what analysts do to patients.

Process versus Change

Obviously, if the patient throws down his crutches and walks, so to speak, we will have to concede that change has occurred. But a niggling critic might ask, "But was it psychoanalytic change?" If we do not, for our current purpose, rely on the correctness of the activity of the analyst to assure us that the change came about in a psychoanalytic way, then what is our recourse? Notice, we have just tripped on another pair of questions: Is there a special psychoanalytic way of changing? Isn't all change in a desired direction equally welcome? Yes, such change is Change, certainly welcome to the patient and hardly to be begrudged by the analyst. But our critic, who is turning out to be more of a purist than I thought continues to object: Change can be caused by many factors, most perhaps having nothing to do with the analyzing that is presumably under way. Agreed.

We might ask our critic to allow for the possibility that a patient who has won the lottery or who seems much better following the death of a tormenting spouse might have been helped by the analyzing to make use of the good luck. But that seems too weak a foundation on which to build a case. Perhaps we would do better to drop the presence of change as an absolute criterion. Of course, if we are lucky enough in our sampling of the analytic material to have observed that the patient responded to a correct interpretation with changes in his subsequent associations, we might infer that the thrust of the interpretation has been confirmed. Our observation would assure us that analyzing is going on, that is, that the process is analytic. But we cannot count on making such lucky observations.

Let us, then, move on to consider several possibilities. Perhaps I was too quick to abandon the criterion of change in judging the presence of psychoanalytic process. After all, it is the purpose of clinical psychoanalysis to promote self-understanding with the expectation that desirable personality change will follow. It is possible that our worried observers noticed that a change in self-understanding failed to occur following a correct interpretation although it might have been expected to occur or that an expectable change in personality did not occur en suite. It might be useful to pursue these possibilities.

But first, for the sake of clarity, let us substitute the phrase "observable change in behavior that might portend a change in personality" for the phrase "change in personality." In that way we may deal with phenomena that all of us can see rather than with private inferences. Second, let us allow that a change in self-understanding or in the resulting behavior might be so subtle as to escape our notice. More likely, changes that did occur were not cumulative. Although the neurotic system of the patient, or of the patient and analyst, might have been disturbed momentarily—that is, changed by some action of the analyst or self-realization by the patient—the systems were subsequently allowed to restabilize. Thus a desirable change, viewed from the standpoint of clinical psychoanalysis, might have occurred and then been allowed to dissipate.

Sadly, such lost opportunities occur all too frequently in psychoanalysis as practiced. If our worried observers had noticed such a sequence in the work of the candidate under discussion, I would have to agree they were on to something. But would their educational diagnosis of the situation properly be labeled as a failure to achieve psychoanalytic process, or could it be described more accurately in some other way, perhaps as failure to capitalize on the effects of an interpretation so as to promote the structuralization of change? A mouthful, indeed, but nevertheless more accurate.

You probably noticed that I sneaked in an additional value judgment: I referred to a desirable change in self-knowledge or behavior that might be ephemeral because of insufficient follow-up. You would not have to be a cynic to point out that not all change is desirable. But, more importantly, I have left hanging the more basic question, Desirable to whom? Those issues also have philosophical and ethical implications and deserve fuller consideration than would fit in a discussion of technique.

Another major consideration arises from the possibility that what the two parties are doing is less than optimal analyzing. Characterizing a process negatively does not promote understanding. Once the phenomena under observation have been dismissed as "not analytic process," the next question would have to be, But what *are* they doing? This is the same issue we raised earlier with regard to resistance. Here, too, we must deal with what the patient is doing, not with his failure to do what we would have preferred him to do. And we must approach in the same way the analyst who we judge is not promoting analysis. If the two parties in a psychoanalysis are not engaged in a psychoanalytic process, they must be engaged in some other kind of process. It is more useful, both for teaching and for evaluating, to specify what the parties are doing rather than what they are failing to do. Typically, at this point in our discussion, some committed analyst will offer the dismissive, "Well, it might do for psychotherapy, but it's not analysis." It should not take a defender of psychotherapy to rule that comment out of bounds. But then, how to characterize the process?

I believe we agree that human processes invariably are governed by intentions. Thus, we may ask, what is each party trying to do to, with or for the other? How did the situation get to this point, and where is it heading? If one wants to help the participants alter the nature of the process, how could one go about it? These are interesting questions from both an educational and an analytic standpoint. They are grounded in a psychoanalytic stance rather than a dispositional one. But, hold up! Have we not ignored that we expect the two parties in analysis to have mixed intentions? The patient, at least, is presumed to be bogged down in conflict and thus inevitably will express intentions that are at cross-purposes. From time to time, so will the analyst, even if, we hope, to a far lesser extent than the patient. To follow this argument to its logical conclusion, we would have to agree that the presence of conflict and mixed intentions in the patient's utterances—or sloppiness in the analyst's technical handling of matters—would not by themselves rule out the process as psychoanalytic.

Criteria for Process?

We seem no closer to a satisfactory definition of psychoanalytic process than we were before. But we do seem to have ruled out several prospective criteria: the content of the conversation, the presence or absence of change, the activity of the analyst and the quality of analyzing. Still, whether or not there is an analytic process is a question that has both practical and theoretical implications. Thus far, we have considered mainly the practical implications: the necessity, for educational purposes, to decide about the competence of a candidate, or, for clinical purposes (although we have given it less attention), to decide if the patient is analyzable, if analysis is the right treatment and, if it is, if the patient is in the right hands.

Does any particular quality mark the process in the analytic session as peculiarly psychoanalytic? That is an important question, and it is amazing and disturbing that there is so little agreement among analysts about its answer. As part of a recent research project (Vaughan et al., 1997) asked senior analysts to specify their criteria for analytic process, and the researchers found no consensus. Given this failure, it may seem bold of me to propose a set of criteria that seem to me to have served the purpose well for many years, even if they have not come to be generally endorsed.

Menninger and Holzman (1973, pp. 154–157) proposed that in a "properly going" analysis (quotation marks are theirs) there is a usual order in the way the patient presents material. The patient typically begins the session with recollections from the day immediately before the session or earlier, often he speaks with a tone of displeasure. As his story winds down it is succeeded by references to the analytic situation, either with the same tone or, depending on the state of the transference, with contrasting tone. These references soon give way to reminiscences about childhood, again with concordant or contrasting mood.

This cycling pattern, in a direction Menninger and Holzman termed "counterclockwise," continues as the patient, perhaps with the assistance of the analyst, gains "insight" into the patterned expectations that govern his life. It is a sequence that fits with Freud's (1914a) suggestion that the material ought to progress from "surface" to "depth," but Menninger and Holzman's (1973) proposal is both more precise and more easily made operational. They proposed that, when the material regularly moves from deep past to present, skipping reference to the analytic situation, or goes out of order in a "clockwise" rotation, or goes back and forth between any two of the three locations, or remains stuck, as it were, in any one of them—the analyst and any privileged outside observer should be alerted to the presence of forces overriding the aim to associate freely, typically some form of "resistance."

Menninger and Holzman make only a modest claim for this schema: that it may help young analysts appreciate that there is an underlying structure to the seemingly chaotic nature of some patients' communications and that there is orderliness in the way an analyst can understand and deal with that chaos. Recognizing the ubiquity of these patterns would take us a long way toward establishing criteria for the distinctiveness of psychoanalytic process. Test the Menninger and Holzman criteria for yourself. I believe you will find them useful for discerning whether the process is going smoothly or whether the patient is struggling with more conflict than he can express easily and perhaps is not getting the help he needs from the analyst.

Let me hasten to correct a possible misimpression. My point is not that Menninger and Holzman's counterclockwise progression defines psychoanalytic process and that other patterns are deviant or less than psychoanalytic. Unless one is prepared to uphold the untenable position that a resisting patient should not be considered to be in analysis, one would have to accept any of these patterns as examples of psychoanalytic process. We may refer to whatever is going on in the analytic situation as psychoanalytic process but still recognize some psychoanalytic process as better than others for therapeutic purposes.

Note also that it is a rectifiable shortcoming of the Menninger and Holzman criterion that it deals explicitly only with the words the patient utters. The analytic material, of course, consists of everything the patient does, of which speech is only one, perhaps the most obvious, channel of communication. It is a challenge to the analyst to observe and to consider the concordance or discord among all the ways in which the patient communicates—words; the "music" of the interaction, that is, the way in which the words are voiced; actions, such as postural changes and gestures, including how the patient enters and leaves the session; and autonomic-emotional messages ranging from tears or rage to stomach rumbles. Outside observers, who generally have only reports of the goings on to evaluate, generally are not privy to these important aspects of the analytic material.

Another possible criterion for analytic process derives from the power of unconscious fantasy to drive the associations of the patient when his mind is not occupied with a task, the desired situation in an analysis. Then the high degree of redundancy in the analytic material becomes obvious. It has been said that a patient with a severe neurosis does not need a hobby. He has only one story on his mind and circles through it repeatedly. Compare the passage of psychological time for the patient with the path of a helix that cycles repeatedly through the same issues while clock time passes linearly, as it were through the axis of the helix, and you will see what I mean. Or listen to such a patient for any length of time. As the treatment progresses and the patient improves, the cycling speeds up. The wide, slow sweep of early cycles, which might have taken several sessions now becomes tightly wound and may take less than a session toward the end of treatment. As the cycles speed up, they become easier for the patient to grasp as a pattern for the futile path he has been compelled to follow.

In addition to these models of the flow of material, other phenomena can inform the analyst about the state of the analytic situation and the analytic process. Roy Shafer (1982) has called attention to the desirability of a mild degree of tension in the patient and in the atmosphere of the analytic situation, tension that refers to the degree of frustrated expectancy the patient typically experiences.

The mild tension of expectancy can, of course, be found in any conversation when the speaker is uncertain about holding the interest of the listener; the absence of mild tension would signify boredom. But in the analytic situation, the at least slight additional degree of tension we expect to find reflects the extent to which the patient's communications are driven by unconscious forces. If this mild additional degree of tension is absent, the analyst may feel that the patient's story sounds "flat." He may wonder with increasing irritation, "Why does he bother to tell this to me? It seems to have no significance to him; it doesn't even interest him." But one would have to observe for a long enough period to see if the lack of tension is characteristic or only momentary. Occasionally, a patient may slip into a kind of reverie or become slightly dissociated or even fall asleep. Absence of tension during such generally brief episodes would hardly disqualify the process as psychoanalytic.

Taken together, these two phenomena—the direction of the flow of the analytic material and the tension of expectancy—may be peculiar to the analytic situation in which one party is invited to associate freely. If we need the term psychoanalytic process—and I still am not sure we do—these two phenomena might serve as a working definition. In combination they do form a satisfactory indicator that the process between analyst and patient is propitious for analyzing.

What, then, has become of the search for criteria for the "process?" Perhaps we may conclude: that the difficulty in arriving at plausible criteria tells us that we may be trying to answer a bad question. Clearly, the term psychoanalytic process is not a discriminating one; it can be only a general descriptive term referring to what is going on between the two parties in the psychoanalytic situation at any time. More usefully, our worried observers might ask: Does the analyst understand the shifting nature, quality, direction, purpose, etc. of the "process" in which he and the patient are engaged? Does he sense the tension of frustrated expectancy that tells him of unexpressed transference wishes? Does he recognize the significance of the direction of flow of the material? Does he have a theory about why it is so and a plan for whether, how and when to intervene?

14

The Place of Regression in Psychoanalysis

Is Regression Necessary?

Both psychoanalysis and the therapies that derive from it recognize that for many patients a degree of controlled regression may be helpful in the treatment process. Transference, which, after all, involves regression, is ubiquitous. Psychoanalysis and the psychoanalytic psychotherapies are distinctive in that they expect the appearance of transference and plan to make therapeutic use of it in various ways.

Questioning the necessity of regression, I think, correctly reflects current divided opinion about the topic. It reminds me of a James Thurber (1929) story, "Is Sex Necessary?" Part of the charm of Thurber's title is the gentle conceit that nature is waiting for us to make up our minds about the need for sex. A further implication is that, if we should decide that neither sex nor regression is really necessary, we could dispense with them and go about our business relieved of any concern.

My position is that regression, like sex, is always *there*, but its presence is not always obvious. Neither sex nor regression, however, has to raise its head very high to exert an influence. Whether or not either sex or regression is necessary cannot be answered categorically, but only within a specific context. I shall not develop the argument further in regard to sex, which after all has many proponents, but as far as regression goes, when the analyst becomes aware of it, he would do well to consider its appearance necessary.

I also take the position that the analytic situation itself, including the behavior of the analyst, does not create regression in the patient (Reich, 1951). The analytic situation is, however, well designed to permit the regressed, but normally hidden, aspects of the patient to show and to allow the patient to experience himself in that peculiarly painful state of being in two emotional positions at the same time.

I have, I admit, put my position crudely. To clarify matters, it is necessary to discuss what we mean by regression and by necessary. Recall that both Sigmund Freud (1900, 1914a) and Anna Freud (1963) observed that regression is not a unitary phenomenon. Perhaps the most common context in which we tend to think about regression is in the view the libido theory gives us of child development and neurosis in which it occurs in the same sentence with fixation. Freud recognized three usages of the term. "Topographical regression" described the retrograde movement of energy through the psychic apparatus and referred to the "psi" systems of his model of dreaming. "Temporal regression" implied a "harking back to older psychical structures;" while he used the term "formal regression" for the occasions when "primitive methods of expression and representation take the place of the usual ones." Freud (1900) suggested, "All these three kinds of regression are, however, one at bottom and occur together as a rule, for what is older in time is more primitive in form and in psychical topography lies nearer to the perceptual end" (p. 548).

It is crucial to my argument that I take issue with this last suggestion of Freud. The issue is partly semantic since we no longer refer to topographical regression in our clinical work. What Freud called temporal and formal regression seem to refer to the same phenomenon, which we now call ego regression. But I believe we now conceive of other important senses of regression, specifically regression in the form of object relationships, particularly as manifested in transference. I believe most analysts today would also take issue with Freud's proposal that all forms of regression proceed together. It is easy to demonstrate in our daily work that, for instance, regression in the form of the object relationship with the analyst—that is, transference—most of the time, fortunately, does not coincide with an equal degree of regression in formal ego functioning, such as cognitive functioning. The logic of the patient's attributions is usually intact, but the premises arise in unconscious fantasy; they are generally wrong. When these regressions do seem to coincide, as in the crises of our sickest patients, we have a difficult technical problem to face.

While regression was generally thought of in the context of explaining psychopathology, Anna Freud (1936) pointed out what many analysts had already come to understand: that regression is a normal and necessary aspect of development. Others (for instance, Frijling-Shreuder, 1966; Yorke and Wiseberg, 1976) expanded that point of view. Backing and filling and retreating in order to advance are commonly seen in the development of children as well as among adults who are coping with changed circumstances. These behaviors are also seen in the analyses of our patients during the process we call working through (Freud, 1914a; Lewin, 1958).

Regression and the Principles of Technique

The idea of regression has been present by implication in all the previous chapters. The phenomena associated with regression are among our central concerns. By way of review: although the preferred medium of communication between patient and analyst is speech, the analyst soon learns that the patient's words must be understood not just lexically but mostly in terms of their intention, as tendentious as well as communicative. The patient's speech and other actions must be heard as somehow intended to influence the analyst/listener to get him to do something to, with, or for the patient (again, as "real" object or as transference object); or to prevent him from taking some undesired action. Whatever the patient talks about, whether relating to something in the past, present, or future and regardless of its "truth"—regardless of its reasonableness, plausibility, or conformity with known fact—must also (and generally primarily) be understood as referring metaphorically to the psychoanalytic situation and the analyst, particularly to the transference figure of the moment. The analyst's listening habitus is always governed by the maxim, "Why now?"

I have reviewed these analytic commonplaces to introduce the topic of regression because metaphoric communication is often cast in a regressive form, and it is important that the analyst appreciate the degree of regression prevailing at the moment. It may advance the argument if you imagine the forms of communication arranged in a hierarchy. At the top would be pure symblic speech, words spoken only to inform the listener. Of course, we recognize that all patient (and analyst) communications are impure in this sense. Patient communication, especially, is suffused with transference, so that "pure symbolic speech" is an idealistic conception needed to anchor the top of the ladder. We would not expect to find examples of such speech in the analytic situation, but we do find them in everyday life; for instance a radio announcer intoning, "The time now is . . ." is giving us information without any direction about using it. Below this ideal point, we can locate speech or another action that is intended both to inform and to act on the listener, as when a patient tells a story and hopes to evoke sympathy or revulsion in the listener. Examples of an analyst feeling impelled by the patient's storytelling to act within its script can be found in my case illustrations.

Closer to the bottom of the hierarchy we would locate speech that contains a message but is mainly intended to get the analyst to do something. Flagrant examples, which also refer to time, are, "Doctor, I just want to tell you one more thing," and "I know you are going to call time on me again just as I'm about to get going." Even closer to the bottom we would locate messages conveyed mostly by action or in which the action component clearly outweighs in importance the symbolic content, as when a patient refuses to pay the bill, misses sessions, or attempts suicide. The content of the message typically is, "I am hurt and angry" while the action component could be stated as, "I want you to know it and feel it; you should suffer also." At the very bottom, we would anchor the hierarchy with another idealistic conception, "pure action." We would not expect to find examples of pure action in the analytic situation since the absence of symbolic content would also preclude addressing the analyst. In everyday life, examples might include falling victim to random violence or to a hit-and-run driver.

The hierarchy also maps the degree to which the patient's communication involves regression. But the presence of an action component alone does not by itself inform us about the amount of regression involved or the degree to which the action should be viewed as acting out. Consider this extreme example:

> If a patient were to walk out of a session angrily saying he did not intend to return, we would regard his behavior as an action and certainly with some communicative intent. But without knowing more about the antecedents to the action, we could not safely ascribe it to transference or describe it as regressive; it might be justified by the patient's realistic disappointment with his treatment.
>
> But if the patient had just related with increasing passion his wife's latest failure to meet his unspoken needs; and told you that his oldest son, whom he has been supporting ever since he dropped out of college, was fired for not doing his job; and said that his brother-in-law had finally gotten up the nerve to quit his job after suffering under an impossible, inconsiderate boss—then we would feel safe in regarding the utterance as also expressing an inhibited action against the transference figure. The justification for our assumption would be the buildup of anger toward other figures on whom the patient ought to be able to depend and who ought to know, without being told, what he needed from them. The analyst in such a circumstance could well feel that he is in the eye of a storm swirling all around him.

I am not indicting acting in general as regression. Rather I am urging that a patient's effort, through transference, to convert a current reality-attuned state to an earlier, possibly fantasized state also should be understood as regression. The regression from largely symbolic, communicative speech to tendentious speech may be thought of as formal regression, or regression in ego functioning, and may or may not be accompanied by regression in the form of defending. Of course, transference itself reflects regression in the form of object relationships and possibly in the level of psychosexual organization.

Acting (Out, In, or Up) and Regression

The term acting out is generally (and, by my lights, improperly) used when the analyst is distressed by something the patient is doing that he believes opposes the work of the analysis and threatens an emergency that will disrupt the analytic situation. Perhaps the patient has stopped behaving "properly"; he seems to have stopped trying to associate freely (that is, in words only) and has lost interest in speaking to express what is on his mind. The analyst is apprehensive that the patient now seems intent on breaking some rule or convention; he is about to make trouble. The patient seems to have forgotten for the moment that he came for analysis; he now has a more urgent program to pursue, a cause to rally, a grievance to right, a peremptory need to fill. He cannot think of resuming the analysis until he has obtained satisfaction.

Matters are not usually as stark as that kind of threatened emergency. More often, the patient may seem to try to associate freely, but something keeps gnawing at him and intrudes itself repeatedly. The patient may say he wants to analyze, but "acts" in such a way as to make it difficult for the analyst to work with him. Generally the patient acts in such a way as to worry the analyst, or, if the analysis is being conducted under the auspices of a clinic, perhaps to get the therapist in trouble with the administration. As we have mentioned, common forms of such misbehavior include not paying bills, or paying slowly, missing appointments, coming late, or staying too long in session. A variety of other annoying and puzzling behaviors also could be included.

The time and frequency of sessions and the fee to be paid are usually considered as part of the "structure" of the analysis. Structure may seem an odd word for anything connected with such a flexible, elastic, and occasionally seemingly formless process as analysis. But the word does convey that the arrangements around money and time are among the very few that are set up as fixed at the outset. It is just these few simple and necessary arrangements, the only matters about which the analyst has as yet taken a clear position, that the patient will challenge if he has a grievance against the analyst, that is, against the transference figure for whom the analyst stands at the moment, and cannot express it openly in words.

The nagging, unanswerable questions, doubts, and resentments that are embedded in unconscious fantasy cannot be voiced more directly because, in the first place, they are not available to consciousness and, secondarily, are in conflict with the need to maintain the good will, or at least the support, of the transference figure. Open rebellion would not do, it would be too dangerous. But foot dragging, sulking, disappointing, and other behaviors guaranteed to catch the attention of the transference figure and analyst are a safer compromise between the conflicting motives. The beauty of the compromise is that, just as in ancient times, when the parent would become more involved with the recalcitrant child to make him behave, so the analyst is likely to be drawn into a corrective stance, into efforts to get the patient to live up to his agreements about time and money so that they can get on with the task of analyzing.

It is difficult for an analyst confronted with such annoying and expensive misbehavior to keep in mind that he invited the patient, explicitly or not, to speak his mind in whatever form he finds possible and for the analyst to recognize that by his objectionable behavior, the patient may be doing just that. This sort of patient behavior is commonly referred to as "acting out," and of course it is, just as is *all* transference-based behavior.[1] If we need a special term for the more extravagant dramatizations of transference that are also conspicuously annoying to the analyst, but also possibly to the police and the Board of Sanitation, we might borrow the term acting up from child rearing.

The main idea, of course, is that, when important messages cannot be conveyed in symbolic speech (which for the patient in analysis is most of the time), they will be expressed regressively in action. The action may include words with strong emotional connotation, physical movement, or disturbance of various somatic systems, but, as is the case for the patient who comes late or withholds payment, the action may simply be wordless negative action, not doing what one is supposed to do. "

To repeat, I am reserving "acting out" to mean a form of communication mostly within the therapeutic session, but elsewhere as well. This term should be taken literally, to mean dramatizing a message that also could be put into words. This is not to say that acting out is necessarily wordless. Even when it is wordy, the essential message is generally conveyed more in what the patient does than in what he says; elements of mime may be employed. And as one reads the actions, they may seem to be at odds with the words. A good general rule is that, when the action component conflicts with the verbal component, the analyst should give primary consideration to the action.

It is one of the universals of psychotherapy and psychoanalysis that all, or nearly all, important messages in psychotherapy—especially those that contain anger, disappointment, fear, resentment, or other "negative" feelings—are first uttered by the patient, and sometimes exclusively, in what might be called action language (Schafer, 1976). The reasons are several, and include at least these few put in the most general terms. As I discussed

[1] Some analysts would prefer to refer to acting out within the analytic situation as "acting in" and reserve "acting out" for behavior outside the analytic situation. To my mind, these are pointless distinctions.

earlier, the patient is not fully aware of what he wants to say, in part because he is in conflict about it. The conflict is, at least in part, unconscious and so he tends to be more aware of one side of the conflict than the other. It is a terribly important question, and he is not sure he wants the answer. It would be better, or at least safer, to remain in conflict than to risk inviting a hurtful answer or an unwanted solution. It is not a new question but one that has haunted the patient for most of his life and concerns his relationships with important, powerful people whom he needs, loves, fears, or hates and who must therefore be controlled.

These reasons draw on the general principle that in psychotherapy, as in life, we tend to repeat, that is, act out, what we cannot remember (Santayana, 1905–1906). The patient's not knowing exactly what he wants to say and his inhibition about finding out also speak to the origins of the problem in an unconscious fantasy that always ends badly. It is the analyst's job to help the patient translate these important messages from action language to verbal language. This process of raising the level of communication, which is one of the most important senses of the term interpretation, is perhaps the main activity of the analyst. I want to stress here that in speaking in this way about what to the analyst seems like the patient's sudden and perverse efforts to mess up the only "clean" things about psychotherapy and psychoanalysis, the arrangements about time and money, I am linking them to everything else that goes on. I also suggest an answer to the question, Why now? what may seem a sudden emergence of misbehavior may be only a flagrant expression of something the patient has been saying or hinting at for some time, but that the analyst has not yet heard and understood. Now the patient has put them in a form that is certain to catch the analyst's attention.

So another reason the patient uses action language rather than words and manipulates the symbols of time and money is: his growing sense of being misunderstood or ignored. It is possible that the therapist did not hear the patient, or did not understand him, when he was emitting these same messages in some less obvious form. Messages that first were unheard when whispered, or even when spoken aloud, finally get through to the analyst when, so to speak, they appear on a billboard. When acting out manifests as acting up, it should be understood that, because earlier, softer expressions were not heard and responded to adequately, the situation has escalated to the point it can no longer be overlooked.

The Language of Money and Time

Thus far I have been speaking about the patient's behavior around issues of money and time as if it were totally a matter of the content of communication. I could say that the manipulation of money and time can be viewed as a language, as a "form" as well as a "content." As a language, time and money can be compared to the "language of flowers"; the choice of flowers a suitor sends his beloved and the size of the bouquet may weigh more heavily than the words on the accompanying card.

To consider time and money only as media of communication and not as important in their own right would invert the values generally placed on these matters in society. Time is money, and money makes the world go round and keeps the analyst solvent. You may have been thinking, "Surely that can't be all of it. It is all very well to advise working psychotherapeutically with acting out, but what do I *do* if the patient doesn't pay, if the patient doesn't live up to agreements about time and money arrangements, whatever the cause of the misbehavior?" That question points to another principle in working with acting out. The patient's acting out invites, or, better, coerces the therapist into counteracting out, usually by being unable to think of any way to deal with the situation other than by "doing something" to counter what the patient is doing or threatening to do. The analyst in that position feels powerless, sensing that the patient has seized the initiative and is dictating the analyst's moves.

A kind of Gresham's Law operates in psychotherapy as well as in economics. To paraphrase Gresham, "Bad money drives out good money," meaning that, if paper money and gold are both circulating and there is any doubt about the value of the paper money, the public will tend to hoard the gold and circulate the paper. The "bad money" drives the "good money" out of circulation. A similar "law" operates in psychotherapy and psychoanalysis. Faced with acting-up by a patient, a therapist feels an almost irresistible compulsion to counteract. If he does indeed resist the impulse to counteract, he will tend to feel paralyzed, for, while restraining the temptation to act (and restraint is itself an [inhibited] act), he can think of no other course. We could also put it as "Regression invites counterregression."

Low-level action language tends to displace higher level symbolic language. This inclination is illustrated in the worried question, "If the patient doesn't pay his bills, what do I do?" The implication is that the therapist does not want to do what he feels forced to do. He is an unwilling actor, afraid to act as he has been scripted to act. Clearly the initiative has swung to the patient; by not paying (or by threatening not to pay) he foresees that the analyst will have to *do* something about it. The analyst may agree that the patient might be sending a message in that painful way, and "maybe" the patient does want to find out if I really am interested in him. "But still, if he doesn't pay his bill, I will have to do something. I will have to stop seeing him even though he might wrongly conclude that I am not interested in him."

As the two essential and "tangible" media of exchange between patient and analyst, money and time are ideally suited to be used as a "language," a "dialect," if you will, of the general action language in which most of the treatment is conducted. Like all actions, speaking through appointments (time) or fees (money) can be highly expressive, but also minimally articulate. The therapist may be uncertain what the message is about, other than that the patient is unhappy with him and seems to want to get even. The work of interpretation can be seen here, as elsewhere, as consisting of raising the level of communication from actions to words; we might call it interpreting upward. The analyst must be aware of the danger that, because his personal and professional life is immediately affected when the patient "speaks" by withholding fees, missing appointments. or coming late, he is likely to take only a "realistic" view of the patient's behavior. When the patient expressed the same message about his anger, disappointment, or distrust in words, even affect-tinged words, or in less conspicuous acting, the metaphoric import was easier to miss.

Interpreting When Acting Out Is Convenient for the Analyst

Consider also: the language of time and money is equally suitable to expressing compliance and hypercompliance as it is to expressing disappointment, anger, and revenge. But an analyst is not likely to look closely at the behavior of a patient who never is late or never misses an appointment, who even crawls out of a sick bed to attend his session or who pays his bills instantly, even when he cannot afford to do so. This patient is not likely to be charged with acting out, although he surely is dramatizing an important message. The analyst will not be disposed to analyze neurotic behavior that is convenient for him. Unless I asked, I have never heard supervisees mention that patients always paid on time if I did not ask. Supervisees are always surprised that patients could have some angry feelings against which they might have erected strong defenses or that a patient might be observing the "rules" so sedulously to keep certain matters out of the analysis. They wince at the suggestion that a patient might silently be saying, "All he is interested in is his fee, and, if I stay current, he'll stay off my case."

Please do not infer from my advice to search first for the meaning of what a patient says or does that you can safely ignore its practical consequences. I do mean that an analyst ought to pay attention to the earliest, softest indications that a patient is shifting to a "language" lower on the hierarchy, that he is slipping toward acting. Acting, as a form of communication, may not be so immediately serious as to shake the structure of the analysis. Unless the patient expresses himself by manipulating the symbols of money and time, the analyst who is not alert to the patient's tendency to shift subtly to a lower level of communication may miss the phenomenon, or perhaps he might prefer to overlook it.

Not infrequently, an analyst first becomes alarmed by acting out only after having ignored for some time that the patient was slipping into action language while the analyst was inadvertently slipping into counteracting. He has been counteracting by overlooking, forgiving, and making allowances for the patient's "trivial" misdemeanors rather than trying to understand what the patient is trying to say and why he has had to shift to another language to say it. The generally benevolent attitude that we bring to our work tends to make us uncomfortable about "making an issue" about lateness and slow paying, reluctant to see ourselves as timekeeper or bill collector. We may accept the distasteful attribution only when forced. We would rather overlook what might "really" be only a minor delinquency, delay, or oversight so as to focus on the more interesting work of helping out patients with their problems. In that way, we collude with patients to put ourselves in an awkward position, a dilemma in which our choices seem to be limited to ignoring their trespasses or become what we would hate to be. If we see these choices as the only moves open to us, the situation would best be viewed as a countertransference dilemma.

The evocation of transference or countertransference feelings in the analyst can also be thought of as a language, or a dialect of action language, a dialect well suited to communicate to the analyst what it feels like for the patient to be stuck in conflict. If you recognize in this situation the familiar pattern that analysts prefer to avoid distasteful transference attributions and hence may miss the most important things the patients have to say, then I will have succeeded in placing in the context of general principles the behaviors we tend to lump as "acting out" rather than viewing them as special situations that require special rules.

Perhaps this is enough in the way of introduction to the problem of patients who communicate with us by pulling the chains of the system.

15

The Challenge of Regression

Setting Limits

Every analyst will recall at least one supervisor who shook his head wearily while saying, "You really ought to set some limits," implying you were being bamboozled by your patient and even colluding in the patient's misbehavior. If you think about it, however, apart from the painful reminder that you were once less skilled than you are now, you might agree that the term does not fit comfortably into the way (I hope) you are coming to think about the analytic situation.

Recall that the main function of the analyst is to construct an analytic situation, a safe place where the patient can experience maximum freedom to associate freely and voice everything that comes to mind. The less obvious function is to make dramatically clear to the patient that he is unable to permit himself to take advantage of this opportunity to experience freedom. Much of the analysis consists of helping the patient to understand why this is so and in that way to relax the defensiveness that stands in the way of his experiencing freedom.

Another way of looking at this issue is that the patient, in his effort to associate freely, is able to "remember" his infantile life only in a regressive mode, that is, through transference; and transference, we understand, is expressed in action. The warning commonly given to beginners, "Watch out for any tendencies toward enactment by the patient," must seem odd if one considers that, in principle, transference is enactment pure and simple. If a patient tells you, "You look just like my father," he may or may not be experiencing transference. But if he treats you as if you were his father, that is, if he acts toward you as if you were the father of his infancy and expects to be treated by you as he is in his fantasies about that period, then you may be sure he is transferring.

As I discussed earlier, the "analytic material" is what the patient *does*, not just the words he speaks. The "language" used by the patient in analysis is closer to pure action than to pure verbalization. The analytic situation is intended to permit the patient to tell his story in whatever language he can, and we expect that most of the time the lingua franca will be of the kind involved in dramatization, the language we call transference.

Still, the supervisor of our youth had a point in warning that *this* patient, at *this* time, seems to be in danger of losing track of the technical purpose of the permissiveness of the analytic situation. He might lose the therapeutic split that permits him to observe as well as participate and might do something embarrassing or destructive to himself or to others. When the analyst examines a patient to determine if psychoanalysis would be the proper treatment, he should estimate whether the patient will be able to make use of the implicit invitation to regress and also be able to withstand the temptation, or perhaps the compulsion, to exceed the degree of regression that is necessary for analyzing.

Before considering this dilemma further, let us stay for a while with the admonition that an analyst should set some limits, the scolding that first caught our attention. That scolding seemed to imply that the analytic situation under criticism was without limits altogether. The analyst so admonished surely understood it that way and that he better get across to the patient somehow to "knock it off," to stop behaving badly and get down to business. He understood the subtext that it was his fault that the patient was acting up.

But what does it mean, operationally, to set limits? One could tell the patient, "Stop it, or the analysis cannot proceed," and many an analyst has done just that. Whether one can conduct an analysis after taking such a stand deserves more careful discussion than I can give it here. Making such a threat or ultimatum certainly sounds as if the analyst "means business." But when the analyst speaks or, more accurately, acts in that mode, on whom is the injunction placed? The analyst has no power to enforce the injunction; his ultimate sanction is to decline to participate further in the attempt to analyze. The only party on whom the analyst can set limits is himself.

Perhaps the supervisor who started us off on this discussion had just that fact in mind, and was too annoyed with the supervisee to tell him so directly. If the supervisor had been less annoyed, he might have said, "I would like you to consider how you might be participating in your patient's dangerous misbehavior. You don't seem to realize that the patient is saying something to you by acting in this way and that you are saying something to him in return by putting up with it silently. You might want to consider that your failure to address matters analytically is forcing him to escalate in order to get his message across. You ought to place a limit on your unanalytic pose of misplaced tolerance." There, we hear useful technical advice: "Don't just sit there, analyze!"

But is there no use for the idea of limits when the patient is not "misbehaving?" Is the concept of limits irrelevant except when the patient threatens a disturbance? A little reflection makes it obvious that limits are inherent in all social situations, including the analytic situation as was discussed in Chapter 2. The analytic situation draws on the physician–patient relationship with an additional, if implicit, proscription against touching and perhaps with other procedural rules. Depending on how the analyst conducts himself in the initial interviews and in the setting of the consulting room, these aspects of the analytic situation might be defined explicitly or left to the patient to define, perhaps by analogy to other encounters with physicians or through imagination and fantasy.

For instance, some analysts make a point of stating "The Basic Rule" as if it were a statute that could be enforced. The analyst also might discuss the schedule of sessions as if it were a legal contract, anticipating, as do all legal contracts, that the party of the second part would be inclined to break it if he believed it to be to his advantage and therefore must be reminded that there will be sanctions for nonadherence. Such sanctions include paying for missed sessions and having to observe a "window" for timely notification of planned or emergent absence so as to avoid penalty. The analyst might also include a requirement that the fee be paid in full within a certain time after he presents the bill. In this way, matters of procedure that merely are convenient for the analyst become set up as aspects of the "structure" of the analytic situation and then are defended as essential to its purpose.

This way of thinking about the structure of the analytic situation is time honored. When Freud was practicing in Vienna under the stringencies of World War I, the foreign patients he had come to depend on were kept away. Because his livelihood depended on what was becoming a steadily decreasing clinical income, he began to charge for missed appointments. But his justification was economic, not analytic. Subsequently, a moral reinforcer was added: the patient ought to be charged a fee sufficient for him to feel pain and certainly ought not be allowed to profit from delinquency, such as failure to attend sessions.

Considerations of the symbolic significance of money and of paying and receiving gifts added to the growing weight of opinion. It thus came to be doctrinal that one could not conduct an analysis successfully without charging a significant fee, a belief still held widely and firmly despite the evidence that it is not true. Lorand and Console (1958), reporting the demonstrated efficacy of no-fee treatment, reminded us that Freud had attempted it quite early and, he thought, unsuccessfully. Nonetheless, he recommended it to the Budapest Congress in 1918 in order to accommodate the broad mass of the population who could not afford a private fee.

When the analyst defines the analytic situation according to rules, despite the coincident invitation to associate freely, he guarantees that the patient will be preoccupied with the rules, will want to heed or rebel against the implied command to "be good," and will both resent the strictures and fear the risks of nonconformity. You can easily demonstrate for yourself that if you do not raise the necessary procedural arrangements to the status of rules, that is, not offer the "basic rule" as a rule, but only as a procedural suggestion or "permission," if you do not charge all the traffic would bear, if you do not charge for missed sessions nor insist on prompt payment—your patients will still be preoccupied with what they construe to be "the rules" and the risks of breaking them. And they would be neither more nor less inclined to conform or rebel.

It is the nature of neurosis to express conflict by projecting one side of the conflict to the external world. Rather then feeling torn by internal conflict, patients find it easier to struggle with external authority, most easily with their analysts. The analytic situation facilitates the expression of such transference, but it is possible to analyze transference only to the extent that the attribution of authority *is* transference and not an accurate perception of the analyst's arbitrariness and the power he has arrogated to make "the rules" to suit himself.

We hold the view that it is the general purpose of analysis to relieve the patient of an excessively burdensome and anachronistic rule structure, a neurosis. It hardly seems to be the most direct way of going about this to impose additional and unnecessary rules. Whether or not casting the necessary arrangements about schedule and fee as rules is necessary in any particular case would have to be considered in that context and justified by the facts of the case.[1]

Inadvertent Limit Setting

It is common practice for some analysts to end an interpretation or intervention of any kind with a "standard closing" having the general form of, "What comes to your mind about that?" It is, of course, a way of saying to the patient, "That's all I have to say at the moment. Now it's your turn" and, in that sense, is reminiscent of good practice in radio communication to signal to the unseen other that one is done for the

[1] Some authorities (e.g., Kernberg et al., 1989) who specialize in treating patients with severe borderline and narcissistic conditions, including those with antisocial tendencies, strongly believe so. My own experience does not confirm that opinion, but I did not treat the patients Kernberg and his associates treated.

moment by saying, "Roger." I think it remarkable that an analyst would have to signal that he is ready to hear what the patient might have to say and would choose a construction that implies the absurdity that the patient might say something that did not come to mind.

Absurdity aside, an analyst who has fallen into that habit probably does not realize that he is setting a limit on the patient by dictating the form, content, or timing of the desired response. The innocuous-sounding formalism is anything but innocuous and is, in effect, a kind of "commercial" for free association that attempts to direct the patient's response. I believe anxiety is at work here, the subtext of the commercial could be read as, "Please say whatever words come to your mind, but don't *do* anything. Just words, please." While I doubt that many patients take the implied injunction of the subtext literally, it does stand as a constant reminder to "talk, don't act."

Would it not be better if the analyst allowed the interpretation to stand by itself? Then the analyst would hear or see what the patient's response might be, not just the content, but also the form it might take. The response to an effective interpretation might be an emotional experience, a stroke of sadness marked with tears, or a sudden relaxation, or a muscle spasm. The response might not be primarily in words at all. What is gained by suggesting the form of his response to the patient other than to remind him to "speak, not act."

Even when that analyst agrees, with some chagrin, that he had never considered the possible effect of these "commercials," he may find it difficult to desist. Partly, of course, habit is to blame, but we should also consider that the message, "Think, don't act," is the more or less unconsciously intended subtext; the analyst, like many patients, may fear that analyzing will release the demons lurking in the unconscious. And so, with one hand, he invites the patient to be free and, with the other, warns him to behave himself. It is a classic version of the double bind and hardly conducive to analyzing.

When Regression Becomes a Problem

Regression becomes a problem when it exceeds what the analyst regards as useful and no longer seems controllable by the patient or, for that matter, by the analyst. It is especially frightening when, for instance, a borderline patient, after a period of seemingly successful psychotherapy, develops an overwhelming transference reaction that threatens to undermine the treatment and disrupt the patient's life outside as well. An analyst who has done any amount of psychotherapy certainly has found himself in the situation in which a patient, at least for the time being, seems to be much worse off than he was, and the patient, his family, and even possibly the analyst believe that the treatment itself is somehow the cause of the patient's disturbance. Such episodes pose daunting technical problems.

Several conceptual problems must be clarified before we can consider how episodes of regression come about, what they mean, and their function in the patient's life and in therapy. Suggesting that there could be a "function" for this behavior begs the questions that we should be discussing: are these episodes to be understood as accidents, untoward interruptions of an otherwise smoothly going analysis, or are they somehow integral to the process? Another way of looking at the same issue is, should we regard the disturbed behavior as representing a failure of the patient's personality structure, an event analogous to a collapse of an overloaded bridge, or is it a misguided attempt to communicate?

I am reminded of a bit of black humor that was current some years ago to the effect that death is nature's way of telling us to slow down. In the same way, clinicians are accustomed to thinking that suicide attempts are a "cry for help," that they are an extravagant, desperate, misguided form of communication. Clearly, the choices are not mutually exclusive. A suicide attempt, which incidentally may be an expression of just the sort of regressive behavior that concerns us, may reflect a desperate wish to communicate with the analyst or other important persons. We also must recognize that the patient may also, and quite independently, have any or, fatally, all the following wishes: to die, to kill, to be killed, to be dead (Menninger, 1938).

We might also ask if a regressive episode is best understood as an expression of conflict, as symptomatic behavior, or as a deficiency in self-control. From a slightly different point of view, the issue could be approached by asking, if we believe the behavior is motivated, are the motives underlying it mostly conscious or unconscious? We could also ask if the behavior is best understood as mostly patient dependent, that is characteristic of only certain kinds of patients, perhaps those with specific ego deficits, or is it treatment dependent, mostly characteristic of certain therapies? Or is it analyst dependent—could such behavior be precipitated by lack of skill or a failure of empathy, a common fear among beginning analysts? Thus, we could ask if we ought to understand severe regressions as just one of the hazards of treating certain kinds of patients. Or perhaps we should regard severe regressions primarily as a technical issue with the implication that analysts should learn to deal more effectively with vulnerable patients so that the incidence of such disturbances is lower and the treatment less turbulent and more effective.

While these antitheses were contrived for heuristic purposes, they implicate important theoretical and clinical issues. For the present, let me simply assert that these severe regressive episodes do *not* occur in all patients, but only in those who have some combination of "talent" and weakness. By weakness, I mean a vulnerability to at least temporary disruptions of ego structure. By "talent," I mean the capacity for making expressive, communicative use of regressive phenomena. Patients without the talent or taste for regressive display tend to experience their vulnerability more or less silently. They defend themselves inconspicuously, withdraw, regroup, and may even conceal completely the internal drama that has been going on. Some of these patients break off treatment at this point, to the surprise and dismay of the analyst. We may understand this action as the dynamic equivalent of interrupting the process of analyzing by displaying severe regression, or the fear of regressing, a fear that, put into words, might sound like, "If I don't run away, you will let me go crazy."

For the broad range of patients who have the necessary degree of vulnerability, it makes a vast difference how the analyst works with them—how sensitive he is to their needs and fears, to their characteristic forms and patterns of decompensation, and to the situations that offer dangerous temptations and are potentially traumatic to them. For each patient it especially makes a difference how sensitive the analyst is to the vicissitudes of transference (and to the resiliency of the patient's defenses against transference) in which all these issues come alive.

Patients may fall into three broad groups with regard to vulnerability. Severe regressive episodes occur frequently with patients whose ego organization is fragile and who tend to slip into episodic decompensation. These episodes may be related to external stressors, but it is not always easy to see what the stressor might have been. The episodes seem to have at least as much to do with endogenous factors, that is, "personality weaknesses." Severe regressive episodes also occur, but with much lower frequency, in patients who seem to be organized sufficiently well to withstand most of the vicissitudes of life but who occasionally experience stress-related decompensation.

The stress that interests us particularly is the temptation to regress in the therapeutic situation. Such a temptation is particularly dangerous when the analyst does not sufficiently understand that the patient is facing a dangerous temptation and how anxious that temptation makes him. The danger is greater when the analyst unwittingly undermines the patient's necessary efforts at defense or makes excessive libidinal demands on the patient. Under these circumstances, the ensuing regressive episode may indeed include a "cry for help." As I discuss later, the cry for help may be mixed with a plea for distance that expresses the patient's wish to get away. As in the group of fragile patients, it may also occasionally reflect a loss of control and to that degree may be free of communicative intent.

There is a third group of patients, those who do not regress in any obvious way, who are sufficiently well organized to withstand easily the temptations to regress in the therapeutic situation. Some of these patients withstand the pressures of therapy so well, and are so rigidly defended against useful regression, that they are well-nigh untreatable. Others, while not rigidly organized, are sufficiently well put together that they negotiate easily the usual vicissitudes of the analytic situation and remain relatively unthreatened by the analyst's inevitable temporary failures to understand them, or even by major gaffes. They either express their annoyance or anxiety clearly enough to help the analyst to correct his stance or,if that seems impossible, are free enough to leave an unuseful treatment.

16

Severe Regression

The Hazards of Severe Regressions in Vulnerable Patients

In this chapter, I focus on the problems caused by episodes of severe regression in patients, described in the previous chapter, for whom a combination of vulnerability and analyst mismanagement brings about the episode of regression. This group spans a broad range of patients and includes those who would be diagnosed among the higher level borderline personality organizations, narcissistic personality disorders, and psychoneuroses.

Although severe regression may be viewed as a disturbance in a hitherto more or less smoothly going psychoanalysis, in short a "middle-phase" phenomenon; such episodes not infrequently occur when a patient fears that the end of therapy, or even a temporary interruption, is impending; or they may occur at the very beginning of treatment (Schlesinger, 1996). Many of the "emergencies" with which the treatment of certain patients begins could be understood within this framework.

A kind of "complementary series" governs the likelihood of occurrences of such regressions in which the patient's vulnerability to severe regressions is balanced against the technical skill and sensitivity of the analyst, and is compounded by the analyst's liability to transference and countertransference.

The sine qua non of this kind of severe regressive episode is an unanalyzed, possibly even unrecognized, dependent, heterosexual or homosexual transference in which the patient feels both propelled toward the analyst and fearful, even panicky, about the strength of his impulses and the alternating (or even simultaneous) likelihood of seduction or rejection. In patients whose self- and object relationships are not well organized, these fearsome fantasies may also contain the loss of a sense of a separate self and the danger of imminent merger with the object. The apparent, that is, surface, content may be sexual or sexualized, or it may be apparently aggressive. It is important that the analyst understand whether, for instance, the "sexual" is the message or the medium, whether it is content or form. Sexual and aggressive behavior, like withholding payment and missing sessions, can be viewed as "languages" to express a range of wishes and fears.

A point to keep in mind is that the content of the fantasies that may be acted out does not discriminate between mild and severe regressions. The problem lies not in the seeming noxiousness of an unconscious fantasy but, rather, in the character, dynamics, and quality of ego organization of the patient. The other indispensable element is that the patient experiences a deep unconscious (though it may partly be conscious) attachment to the analyst as part of the transference. The importance of the element of unconsciousness is that, if the patient were aware of his feelings, he might find it possible to use actual flight to resolve the fear of temptation, frustration, rejection, or merger. At these points, such patients may break off treatment, at least temporarily. A patient who cannot flee geographically, that is "horizontally," may feel forced to flee psychologically, or figuratively, "vertically," in the form of a regressive episode. A patient may regress in both senses by, as it were, jumping into the therapist's lap to avoid the dangerous wish to be close.

My referring to talent and vulnerability as indispensable in these patients amounts to a theoretical, as well as a clinical, commitment. It is a way of asserting that, in this patient group, episodes of severe regression are to be understood neither as accidents nor as inevitable occurrences, but as emergent phenomena having to do with a failure of both patient and analyst to appreciate the nature, intensity, and significance of a shift in the transference. I use the word transference here as an omnibus term to include not only the patient's transference toward the analyst but also the analyst's transference toward the patient.

I have avoided describing regressive episodes as "sudden"; I prefer to describe them as emergent. They usually appear to be sudden to the analyst, who may be surprised, if not shocked. But the patient may not have experienced the episode as sudden. He may say, "I was trying to tell him [the analyst] for weeks, but I couldn't make him understand." At other times the patient, will report (I believe in collusion with the analyst) the episode as having had a sudden onset, as, "Unpredictably, it came out of the blue." I believe the attribution of suddenness may represent an effort to forestall blaming the analyst, as in, "It went by too fast to notice." A careful review of the material generally indicates that prodromal indicators were available to be seen and heard by both parties; that a shorter or longer period of strain and successive misunderstandings preceded the regression.

I must qualify the flat statement that severe regressions are not inevitable events in the treatment of vulnerable patients. Doing psychotherapy with such patients does run the risk of unwanted regression if the treatment is at all involving. If the relationship with the analyst develops in depth, the patient will experience a temptation to regress. He may even be partly aware of the temptation, especially later in treatment. As the patient's conflicts are mobilized, tendencies to act in and out of the treatment situation are as likely as with any other patient, but the danger that the regressive swings may get out of hand will be greater. Often the most effective therapeutic work can be done, as it were, on the risky edge of the patient's feeling tempted to act up or regress, which may amount to the same thing. The task, here as always, is to maintain the therapeutic situation and to help the patient experience and verbalize what he is experiencing rather than short-circuiting the expression of fantasies by regressive acting. For the analyst these tasks devolve into the usual issues of tact, dosage and timing, and sensitive awareness of the nature and depth of the patient's transference involvement, on one hand, and, on the other, the nature and state of the patient's defenses, particularly those against awareness of transference.

The following example is not unusual:

> A recovering borderline patient came into the session angry and chagrined: "I sat up half the night trying to cut myself and I couldn't. I wanted to and yet I thought it was silly, but I couldn't stand the idea that I wasn't able to. I've always been able to control things and put an end to things, but you've interfered with my will."
>
> The therapist nodded understandingly and reminded the patient that in their last session, for a few moments, she had felt an unaccustomed sense of freedom and did not know what to make of it. She had felt like looking around the office instead of keeping her eyes fixed on the floor, with only an occasional furtive glance at him. Unusually for her, too, she had cautiously said that it felt good, but then she fell silent and looked worried. A few minutes later, leaving the session, she slumped over again and did not say goodbye. "So?" she asked, challengingly.
>
> The therapist went on: "So, I think by the time you left you must have felt that you had sold out, regretted that you might have given up your prized independence just to feel good for a few moments. And, of course, as soon as you got home you had to make sure you were still in control of yourself, and cutting has always worked for you. But this time you didn't cut—that doesn't mean you won't ever be able to resist cutting again. I think you half-believe that it may be possible to feel a bit freer and keep your sense of being an independent person. And I think you want to be sure that, just because you felt good for a moment, I won't take you for granted and lose interest.

With that, and without indicating agreement or disagreement, the patient changed the subject and went on with no further reference to the matter.

Note that the therapist's intervention was directed toward the patient's shaky sense of self and her fear of becoming close to and dependent on him. But his words were chosen from her idiom and avoided the word dependency that she dreaded. His intent was to "normalize" her reaction, to make it reasonable for her to have feared loss of her sense of being in control and loss of him and to have tried to find a solution. And he hoped to minimize the importance of her inability to cut. His unworried, matter-of-fact acceptance of her story and her challenge to him also reassured her. And he supported her ability and willingness to deny the significance of her increasing tolerance for remaining in a nonabusive relationship (Schlesinger, 1993a, 1996).

The obvious technical advice, then, seems to be that of perfection: Don't make any mistakes when working with brittle patients and all will be well! I often received such advice, particularly in earlier days, but I no longer give it. For merely to warn an analyst about the risks with such patients and the importance of tactful and sensitive handling generally produces only apprehension and excessive caution. An uptight analyst, fearful of what might go wrong in the treatment, is in a poor position to help his patient. Yet the opposite position—since we can't prevent these regressions, relax and enjoy them—can be equally harmful. The answer is not a middle ground of "alert relaxation" or "relaxed caution," but, rather, a commitment to stay in touch with the transference and being able and willing to interpret and support the defenses against recognizing and experiencing transference vigorously, accurately, and empathetically in order to maintain the therapeutic situation.

Is there not a contradiction between interpreting and supporting? Can one interpret and also support a defense at the same time? We can and do reduce the intensity of a patient's anxiety by interpreting, empathetically, the *need* for defense as it emerges in the transference. The need is perhaps better put to the patient as a need to feel safe. By naming the patient's experience, by identifying the proximal stimulus for the patient's anxiety and the resulting understandable defensiveness, we can help the patient keep the pressure to regress[1] within tolerable bounds. When the analyst interprets in this way, the patient may feel supported sufficiently to reduce the need for emergency measures, such as severe regressions.

[1] Pressure implies either temptation to repress or the patient's fear of regressing excessively.

Thus, the advice to interpret *and* support is of the essence. It also implies that, as the analyst advances the process of interpretation, he should avoid implying the subtext, "You are doing something wrong. Stop it." Rather, the thrust of the interpretation should be to help the patient understand and appreciate his perceived necessity to pull away and in that way to share with the patient the increased burden of defense. I hope it is clear that it is not one of the goals of the analyst to eliminate acting out, for that would eliminate analyzing, but rather to interpret so as to explicate what the patient is trying to say by this troublesome behavior. Consider the following example:

> The patient was a talented artist, a woman in middle age, whose occasional exhibitions were dragged out of her by well-meaning friends who could not stand her procrastination and overpowering self-criticism. Her paintings sold but not enough to support her through her art alone. Her shows received warm critical reviews, all of which remarked, sadly, on this fine artist's slender portfolio.
>
> Both her parents had suffered from severe depressions. Her mother, who was critical of every aspect of the patient and her ambitions, was hospitalized repeatedly during the patient's childhood, with the effect that the patient had to raise herself as well as her younger brothers, all of whom turned out "peculiar." Still, the patient remained intensely loyal to her mother; she defended her against relatives who accused her of neglecting her children and household.
>
> The patient sought analysis at the urging of her friends and out of awareness that she was always getting in her own way. During the second year of analysis, the patient was getting ready for another show and becoming increasingly anxious, certain that it would be no good, that her work had not advanced, that she was just repeating the same old stuff, which wasn't even any good the first time. She could hear her mother's voice telling her she would never be any good, and lamenting," If only the baby boy who had died before she was born had lived . . ." Partial understanding of the burden of guilt she carried permitted her to complete enough work to let her apply for a show but, as the opening drew near, her anxiety mounted. She could not sleep; she felt that she would have to withdraw from the show or destroy the work—better that than to be ripped apart by the critics.
>
> In many phone calls at all hours, the patient repeated the same litany of fears and woes, seemingly without awareness of the repetitiveness. She would always feel somewhat better after the calls, during which the analyst would mainly listen and then link

> her fears to the work of the previous sessions, which were increasingly about the function of her guilt as a guarantee of attachment to her mother. Loyalty to her mother implied both identifying with her critical attitudes and suppressing her own rage. If she were to allow herself to be successful, she would lose her mother and be alone. The phone calls were a regressive enactment of staying in touch with her childhood mother, keeping her awake with professions of loyalty through the misery she was feeling and reminding her of the expectation that she was about to fulfill her mother's prophesy that she would fail.
>
> Through constant interpretation of the meaning of these regressive enactments, the patient gradually was able to separate her ambivalent attachment to her mother, which had led to her obligation to fail, from her ability to exercise her talents and enjoy the fruits of her work. The show was a huge success and the patient was able to enjoy it, although she admitted that she kept looking out of the corner of her eye for her mother, who often would blindside her with a slap to the head just to remind her not to be uppity and think too much of herself.

It should be clear from that example that adhering to an interpretative stance does not preclude the analyst from extending himself in times of crisis. The analyst should also be ready to do what may be necessary to maintain the patient's sense of safety while interpreting first "upward" toward the current function of her behavior in the transference. The combination of support and greater understanding, with the implied expectation that the patient could do it, also promoted the patient's activity. Paradoxically, offering support through reassurance but without interpretation tends to deepen regression and invites the very trouble one hopes to avoid.

Severe Regression and Countertransference

There is a hazard for the analyst as well as the patient in that transference is coercive. If the patent's conflict resonates with one of the analyst's, the analyst will tend to become polarized by the patient's transferring and be forced willy-nilly into a position of acting with or against the patient. We have all been in this situation, feeling "over a barrel," feeling, "I can think of only two things to do, and both of them are wrong." At such times, we feel therapeutically impotent, perhaps seeing fairly clearly what the patient is doing but feeling unable to help the patient or ourselves. And we may come to hate the patient for putting us into this painful situation. We wish for some way to get him to stop it, but we sense it would be futile to try. Thus, whether the analyst expresses his counterwish positively or negatively, in action or in inhibited action, the analyst has joined the patient on the level of acting; he has lost his "therapeutic split." All these analyst emergencies can be thought of as analogues or counterparts to the devastating experiences of the patient, but as experienced by a person less vulnerable to severe regression. The ingredients are the same, and the experience, while embarrassing, is far less painful.

Calling attention to the parallel between the patient's severe regression and the analyst's crisis of impotence may help to underscore the generality in what would otherwise be a collection of particulars. If we understand that, when we are feeling "in a bind," our patient may also be on the verge of an experience of unbearable helplessness, or that the patient may have pushed us into this uncomfortable position so as not to be exposed to that danger himself, we may be in a better position to help both our patient and ourselves. For an example, let us return to the vignette of the frustrated self-cutter:

> In the previous year, whenever there was some "progress" (in common, life-promoting values), the patient would regress, typically by cutting or some other conspicuous, self-destructive act that required that the analyst help to "pick up the pieces," and put the therapeutic situation back together again. By the time they were ready to resume, both parties would have forgotten what had been going on in the therapy when it was so rudely interrupted.
>
> Feeling frustrated, impotent, and silently furious at the patient for "messing up the treatment," the therapist sought consultation. He was helped to see that while the patient, in a sense, subscribed to the therapist's wholesome ambitions for her, he did not appreciate that these goals were fraught with danger for her. To strive for these goals implied that she was rejecting the figures who populated her persecutory unconscious fantasies but who nevertheless were the only "family" she had, and their presence permitted her a degree of painful stability. Subscribing to these goals also risked the certainty that the therapist would abandon her when "his" goals for her had been achieved. The therapist began to see that he and his ambitions had become the "problem" that the patient was solving by interrupting the relentless march toward health.
>
> Taking courage in hand, in the next session—in which the patient seemed to move toward a better understanding of the dilemma of her life and, as usual, eventuated in what he formerly had taken to be a comfortable silence—the therapist noted that the patient's face had darkened and her jaw had clenched; he took these signs to mean

that something important was not being said. Saying nothing, she looked away. He said that he thought that, like him, she had been pleased with what they had just come up with, but then she remembered that the session would soon be over and she would be left alone with her "family." They would be furious with her for neglecting their possessive interest in her and could be pacified only by her "destroying the treatment," derailing it by cutting herself. He guessed that right now she was silently rehearsing how she would go about destroying what she had just accomplished while bitterly thinking that he had no idea how much trouble he had caused her.

The patient slowly began to reengage and, for the first time, was able to say how much she resented and feared his "obliviousness," though she had never before mentioned its role in her cutting. This approach brought the acting out, which, as an unfolding plan, had already begun, into the session before it had fully flowered as acting-up. The therapist ended this session by adding matter-of-factly that he thought she would not feel she had to cut herself tonight, but she probably would want to, if only to make sure she still had the "right" to do it. Reflecting on the incident, the therapist realized that what the patient had labeled obliviousness was his sitting back in his chair and looking pleased with himself after offering an interpretation. He had not been aware of this postural change.

We use the designation, episode of severe regression, to cover a multitude of undesirable patient behaviors: attempted suicide, transient psychotic episodes, paranoid outbursts, acting up, all behaviors generally with a self-destructive character. Not all these behaviors may seem manifestly regressive on the surface. Indeed, some of them are better understood as defensive against regression. But, then, any piece of behavior includes aspects that are expressive as well as defensive, and knowing whether the behavior is mostly *dis*organized or *re*organized is not essential for the present argument.

The patient's experience, particularly early in such an episode, generally has the quality of an "attack" of helplessness, hopelessness, and rage. There may be a coloring of homo- or heteroerotism as well. The patient will be feeling "in a bind," "over a barrel," "in a crack," let down, and also furiously disappointed. At the same time, or alternately, the patient will be feeling guilty for failing the analyst's high expectations of him and enraged about the injustice of it all. The invariable component is rage, which may not be expressed as such and may not even be understood as such by either patient or analyst.

This very ambiguity and lack of clarity may reflect the unwillingness of both parties to face up to the nature and intensity of what is going on. As in the foregoing example, the collusion of the therapist in the patient's defense against recognizing her rage, while swallowing his own, intensifies it. It also increases the patient's sense of helplessness and the growing conviction about being betrayed by a loved and needed person who has, "suddenly, for no good reason," become heedless or uncaring, and perhaps always was so. The patient experiences a fluctuating conflict between memory and perception: "Is this therapist the cold, unfeeling person I think I see now or is he the kind, caring person of last week? Is he the cold, unfeeling parent of childhood, or the kind, caring person who is sitting with me now, obviously concerned with my pain and distress?"

As the episode of severe regression develops, it changes rapidly. In the prodromal stage, it may look quite different from what it later becomes. The longer the episode persists, the more it develops its own momentum, its own "reasons" for being, and the more detached it becomes from its origins. As one patient put it, "I see now that I started to drink because I was angry at you and couldn't stand it, but I kept on drinking because I was drunk." It follows also that these episodes are easiest to deal with in their prodromal or earlier phases and when they have nearly run their course than when they are in full flower. Early intervention is, of course, preferable; later on, there may be more damage to undo and much debris to clean up. By that time, the mess in which the patient has gotten himself may have harmed other persons, and the consequences will have escalated in complexity. It is likely that everyone involved will have lost track of what the episode was all about in the first place, and nothing will have been learned. It is difficult, logically, to demonstrate prevention, but here is an example of early intervention that, like the therapist's intervention in the previous example, I believe precluded an impending regression:

> It was relatively early in the analysis. The patient had kept all his appointments, was invariably on time or even a little early, and paid his bill promptly. Then came a session during which the analyst had, unusually for him and in a quite mild tone, remarked on the patient's pride in the activity he had been describing with such gusto. The analyst was then surprised that the patient fell silent, discontinued the account of the activity that had occasioned the analyst's remark and, seeming in general to be quite disengaged, filled the rest of the session with matters in which he had no obvious interest. He interrupted frequently. The analyst did not comment on the change in the patient's attitude and behavior.

The patient was right on time for his next session but, differently for him, was puffing as he entered the consulting room. He began to speak in the same desultory way in which he had ended the previous session. When the patient paused, the analyst said that it must have taken a special effort to get here today. The patient was silent but seemed stiff and then spoke sharply, "But I was on time, wasn't I?" The analyst agreed that he had indeed been on time and added that the patient must have felt criticized by his observation. Openly angry, the patient retorted, "You doctors all know everything about everyone." And he fell silent again.

After a bit, as it seemed the patient was becoming more sullen, and recalling the disturbance that had followed his "innocuous" comment during the last session, the analyst said, "I think you were offended by my remarking on how proud you felt about handling that situation at work."

"Damned right!" said the patient.

The analyst added, "Then I guess the special effort it took to get here today reflected uncertainty about whether you wanted to come at all."

After a brief silence, the patient concurred, "Who needs this? I felt just as deflated as when I graduated *summa*. They were more concerned that I would think too much of myself than about how hard I had worked to achieve it."

A new bit of history emerged as the patient detailed growing up in a puritanical household in which showing or even feeling pride was an anathema. He had had to hide any evidence that might lead to the accusation that he thought himself better than his parents and siblings.

Ordinarily such a commonplace example would not be classed as analysis of acting out, or as aborting potential regression, but it is both.

The Analyst's Transference versus the Analyst's Countertransference

It is useful to recall the distinction between analyst transference and analyst countertransference I drew earlier. The topic has plagued analytic thinkers for some time, and I shall not attempt to review the controversy about whether or not all unconsciously driven responses of the analyst should be lumped as countertransference (for example, Reich, 1951; Kernberg, 1987).

Consider first the feelings, attitudes, and ideas that arise from the unconscious fantasies of the analyst and that are available to be expressed in a wide range of situations. They are typical of the analyst and are organized into what could be called the character of the analyst. For instance, we may recognize in ourselves and in others a generally nurturing attitude, or a "soft spot" for troubled youth, or distaste for clinging dependency. These and other unconscious commitments of the analyst will likely give rise to a transference toward patient and non patient alike. These attitudes mostly are comfortable and thus may not be recognized as transference unless a supervisor points out how they are getting in the way.

Second, and distinct from the foregoing, are perhaps similar feelings, which, although not characteristic of the analyst, can be evoked episodically in response to a specific transference of the patient. Often they are experienced as unpleasant, if not repugnant, and, even if tempting, tend to be ego alien. These evoked emotional responses deserve to be distinguished by the term countertransference.

It could be argued that, since nothing can be evoked in a person that was not there in the first place, there is little difference between the two kinds of experiences. It is true that there is enough commonality in the genetics, culture, and upbringing of all of us so that, to one degree or another, we can resonate with a wide range of human experiences. But it is important for the conduct of a treatment whether the analyst is imposing on the patient *de novo* a transference disposition that originated in his own psychic development or is responding in action to transference of the patient. The consequences for the treatment may be different, and correcting the distorting power of such feelings requires different approaches and operations.

When alerted to his transference, the analyst must consider his involuntary contribution in the treatment of all of his patients. He must also consider the ways in which his own attitudes and needs complicate the treatment of the kinds of vulnerable patients we are considering. When an analyst becomes aware of countertransference, the focus of his attention will tend to be on what is emerging from the patient that evokes the particular response in him.

Consider, too, that transference in the analyst tends to blind him to what is actually going on in his treatments in general, whereas countertransference may alert him to the presence of trends in this patient that are not yet obvious through other channels. In this sense, countertransference may be thought of as a channel of communication (Kernberg, 1987). In practice, of course, analysts' transference and countertransference, like patients' transference and countertransference, tend to occur together and it may be difficult in any particular instance to tease them apart. A supervisor frequently can be helpful in calling an analyst's attention to the intermingling of the two, but the help of the analyst's analyst may be needed to disentangle them effectively.

Complications in the Treatment of Vulnerable Patients

I asserted earlier that a patient's attachment to the analyst is a necessary precursor to severe regressions. Becoming attached may not take much time for vulnerable patients, as it may for many others. The volatility of vulnerable patients reflects the rapidity with which they make attachments, at times instantly, and helps to explain the instability of the resulting relationships. It is not uncommon for a patient to enter treatment during a disturbance that can be understood as expressing the patient's anticipatory reaction to the probable failure of empathy by the therapist he has not yet met. Unsurprisingly, we also find low object-constancy in these patients. Some patients become firmly attached to a therapist they have not yet met but have only been referred to. During the initial phone call to make an appointment, they announce to the therapist-elect their willingness to wait for an opening even though they are told she has none at present and foresees none in the near future. No matter. For this would-be patient, no other therapist will do.

Another important element, though less frequently acknowledged, is the analyst's attachment to the patient. The analyst may be unaware of the depth or the nature of this attachment, or he may rationalize it as an aspect of his legitimate therapeutic intent. The analyst who signals covertly that he desperately needs the patient to get well, that his self-esteem so rides on therapeutic success that he is unwilling to hear how things really are with the patient, can place an unbearable libidinal demand and a burden of obligation on the patient. It is not just the analyst's excessive investment in the patient's improvement that is the problem. More troublesome is the failure to recognize it and acknowledge it at least to himself, while insisting that everything he does is for the patient's benefit. All too frequently, this situation repeats a familiar childhood experience of the patient, of having his own sense of self bound to the expectations of another.

The analyst's attitude may also resonate with the mixed feelings of a patient who desperately wants to please the analyst lest he be abandoned, yet is afraid of progress lest it lead to the end of the relationship. He equally desperately fears being swallowed up by the analyst if he does not manage to get away (Schlesinger, 1996). Thus, both patient and analyst can be caught in "double binds." The expectable testing by the patient of the nature and strength of the analyst's interest may be countered by the analyst's insistence on his virtuous intentions while failing to hear that the patient's covert pleas to "Let me go" are escalating to screams.

Thus, the analyst's own need to see himself as helpful may interfere with his clinical sensitivity and make him less able to sense the patient's angry despair about once again having become engaged with an inevitably neglectful parent-figure while the analyst vigorously, if unconsciously, rejects this attribution. The patient's uninterpreted transference may then escalate until the disturbed and disturbing behavior reaches proportions impossible to ignore. This eventual development then is named a severe regression, as if it were a distinct and separate phenomenon, rather than the outcome of a process of continuing neglect.

Some analysts have a strong need to keep patients attached, but they have an equally strong aversion to hearing patients express their feelings openly. They send a complex message: "Stay close to me, but don't embarrass me with your feelings." This kind of double-bind can interfere with therapy for any patient. But with vulnerable patients, the capacity to remain safely related may easily become exhausted as they feel pulled to respond to the conflicting messages.

A version of this problem can be seen in the analyst who, as the transference heats up, redoubles efforts to interpret toward the past. The covert message is, "I don't want to deal with your feelings about me. Let's agree that they are really about your father." The underlying attachment of the analyst to such a patient may have complex origins. Rather than holding excessive ambitions for the patient, the analyst may be fearful of letting go a patient who threatens unwelcome libidinal demands, or demands limitless dependency, or harbors a wish to merge. To experience himself as the target of such wishes may arouse conflict in the analyst between a desire to save himself by escaping and a sense of responsibility for the welfare of the patient.

The technical advice that can be derived from these considerations, for any patient and at any time is to pay close attention to the state of the transference and the patient's attachment to the analyst. In particular, the analyst should be attentive to the state of the patient's defenses against premature and overwhelming awareness of the transference and the sense of helplessness that accompanies it, matters that are "on the analytic surface." The analyst must also help the patient maintain an adequate level of defense. The more poorly organized the patient's personality structure, the more likely it is that denial and identification will be the ways of defending. The main tool of the analyst is early tactful and empathic interpretation, beginning "upward," to help the patient understand that the temptation to retreat he experiences fearfully is something he is doing, not something that is happening to him, and, under the circumstances, it makes sense.

A regressive episode or impasse may develop when a patient has progressed sufficiently so that he fears he will "improve his way right out the door" and in that way lose more in the relationship than he possibly could gain in health. Improvement based on identification with the analyst may threaten the patient's attachment to internal objects, which, destructive as they may have been, have nevertheless provided a sense of belonging and a degree of stability that seem indispensable to the patient. I have discussed elsewhere this subset of patients for whom the regressive episode is a predictable phenomenon in the course of getting well (Schlesinger, 1996).

17

Analyzing in the Middle Phase

Intervening in Conflict

Each of the earlier chapters has been, in one way or another, about intervening in conflict, but to continue to discuss intervening as we get further into an analysis, we need to refer to the previous consideration of regression. We recognize that the patient came because he was in conflict. Now, his conflicts are more obvious and they seem to have invaded the analytic situation as well. Conflict implies at least two antagonistic parties. How can the analyst who wants to preserve his technical neutrality intervene without taking sides?

To get started, let's assume that there is only one conflict and that the portion of the self that guards it so zealously is not fully aware of its organization and details. One party to the conflict is the sense of self of the patient, which is organized around (fear of) the material that we inferred earlier has been excluded from the continuous stream of consciousness. That part is like a bank guard who patrols his beat with only the slightest knowledge of what is in the vault. The other party to the conflict we have called the "therapeutic ally," the aspect of the self that is organized around the stream of consciousness, and that desires relief more than it fears exposure of what has been excluded from consciousness. We regard it as the agency responsible for bringing the patient to us in the first place, but this "ally" is only partly responsible for keeping him coming. The balance of forces keeping the patient in analysis versus those urging him to flee varies during the course of the analysis; indeed it may vary during the course of a session.

In any intervention, we can see that what might be considered useful by one of the contending parties in the patient's conflict is likely to be an anathema to the other. The problem in evaluating the usefulness of an analyst's interventions seems, then, to be that he cannot direct his remarks to only one of the parties, for both are listening. Most of the time the part of the patient that fears change listens more carefully than does the therapeutic ally, for there is more at risk for that first party. Indeed, the therapeutic ally's interest in the proceedings may flag from time to time; many analysts have observed that occasionally they have gone to sleep. You might well suspect that the therapeutic ally is not always steadfast, and even might be corrupted by his not fully conscious opponent.

I hope you will agree that we cannot take the seemingly easier, but actually impossible, course of appealing only to the therapeutic ally. We must direct our intervention to the whole patient and expect that the two parties on the same couch will hear it differently. This idea is, of course, not original. Some schools of psychotherapy carry on ad nauseam about the adult self and the "inner child." Of course, the contending part of the patient isn't always a child, nor is it always inner. One of the reasons why analyzing requires such lengthy training is that an analyst has to learn to listen empathically to both sides in the conflict as well as to the corresponding portions of his own self. The analyst's inner voices include contributions from transference and countertransference, contributions that could muddy things badly if allowed to prompt unconsidered action. But they also can help to clarify matters, if the analyst has learned how to listen to and evaluate his inner musings and can identify the inner voices and their current motives (Schlesinger, 1981b, 1994a; Kernberg, 1987).

To speak of intervening in a single conflict grossly oversimplifies the situation to be found in any analysis. This description omits the crucial fact that conflicts are embedded in an unconscious fantasy. They are not separate issues, but like the handkerchiefs of a magician, are connected, end to end. While they are not connected seamlessly, they do seem inseparable. When the analyst touches one with an interpretation, it seems to metamorphose into the next one. Each time an interpretation hints that there might be a solution to one of the conflicts, the next version shows why that solution would not work, in fact it would only make things worse.

Finally, if the analyst were not already aware of the desperate nature of the struggle he has gotten into with the patient, he would realize that *he* has become the problem of which the neurosis now seems to have become the solution. What I have described to this point would hold as much for psychoanalytic psychotherapy as for psychoanalysis. The major difference between the two applications of psychoanalytic principles is that the analytic situation, designed to permit more regression than would be useful in psychotherapy, favors the development of a transference neurosis. The analytic situation thus favors the analyst's becoming, in the patient's mind, if not we hope in actuality, a party in the patient's conflicts.

The Transference Neurosis

In Chapter 2, when I first mentioned the term transference neurosis in connection with a situation between analyst and patient that had the form of a frozen argument, I may have seemed to deplore the patient's apparent reluctance to associate freely while, sadly, the analyst had become part of the problem. We might recall, however, that the analytic material is what the patient does, not just what he says. With this reminder, perhaps we can allow that the silent, sullen, uncooperative, unhappy, and unmovable patient is doing the best he can under the circumstance that he has accepted the invitation to regress. Perhaps we can allow, too, that he is associating freely but is doing so partly in "action language" as well as in symbolic speech. And the analyst, while perhaps feeling frustrated and impotent to influence matters, is now actually in a position that permits him to experience first-hand what it feels like to be the patient, stuck in an unwinnable conflict (Freud, 1914a, Glover, 1971).

I hope it is clear that I am suggesting an alternative and more useful way to look at the apparent mess into which patient and analyst have gotten themselves. Let us "normalize" it. Consider that this is the way analyses tend to develop if they are going "properly." If the patient was selected properly as one who could safely be allowed to regress and if the analyst does not interfere, the patient will regress and this is what the situation will look like when he does. The problem the patient was talking about, which was so disturbing to him in life "outside" is now "inside." Patient and analyst have become actors in a painful, wearing, and conflicted replaying of the patient's chronic neurosis. And, like the original version of the neurosis, the transference neurosis is a self-stabilizing system that resists change.

The hopeful aspect is that the analyst, who earlier was only hearing about events occurring "outside," and hence was powerless to influence them, is now very much part of the events. As an "insider," but one who still has one foot "outside," he has more leverage to influence matters.[1] An additional indication that the transferences have consolidated as a transference neurosis is that things "outside," that is, those in the patient's larger life, will seem better, calmer, the patient's life less intruded upon by his neurosis. But in the analysis itself things may seem stuck and often there is a veiled threat in the air that things could get much worse.

The analyst who allows the treatment to enter this "middle phase" will be grateful for the educational requirement that analysts have their own analysis to help them function as analysts. For to analyze in the

[1] That is, "inside" as transference object, "outside" as analyst.

setting of the transference neurosis requires something like a "bootstrap" operation; the analyst figuratively must lift himself up so that he can look down into the consulting room to watch how these two—analyst (that is, as transference figure) and patient—reenact as a twosome the patient's internal conflict. To disentangle the two versions of himself—as analyst and as transference figure—while experiencing himself as both, and to sort out the various temptations to respond to the patient's enactments with counteractions, the analyst will have to call on his self-analytic capacities to maintain his analytic split.

In short, most analyzing takes place in the context of the transference neurosis. The various infantile relationships that are the source of transference and have fed into the analysis from the beginning now have coalesced around the person of the analyst. They imprison him, and the patient, in an ever-changing, but always the same, "dance" that cycles endlessly, if erratically, through the same succession of stages, sometimes excitingly, but ultimately wearily. The lesson the patient seems to be trying to get across is that, awful as the neurosis is, it is the lesser evil, far better than any solution that could come out of the analysis. Consider the following example:

> The patient was a graduate student in the humanities who presented to a clinic with an anxiety attack when he heard that a former girlfriend had tested positively for HIV. He was certain that he also had HIV and soon would die of AIDS. The clinic helped the student realize that he had been troubled for some time by an inability to maintain any relationship and that he always seemed to get himself dropped by the women with whom he connected. He felt victimized by these women but was bored with those who were willing to stay with him; he felt that they were "beneath him."
>
> He accepted the recommendation for analysis. It turned out that he had done a great deal of reading about psychoanalysis and had long been both tempted and threatened by the idea. He had decided that, if he could not solve his "problem" by himself in five years, he would let an analyst work on it. The HIV scare had forced his hand.
>
> In the early analytic sessions, the following themes emerged: 1) I am drawn to women I want desperately to love me, but who mistreat me and victimize me. When they have taken me for all I can do for them, they run off with someone else. 2) Women who are attracted to me and want to make me happy are boring; they want to latch on and smother me. After a while, I can't stand them. 3) I am a "good" person. I never get angry, and I wouldn't want to hurt anyone. That's why I can't break off a relationship or reject anyone but have to be the one rejected. 4) I can't let myself compete openly,

because anything I got that way would feel as though I had taken it from someone else, and a "good" person wouldn't do that. So good things have to seem to come to me by accident.

As the analysis progressed, these themes, which had appeared singly in stories of current life, in dreams, in historical material, and occasionally in direct reference to the analyst, became more tightly organized. The analyst could sense the regularity of succession of the several positions as the patient "marched" through them. He then directed his interpretations at the patient's fear that he might allow himself to be influenced by the analyst. If he were seriously to consider that any of these "givens," these basic assumptions about himself, could be relaxed, he would be tampering with a structure that had always worked for him.

In time the dangers the patient was warding off appeared to be equally balanced: either AIDS would kill him, or the analyst would succeed in "curing" him and in that way get rid of him. In the transference, the analyst was perceived as inviting his trust, but only in preparation for betrayal. If the patient allowed himself to be analyzed, he would first "lose his humanity" and then lose the relationship with the analyst. He would no longer be "good" and thus no longer would be entitled to be the beloved "victim," safely powerless in his mother's arms.

The analysis of these successive positions in the "resistance" connected the current versions and the metaphoric presentations of the patient's unconscious fantasy with its historical justification. The patient slowly came to appreciate that he now had choices open to him, anxiety-ridden ones, to be sure, but choices nevertheless. Formerly he had felt trapped in a repetitive pattern of failure that somehow was also its own reward. Working through these issues became the focus of the analysis as it wound its way toward termination.

That example illustrates the position and attitude of an analyst who was aware that he was intervening in a system that had its own integrity and reason for being. He understood that he was attempting to interfere in the operation of a system rather than in the collection of isolated symptoms and complexes and that one effect of an accurate interpretation would be to increase the patient's defensiveness. By loosening the patient's grip on each successive defensive position, his interpretations speeded the patient's "march" through the stations, gradually allowing a fuller view of the unconscious fantasy that generated the conflicts.

This work was accomplished in the context of the transference neurosis, when the miserable, hopeless struggle seemed to be confined to the analytic sessions while the patient's life became progressively unburdened. By following up, "going with the resistance," and slowing the patient's automatic shifting to a new defensive position in response to each interpretation, he also prolonged the period during which the patient remained in the uncomfortable state of realizing that he was in an absurd position, stuck with ideas he wanted to believe but that clearly were unsupportable. Instead, the patient had to examine, painfully, how he had come to each of these false beliefs.

From the conceptual position I have been advancing, we could say that the analyst's successive interventions first disturbed the neurotic system and then interfered with the patient's defensive efforts to repair the damage. Thus his neurotic system was less able to slip back into its former state. Following up the interpretation by attending to the patient's subsequent defensive efforts increased the likelihood that the system would be changed by the intervention, that is, that the change would become "structuralized" (Schlesinger, 1981b; 1995a).

Interventions Disturb the System

We can return now to the idea that, in principle, all accurate interventions disturb the neurotic system. The neurotic organization, for all the pain and misery it causes the patient, is remarkably resilient and stable against the wide range of external forces. These seemingly opposed ideas are not contradictory. Still, much of the time patients seem fearful that the analysis might actually bring about change—after all, "The devil you know is preferable to the one you don't know."

I am sure all analysts were warned, in the more activist moments of their training, not to disturb the transference. I have often thought that, if only I knew an easy way to disturb the transference, I would bottle it and get rich. Beginning analysts are also cautioned about the care they must take when framing interventions. How discouraged they become when they find that nothing that they say, no matter how carefully framed, seems to make any detectable difference in the condition of the patient! If a candidate complains to his supervisor that nothing seems to be happening, he may be counseled that it takes a long time to bring about "structural" change and that he should learn to be patient. In this way the wrong idea is inculcated that, in psychoanalysis, nothing good should be expected to happen in finite time.

How can we reconcile the principle that correct interpretations disturb the system with candidates' correct observation that their, presumably correct, interpretations seem to have no effect at all? First of all, consider that a more or less correct intervention might cause such a minute disturbance that the analyst easily overlooks it or, just as likely, that the analyst does not recognize the various ways in which his disturbance of the system manifests itself. It is essential that the analyst expect a response to *every* targeted intervention; he must train himself to detect and recognize that whatever the patient does next is the response he should be expecting.

This dictum should be taken seriously even when, or perhaps especially when, the patient's response seems negligible. (Recall our earlier discussion of the "analytic surface" in Chapter 4.) We could say about the patient's seemingly null response that its *form* was minimization or trivialization, and that the likely *function* of responding so minimally was to keep both analyst and himself from knowing that he had been affected by the interpretation. The analyst might pick up a great deal of useful information from such a minimal response if he is prepared to notice, as did Sherlock Holmes, in "The Hound of the Baskervilles," that the vital clue was that "the dog did not bark." Similarly, the analyst should be alerted when "the patient protests too little."

As noted in Chapter 9, the patient's reaction to an interpretation may be as little as a momentary pause, after which he continues as before. Or, he may change the topic without comment. Or he might acknowledge the intervention with a vague, "I guess so," or "Uh-huh." You might think, "If these reactions are legitimate responses to what I worked so hard to formulate, they certainly are not anything I could take to the bank." The analyst's acceptance of the devaluation of his efforts, which is inherent in these reactions, stems, in part, I believe, from the tendency to overvalue the *content of* what the patient says. This overvaluation leads us to ignore the principle that the analytic material is what the patient *does*, which, of course, includes the form of the patient's response as well as the words he speaks, and much more.

That a patient reacts to the analyst's carefully thought-out and well-presented interpretation with a monosyllabic grunt is in itself highly informative about the function of responding that way. We might safely infer that the analyst's comment was not entirely welcome, that it did not inspire warm and congenial thoughts, and that it probably did not make the patient feel more comfortable. In short, the negligible response should tell the analyst that he disturbed the system of the neurosis and aroused resistance.

Resistance at this point has several *functions:* "damage control," giving the patient time to undo the harm done to the neurotic structure by the interpretation, soothing the anxiety aroused by it, and discouraging the analyst from intruding further while the patient busies himself to put the neurosis back together again. Consider the beauty and efficiency of the patient's response. We can see that the *form* the resistance took served two of the patient's immediate defensive purposes: first, to hide from the analyst, and also from himself, the fuller significance the analyst's intervention might have had for him; and, second, to discourage the analyst from pursuing that line of approach.

Patients often succeed in discouraging the analyst by such maneuvers. If, for his own reasons, the analyst needs immediate and strong (that is, verbal) confirmation that his interpretation was correct, he will likely desist, back off, and wonder what his error might have been. The error, of course, was not necessarily in the interpretation, but, rather, in not understanding that the patient's reaction was indeed a response—the best response the patient could muster under the circumstances. If he were to apply the working principle that "the patient is always right," the analyst would wonder what the circumstances were that made "Uh-huh" the best possible response for the patient, and how to help the patient appreciate how much meaning he had condensed into that simple grunt (Schlesinger, 1981b, 1994b, 1995a).

Calling a bit of behavior resistant is potentially misleading if we stop at that point. "Resistant" only categorizes the behavior as *against* something, usually against the analyst's immediate agenda. The more important issue for the analysis is what the behavior is *for.* What is it doing for the patient? It is another application of the principle, "The patient is always right." It is also an expression of the principle that the analyst should place *function* close to his notion of the analytic "surface" when planning an intervention.

The patient's minimal, nonspecific utterance does not usually exhaust his reaction, which generally will also include other expressive behavior. The patient may shift position, cross or uncross his legs, fold his arms across his chest, cover his eyes, or hold himself more rigidly, any of which will help the analyst to infer more accurately what the resistance says, that is, how the patient "took" the intervention, rather than that he rejected it. These signs of disturbance are *always* there to be seen and heard and can be used by the analyst to inform his follow-up intervention (Schlesinger, 1995a).

A correct interpretation not only disturbs the neurotic system but also yields at least a small measure of relief. As the grip of the neurosis loosens even slightly, the patient may taste a moment of freedom. Of course, the unfamiliar sense of freedom may itself arouse anxiety, and the analyst may find occasion to call the patient's attention to the paradoxical simultaneity of feeling anxious and also a bit lighter.

You may wonder if I claim that a negligible response to an interpretation is a reliable indicator that the interpretation was correct, well dosed, and well timed. Hardly, a mild "Uh-huh" might merely reflect the good manners of a patient who had suppressed a "WHAT?" But following up the patient's response will soon enough reveal the process of the patient's response and thereby decide the issue.

Even though the patient may object indignantly to an interpretation, as did the patient who was complaining about her boss (chapter 3), even altering the neurotic system slightly brings a measure of relief to the patient. An analyst might well choose to comment on such a shift in the patient's feelings and on the resulting increase in emotional complexity. At the very least, it would imply that the mess the patient is in is understandable. As always, the principles of tact, dosage, and timing will govern what the analyst chooses to do.[2]

But why propose that kind of comment? As I touched on in the several discussions of activity, the point of intervening, particularly interpreting, is to facilitate change. Whether an intervention leads to change depends in part on what the patient does with it—it depends on the nature of the patient's activity in relation to interpretation or in relation to seeming minor change. That kind of comment implies a note of encouragement, helps to focus the patient's attention on his response as noteworthy and helps to slow, if not abort, the return to the status quo ante.

By whether or not an intervention ought to be considered an interpretation I do not mean that the analyst's intentions are irrelevant or that the phrasing is unimportant. It is always good to be aware of one's intentions, while the phrasing of interventions for maximum effectiveness and minimum pain is an art all analysts want to develop. But, regardless of intention and artful phrasing, the analyst still must listen for the effects of his intervention and be prepared to deal in his next intervention with how the patient took it. Generally, this requires that the analyst deal with the "resistance" that inevitably follows an intervention that has any technical weight.

My experience in supervising is that it is not usual for beginners to think this way about what they do. Mostly, young analysts seem to deliver scatter-shot interventions, hoping to hit something. They do so tentatively, and then they retire exhausted, not expecting much to happen, but hoping, at least, that they haven't given offense. And then they go into a refractory phase, turn off, and fail to observe what the patient did next. I wish I had a nickel for every time I asked a candidate, "What did the patient do when you said that?" only to be met with a blank stare, a shrug of the shoulder, as if to say, "What would you expect?" Nothing.

It is important that the analyst expect that something *always* will happen when he offers an intervention with analytic intent; the patient always

[2] A study validating the importance of dosage and accuracy of transference interpretations was reported by Azim (1998).

responds in some way. The analyst who has a theory about what is going on with his patient at the moment and an idea of what might be useful to comment on will generally have some expectation about how the patient might respond if indeed the idea is correct. In this sense the analyst can aspire to the confidence of the surgeon who knows his way around the body. The trouble is that few analytic beginners believe that they are able to, and indeed ought to, have explicit expectations, not even that the patient's immediate behavior may be considered a response and that it will have significance. Without that conviction, an analyst would hardly be able to follow up his first intervention with another on the basis of his understanding of the patient's response as it is seen to relate to the analyst's expectation (Schlesinger, 1995a).

My plea for expectation is not a plea for precision. I do not hold an absolute view of precision. What we are aiming at can be put in process terms, that is, we expect to improve our aim with successive approximations and with the help of the patient (see Strachey, 1934). Another justification for fractionating interpretations that it is likely to improve one's precision because it is easier to gain confirmation of smaller chunks of information. I believe the term interpretation should be reserved for this process of successively refined, partial interventions the analyst offers to enhance the patient's awareness of the cognitive and emotional significance of his behavior, to help the patient appreciate the reasons for the reluctance to broaden his understanding of it, and to invite the patient's active participation in the interpretive process. To capture the idea of interpretation as a process of successive approximation, one could put it aphoristically as, it matters less what the analyst says at any moment than what he says next.

18

Whether and How to Begin a Psychoanalysis

You might question why beginning an analysis comes so late in this book. Perhaps it is a way to say that there is no good place to take up beginnings, for all the matters discussed to this point need to be considered at the very outset of treatment. Beginning is not for beginners; beginnings are complicated and call for a great deal of clinical skill. My aim is not to discourage you, but to counter the common assumption that the beginning is something to get over so that the "real analysis" can take place.

Although, for convenience, we speak of the first interview as the beginning, actually the patient can be said to have begun as soon as he was forced to the conclusion that he had something to do with producing his misery and followed advice to seek an analysis. At that point, if not sooner, he became preoccupied with worries about who the analyst would be, would he be any good, would he accept the patient? The patient found himself asking himself, "How can I tell all the embarrassing mishaps of my life?"

If this is to be the analyst's first case, he will be similarly preoccupied. Even if the beginning candidate is already a skilled clinician, and most are, he will feel once again like a rank impostor, fearful of being exposed as a novice. Consider too that both parties are strangers to each other and are properly uncertain about whether they will have a future together. How are they to find out if there is any point in getting together? Finding out who one is as one's first task in opening a relationship is not all that strange, if you think about it.

Take the experience of going on a blind date. Most of us have accepted at least one blind date on the urging of a close friend who assured us, "She is intelligent, serious but fun loving, very good looking but not stuck up, and extremely popular. She just happens to be free this Saturday." As our anticipation mounted, so did our anxieties. The more we believed the selling job, the more eager we became to be liked by the unknown other and the more we wondered if we could meet her expectations. "How will I stack up among the others she has dated? How can I possibly meet the expectations of such a paragon? What sort of person would she like to find in me? What will she think of me when we go out together?" In short, as we prepared for this first encounter with an unknown other, we fantasized about what the other person might be like and also about ourselves. Will I fail to meet her expectations and lose her interest? Will she find me dull, uncouth?

Both going on a blind date and beginning therapy or analysis involve what amounts to a mutual diagnostic examination. Finding out who the patient thinks the analyst is, is a high art. Separating out (that is to say, analyzing) from this turbulent mixture the person the patient perceives us to be from the fears and expectations the patient imports into the relationship is perhaps the main job of the therapist-elect.[1]

Initial meetings, then, are about finding out who the other person is. Each one disabuses himself of his worst fears and hopes about the other and differentiates that other from the stereotype he has brought in. In psychotherapy, this essential getting to know each other is generally downplayed in the diagnostic process formally designated as "evaluation." This aspect of the process is also diagnostic, in the broadest sense of the term; it is a mutual finding out about the human as well as the psychopathological (or professional, as the case may be) other. While the analyst is finding out if the patient is suitable for analysis, the prospective patient is finding out if the analyst is suitable for him and if the prospect of interacting with this analyst is congenial.

Describing this engagement as a process might leave the impression that a good deal of time is involved, but some processes, like forming first impressions, are almost instantaneous. This is not to say that first impressions are not modifiable, but, at least for some patients, they are lasting and form a relatively fixed reference point that may endure. I must I add that the situation is paralleled in the therapist or analyst, who must, of course, have a good idea of the kind of first impression he makes; but I have never seen anything of the sort recorded in any report written about an evaluation. A story told about my old friend and colleague Lou Shapiro[2] is apropos.

> By any description, Lou cut an unprepossessing figure. He was short, a bit paunchy, dignified and benign-looking. One day, he

[1] It is also instructive to analogize the opening of an analysis to other encounters in which power to accept or reject is either actually held by, or is imputed to, the "other," as in a job interview or selection interview. All beginnings have much in common.

[2] Louis B. Shapiro, M.D. was one of the leading teachers in the Institute for Psychoanalysis, Chicago.

> opened the door to his consulting room to greet a new patient who had called urgently for a consultation. The stranger, a tall handsome man in a well-cut western suit, wearing boots and with Stetson in hand, hesitated for a moment, staring at Lou. Lou broke the moment of uncomfortable silence and captured the dilemma of the patient with his welcoming remark, "Come in, anyway."

Let us take up beginnings from the point of view of a candidate facing his first supervised case. The venue is the clinic of a psychoanalytic institute, but the issues would be the same for a graduate in private practice, even if the requirement for record keeping is less strict.

Evaluation of the Patient

I shall not repeat the criteria and desiderata for analyzability; they are widely available. I only stress that being analyzable is not the same thing as requiring analysis. I believe it is a sad commentary on the current state of the field that so many clinicians who have taken the advanced analytic training required for practicing this powerful method prefer to treat only those patients who they believe will give them the least trouble: patients who are well-behaved, pay on time, and never need to be hospitalized. Many of those patients could also achieve their therapeutic goals with a less arduous form of psychotherapy. Nevertheless, a position strongly held by some in the field (e.g., Rothstein, 1998) is that anyone who can be analyzed ought to be.

When a candidate evaluates a patient for psychoanalysis, he hopes to have found an "ideal" patient, one with not too much wrong but willing to do a great deal about it. Candidates are encouraged in that search by the institute on the somewhat shaky grounds that these patients, so unrepresentative of the general run of needy patients, are more suitable for training purposes. This position is not entirely without merit, for it is easier to demonstrate the important phenomena in psychoanalytic process and the effects of interpretation under the leisurely conditions of a psychoanalysis conducted with multiple sessions per week than in the hurly burly of the ordinary outpatient clinic. (I shall leave aside the public policy concerns embedded in these considerations.)

Let us return to the technical aspects of the evaluation process. The candidate will want to interfere as little as possible as the patient tells the story of his life and how he came to this point. For not only is he gathering information, he is also acquainting the patient with how it will be if they are to work together in analysis, and he is estimating whether or not the patient can engage in a way that augurs well for analyzing. The candidate should expect that the patient's life story will have lacunae, and he will have to decide if the omissions are deliberate or unwitting and whether or not to call the patient's attention to them and how. As will be discussed later, in general it is preferable, instead of probing for missing information, to assume that the patient is doing the best he can, that he may have a reason for omitting it and might become curious about it too when he becomes aware of the omission.

It is common doctrine in all dynamically inspired psychotherapies that the past determines the present. As a blanket statement, of course, this dictum is only partially correct, but it is true enough for us to consider the technique of finding out about the determinative past. In psychoanalysis, we look for causes in the patterning of events, and we attempt to show the patient that he tends to repeat his errors because he does not understand what he is doing. From one point of view, one could say we "cure" the patient by restoring his memory and, through that means, help to reconnect past with present. We generally follow Santayana's (1905–1906) admonition that those who do not remember the past are condemned to repeat it—our understanding of the past helps us to understand the patient's current situation and to predict where he will eventuate if he does not change his view of himself and behave accordingly.

Getting a History versus Taking a History

Because the past determines the present, should the analyst not attempt to understand the past as thoroughly as he can before he begins the treatment? This notion, though plausible, will mislead the analyst if he construes it as requiring that he "take a history" before he begins. The urge to take a history usually is based on the therapist's prior clinical training or on the actual or perceived necessity to demonstrate to an authority that he has thoroughly examined and understands this patient and therefore ought to be allowed to begin the treatment (as if it has not already begun). Another reason for beginning by taking a history can be found in our earlier discussion of questioning: it is to establish who is in charge.

There are counterarguments to obtaining a history by extracting facts through direct inquiry. Particularly if the examiner is later to be the patient's analyst, quizzing the patient at the beginning establishes a wrong model for the subsequent interactions. Interrogating the would-be patient conditions him to await the analyst's queries and to expect the analyst to take the lead. This procedure may also reinforce the myth that the analyst knows all the answers or, at least, all the proper questions. If the analyst follows this route, he will have to reverse his style to establish the analytic situation, and it will take some unlearning by the patient to enter a working relationship with more useful anticipations (Deutsch, 1955).

With these reasons to avoid obtaining history through interrogation, there must be powerful forces to make the habit persist. I mentioned the influence of traditional clinical history-taking in the background of many clinicians. But that background also embodies dynamic reasons, not merely technical ones or reasons of convenience (for instance, allowing a patient to tell his story in his own way would take too much time).

One of the implicit purposes of the opening moves in a clinical interview, as in any interview, is to define roles, to assess and confirm the relative power of the participants, and, in the clinic, to socialize the prospective patient to be ready to meet the doctor's expectations. The most common way in our culture to establish a power gradient between persons is to demonstrate which of them has the right to ask questions and which has the obligation to answer. Recall that the explicit purpose of psychoanalysis is to reempower the patient to resume control of those areas of his life that have been denied him because of illness.

To conduct the initial interview along traditional, interrogatory lines seems to point in the opposite direction—to lodge power unnecessarily in the interviewer. The operative word here is unnecessarily. Many therapists and clinical examiners believe that it is essential to control the interview; they fear that some patients, at least, will attempt to seize control and thwart its clinical purpose. This issue, already discussed in Chapters 11 and 12, has particular relevance for the evaluation phase, when anxiety may increase the analyst's temptation to put the patient on the stand. It may suffice to say that most analysts soon discover that control is hard to give away, and it is difficult to convince some patients that the point of the analysis is to restore to them control over their own lives. The fear of losing control over the therapeutic situation is best viewed as a transference or countertransference issue of the clinician.

Does the Past Determine the Present?

Although psychoanalysts subscribe to a general belief in psychic determinism and the dictum that those who do not remember are doomed to repeat, from a technical point of view, the aphorism, the past determines the present, would make as much sense if it were inverted: (our view of) the past is determined by the present. I suggest this inversion not merely for shock effect; I mean it to be taken literally but in context. A patient cannot tell you history that he does not remember, and memory is one of the cognitive functions most likely to be affected by emotional illness. Moreover, what the patient does remember of his past will have a special functional relationship to the present. The function of recalled personal history, like the history of nations, is to rationalize and justify the present state of affairs. With much justice, it has been said that all history is forgery. Official history is designed to glorify, idealize, and make inevitable the status quo. The opposition's history is designed to tear down, nullify, and delegitimate the status quo and therefore justify resistance.

Clinicians soon realize that a patient's recalled history is confounded with personal myth and family romance. It is a commonplace, though not often commented on, that the history that one "takes" at the beginning of therapy is quite different from the history one might obtain at the end. The despised, resented, and rejecting parents of the beginning of therapy somehow become the benign, concerned, perhaps faulty, but quite human figures at the end. It is most important that a young analyst recognize that the history related by a new patient must be understood as reflecting and justifying the state of emotional affairs at that moment. It is the history the patient has to give to justify his presence in the analyst's consulting room. It also will contain significant expressions of transference, at least in the form of conscious omissions and favorable personal coloring that reflect the patient's belief about what the analyst expects to hear. It will certainly be slanted to present the patient in the best light (or, if the patient is depressed or afflicted with pathological honesty, in the worst light).

Should we understand, then, that the history the patient tells at the beginning of treatment is worthless? Far from it. It is valuable, simply because it is only a partial history, because it also is a function of the patient's defensiveness, myths, fantasies, and need to justify himself. As long as the analyst understands the relativistic nature of the history and its dependent on the stated and current purposes of the teller of that history—as long as he understands that the history does not explain, but rather that it must be explained—to that extent will he be prepared to conduct a psychoanalysis.

Those last observations are only another way of saying that the major area of interest in a psychoanalysis or dynamically oriented psychotherapy is the patient's psychological reality. I do not mean to imply that it does not matter if an event (even including sexual abuse in childhood) actually happened or is only fantasy. Although there may come a time when it is important to determine a memory's basis in actuality, vetting memories should not be the primary focus of the analysis. The veridicality of a patient's belief, be it couched as an assertion or a denial, may be difficult to determine at the outset, whereas, in time, conviction pro or con may emerge in a way that also carries conviction for others.

We could coin another aphorism to accompany "All history is forgery"—or, in other words, all history is a lie. With some justice we could aver that all lies are true. By this paradox I mean that it is part of the therapist's task in attempting to understand the patient to recognize that some of the patient's assertions of fact are best taken as wishes, that some statements offered as truth are best understood as fantasy, that a lie may be something that the patient devoutly wishes were true. To understand the truth within the lie may thus be more important to the patient's therapy than to reject the lie because it does not square with other known facts. In the clinic, the question of validity may devolve into discovering the context within which any particular statement *might be true*, rather than attempting to test the truth-value of a statement by presuming that the only legitimate contexts are social consensus or physical fact. (You may notice in this argument a restatement of the principle that the psychoanalytic "material" is what the patient does, including what he says, and does not say.)

As the analyst assesses the factors and qualities of the patient's history and current life circumstances he needs to know in order to prescribe any treatment, especially psychoanalysis, he ought to pay particular attention to several issues that were neglected in the reports of evaluations I have read. These include the patient's conditions for, and limitations placed on, loving and working; his characteristic ways of entering and leaving relationships; his tolerance for intimacy; and his ability and interest in collaborating in the process of exploring how his mind works.

To evaluate these capacities, the analyst will need to observe how the patient interacts with him during interviews and how the patient reflects on the process of the evaluation between sessions. Does he see himself differently in any way, now that some light is being cast on previously obscure issues? Again, such observations are most easily made if the analyst has allowed the patient to function much as he would be expected to do during the analytic sessions, that is, with minimum constraint and with the analyst supplying only the amount of explicit support that would permit the patient to experience the possibilities of the analytic situation. If the analyst is overly concerned with maintaining control of the interview, as he might be if anxious, he may regress toward the kind of diagnostic interviewing favored in the medical clinic and question the patient relentlessly.

The analyst will recognize also that the patient feels needy and, because he wants to be accepted, will tend to be deferential and willing to conform to what he imagines to be the interviewer's explicit or implicit wishes. It is also possible that the patient may open with a defensive posture against feeling needy and one-down in the relationship. It is essential that the analyst be prepared for whatever ready-made initial transference appears; and transference is more likely to show clearly if the patient is allowed to take the lead in telling the story of what has brought him to this point in his life.

The analyst will want to learn why the patient is seeking an analysis. What does he say he wants to accomplish? These seem to be simple questions, and yet we know that what patients say they want is not necessarily all that brings them to treatment. Even the word problem deserves clarification. We tend to dignify the reason the patient gives for coming in by calling it "his problem." But it is not usually a problem in the literal sense of the term; it is not an unsatisfying state of affairs for which there is a solution. The oft-ignored implication of this definition is that if there is no solution, there is no problem. Many of the unsatisfactory situations all of us face are not problems in that sense. Some are "existential"—that's the way life is. One could have an unrealistic and troubled attitude about such a situation, and that attitude might be construed as a problem within our purview.

But it is usually safest to assume that what has brought the patient to us is that he is in a "mess," a painful situation he does not know how to get out of, or is unwilling to do, or feels unable to do, what would extricate him. And, as the analyst will discover, the initial complaint may turn out to be largely a "ticket of admission," a rationalization that justifies the patient's seeking treatment. The initial complaint states a reason, not necessarily untrue, that the patient thinks the analyst will understand and accept. We can assume that if the person had gone to a religious counselor, the problem would have been put in religious terms; if to a physician, in medical terms. For psychotherapists, the problem is most often cast as an emotional difficulty, an interpersonal difficulty or the like.

An old joke puts it, "Anyone who goes to a shrink should have his head examined." While the intent of the joke is dismissive, we can take a useful hint from it. Anyone who presents himself to a clinician should be taken at face value at least long enough for the clinician and the patient to discover why the patient has presented himself in perhaps an odd way. Another aphorism is apropos: if there is a disagreement between the tongue and the feet, give credence first to the feet. If the patient is here, he probably has good reasons to allow his feet to bring him here regardless of what he says.

Of course, you will already have come to the conclusion that peculiar presentations result when the patient is in conflict about whether to come at all. The temporary compromise to such a conflict might be to come late or to try to change the appointment time—or to make an odd presentation that he half-hopes will lead to rejection. Whatever the initial presentation, it is incumbent on the analyst to make his own diagnosis of the circumstances that brought the patient. Is the "problem" isolated or situational, or is it one of a series of such contretemps indicating the patient has been driven repeatedly into such maladaptive behavior, one indication that analysis might be required?

If the patient has not been preselected as suitable for analysis, the evaluation might lead to a recommendation for psychotherapy or treatment with medication and support, or perhaps for a behavioral treatment. Still, the analyst will want to discover how ready the patient is to enter a therapeutic situation in which he will be expected to be an active and cooperative participant.

The Limitations of the Chess Metaphor

Freud (1913) compared the beginning of psychoanalysis to the opening gambit in a chess game. His main point was that it is relatively easy to describe the opening game and end game of chess, and the beginning and ending of psychoanalysis, whereas the middle game of chess and the middle phase of psychoanalysis are too complex for systematic description. I believe that comparison is valid but that the chess metaphor has too often been stretched far beyond Freud's simple intention. The opening of psychoanalysis or psychotherapy is very little like that of chess other than it involves two persons. There is nothing, after all, that corresponds to the well-defined chess board, which restricts one's moves. And there is nothing that corresponds to the fixed number of chess pieces, each with prescribed movement capacities. Most important, there is nothing that corresponds with the essential purpose of chess—to defeat the other player. In fact, in all these respects, psychotherapy is quite the inverse of chess.

Let us then, invent a game of "inverse chess" as a possible model for psychotherapy. In inverse chess, we also have two players sitting across a playing surface, something like a chess board but with no squares, perhaps an empty desk, a relatively undefined space, both physically and emotionally. The players—let us call them P and T— are meeting for the first time. P thinks he wants something that T has, but he is not quite sure what that is. T thinks he may have what P wants, but he too is not quite sure what it is. He does know that he has been able to "play the game" with others who approached him in this same uncertain way.

Each player has many conversation pieces that he has used in other conversations, but neither player is sure what the value of these pieces might be in this game. There are no explicit rules in inverse chess, only a kind of working suggestion that each player move at least one conversation piece now and then when he feels like it. Then the other player may respond by moving one or more of his pieces in ways that make sense to him and that he thinks may make sense to the other player as well.

Lastly, we need some purpose for this odd game. It is not the purpose of the game of course, to defeat the other party but only to continue to play long enough for P to find out what he wants from T and whether T can provide it, and to decide whether it would be worthwhile to continue to play this kind of game. Another purpose is diagnostic, to let T find out what pieces P is holding and how he means to use them, that is, to discover what implicit rules P follows when conversing.

This inverse chess metaphor highlights both the uncertainties and ambiguities, as well as the diagnostic opportunities of the opening phase. The ambiguities and uncertainties are of two kinds. They refer in part to the circumstances that brought the patient, or, better, that forced him to come. We should consider that the patient came under some form and degree of coercion. He may say he thinks it is a good idea for him to come now, but the analyst would be safe in assuming that it has been a good idea for some time and that some event, or some new appreciation of old events, makes it urgent to seek help now. The topic of coercion versus volition in psychotherapy deserves fuller consideration, but I will leave the topic by noting only that every patient is in conflict about coming.

The other kind of ambiguity may be captured aphoristically; we might say that, whatever issues led the patient to the analyst's office, once he gets there his immediate problem is the analyst. He is in a room alone with a stranger. He does not feel free to leave and is equally fearful that the analyst will dismiss him as not worth bothering with. Thus, the first thing the analyst has to help the patient with is the problem that he himself represents to the patient.

It may seem paradoxical that the would-be helper has become the first problem. But consider: the patient thinks the analyst may have something he wants, but the patient isn't sure what that is. He suspects that, if the analyst doesn't have it, he won't tell him; and, if he does have it, he might withhold it. Even if the patient got it, he might be disappointed. He might find out something he would just as soon not know, for instance, that he ought to be labeled "crazy." If he trusts the analyst, he fears he will likely be abandoned as he has been by every other person he depended on. Conversely, if he puts even a toe in the water, he might be sucked in and never get out. These dilemmas are typical of the fears, fantasies, and expectations of a patient facing his first appointment. It takes a high courage for a patient to appear in your office for a first appointment. Is it any wonder that so many don't make it?

After you have been doing psychoanalysis for a while you may tend to regard first appointments as "routine"—just one more patient. It is easy to forget how you felt when you were in the analogous position as a newly anointed therapist facing your first patient. Recall how fearful you were that you might forget your own name, how you hoped the patient wouldn't notice your nervousness, how anxious you were that the patient would unmask you as an impostor and certain that it would be only a matter of time before you made a fool of yourself or were fooled by the patient. It is important to stay in touch with those ancient and uncomfortable feelings. One of the worst sins a therapist can commit is to become jaded to the excitement and anxiety of beginning with a new patient, to see it merely as a routine affair that has the patient all stirred up, but if you wait a while, the dust will settle and the patient will get around to telling you what is "really" troubling him.

The Responsibilities of the Patient

The main responsibility of the patient is to try to associate freely during sessions and to maintain the general sincerity of purpose that accepting the task implies. When patient and analyst have agreed to continue to meet in psychoanalysis, a schedule of visits must be set up. Generally, the analyst has only certain times free but will try to accommodate the convenience of the patient, who probably also has a fully committed life.

The issue of how many visits per week are required is a much-debated topic among analysts. Opinions are rife and are expressed vehemently, but data are scarce. We may recall that Freud preferred to see patients six days a week and would take some of them along on his yearly vacations. For many years, the American Psychoanalytic Association upheld the "4–5 rule," implying that five sessions per week were preferred for the training analysis, whereas four sessions would be tolerated. The institutes associated with that organization still require a minimum of four sessions a week for training analyses and for patients in psychoanalytic clinics. Institutes abroad are, in general, more flexible on this point. Other psychoanalytic organizations use this issue to establish either their modernity and liberalism or their conservative, traditional, and standards-upholding positions.

Although in the training setting the issue is decided by fiat, from a technical point of view, the matter should depend on the abilities of analyst and patient to maintain the momentum of analyzing, How closely must sessions be spaced to keep the analysis going? The issue is not trivial, for real matters of convenience and expense for the patient must be balanced against the desirability to maintain continuity. I have divided the responsibility between analyst and patient, in fact the actual division depends mainly on the ability of the patient to carry over from one session to the next. You may recall a patient, seen perhaps only weekly, who could pick up at one session where he or she left off last time and whose occasional inability to do so signaled an important defensive intrusion. This phenomenon raises the interesting possibility that these "naturals" might also have an analysis on that schedule, provided, of course, that they need an analysis at all.

On the other hand, the phenomenon of the "Monday crust" is well known. It describes the plight of patients who have difficulty resuming analysis after a weekend. Some few patients, perhaps those on the edge of suitability for analysis, suffer a "daily crust" and need a great deal of time each session to resume. It is, of course, for the analyst to understand whether such a pattern represents analyzable resistance or an irreducible quality of the patient. Some analysts have resorted to double sessions, accommodating the latter presumption. In real life, if the patient is willing, the issue is generally decided by the preference of the analyst.

My own experience is that, in the absence of pressures to do otherwise, four sessions a week seems to work well for most patients. Occasionally a patient who requested a regular fifth session felt that continuity was improved, but in retrospect, I could not say with conviction that I would have thought to recommend it. Occasionally, too, a patient has had to drop back to three sessions a week for an extended time; for those patients at least, I did not think the analysis was compromised. As in most areas of life, it is easier to fall back on a "policy" than to think through the issues for what truly is necessary or what would work.

Fees

By the time the analyst has heard enough of the patient's story to feel comfortable about recommending analysis, he should also have come to an understanding of whether or not the patient's circumstances—his assets, income, and obligations—will permit it and whether the analyst's usual fee expectation can be met or if some adjustment will be required. The analyst may have to raise the question directly if the patient seems to be planning to make too much of a sacrifice. Some authorities, for example, Menninger and Holzman (1973), believe the fee should be significant enough so that the patient experiences some deprivation; they view analysis as a capital investment that can be expected to lead to an improvement in the quality of life and earning power.

In contrast, as noted earlier (see Chapter 15) research has shown that analysis can be provided successfully without charging a fee. Also, a fee that is unfairly high (not that just seems high to the patient), but that the patient feels forced to submit to can be untherapeutic. These days, analysts realize that there are more patients who could profit from analysis than have the means to afford it under private care. Because these clinicians want to practice their profession, they lower the hourly fee enough to make it possible for patients to have analysis at roughly what psychotherapy would cost. Some analysts mention early on that they expect to raise the issue of the fee again if the patient's fortunes should improve. (That possibility raises a question of conscience and ethics for the analyst should the patient's fortunes decline to the point that he no longer can afford the agreed-upon fee.)

As both analyst and patient will discover, if the analysis goes well, the process will continue between appointments. Still, it is customary to charge only for the appointments themselves. While it is necessary at the outset that the analyst help the patient understand clearly the analyst's expectations with regard to payment, the analyst must understand that "clear" is not an absolute value.

At any rate, the analyst should make a simple statement of how he will bill the hourly fee the patient has agreed to. It is a matter somewhere between taste and technique whether or not the analyst adds the kinds of business-oriented provisos that I have heard are becoming increasingly common. These include announcing the expectation that the bill will be paid in full by a certain date; that sessions missed for any reason will be charged as if they had been attended, or that sessions missed for other than emergencies will be charged, or that sessions cancelled fewer than 24 or 48 hours beforehand will be charged, and that the analyst expects the patient to schedule his vacations or other extended absences to fit the analyst's convenience.

The recital of these troubling possibilities sounds as if the analyst expects the new patient to be an irresponsible deadbeat and will have to be reminded to behave himself. It might also properly lead the patient to muse resentfully that the only thing the analyst has chosen to be precise about is the collection of his fee. My experience is that none of this "fine print" is necessary. In general, patients understand that the analyst must charge a fee, and they expect to pay it as promptly as they pay other bills. They expect to attend sessions regularly for the sake of the analysis they want, not to avoid penalty. Handling the fee in this way, as a matter of course without trying to head off possible misdemeanors, also fits better with the principle of promoting the patient's activity and being prepared to analyze the patient's fantasies about the analyst's demands. Besides, such warnings are ineffectual and serve mostly to advertise the analyst's areas of vulnerability.

Earlier, I discussed how money and time, which are the only "tangible" media of exchange between patient and analyst, come to be used as a "language," a "dialect," if you will, of the general action-language in which most of the analysis is conducted. Like all actions, speaking through appointments (time) or fees (money) can be highly expressive of dissatisfaction, but it is also minimally articulate. The work of interpretation can be seen here, as elsewhere, as consisting of raising the level of communication from action to words, another sense of "interpreting upward." At this point, I have come to expect the plaintive question. "But what do I do when the patient is months behind in his payment or misses every other session or always comes late and wants to stay on?" I refer the questioner to Chapter 14, where the matter was discussed as an aspect of regression.

This is not to blink at the anxiety that can be aroused in the analyst who fears that his income will immediately shrink if the patient chooses to "speak" by withholding fees. The analyst should reflect on his own contribution to this impasse and bring that understanding to the analysis. He must be aware that he has no power to enforce payment, other than to withhold treatment, with all the complications that would follow. Both the analysis and his income will be served by helping the patient understand why he is not paying.

Who Owns Time?

"Owning time" refers to the "tangibility" of time. When we stop to think about it, it is remarkable how often time is referred to as if it were a commodity by both patient and analyst. Patients often develop a proprietary feeling about the hour of their sessions. They think of their sessions as "my time" and develop strong feelings about wanting "more time" or having had "time taken away." We pay special attention to "being on time," "losing time" by being kept waiting, and "staying over time." The analyst's and the patient's characterological attitudes toward time—Are they punctilious, or are they relaxed?—play a prominent role here. Does the analyst regard himself as a time-keeper or clock-watcher in sessions? Does he keep a clock where the patient can see it? Who "calls time"? Must sessions end precisely "on time"? Does the analyst make the traditional "50-minute hour" a 45-minute session so as to squeeze four sessions into a three-hour block?

Clearly, a great deal is communicated to the patient about the analyst and his values by the way the analyst deals with "time." Of course, even if the analyst is quite relaxed about it all, the patient is likely to attribute strictness to him as a function of transference and the specifics of his unconscious fantasy. But analyzing is much easier when the patient's perceptions are only a function of transference.

What to Do About Missed Appointments?

I referred the plaintive question about the nonpaying patient to an earlier discussion of regression. But one aspect of the topic also deserves discussion in its own right. The analyst's attitude toward and policies about, missed appointments will say as much as any other aspect of his practice about his general outlook toward analysis.

It is interesting that the American Psychiatric Association (2001) gives guarded approval to charging for missed appointments only when it

> falls within the terms of the specific contractual agreement with the patient. Charging for a missed appointment or for one not canceled 24 hours in advance need not, in itself, be considered unethical if a patient is fully advised that the physician will make such a charge. The practice, however, should be resorted to infrequently and always with the utmost consideration for the patient and his/her circumstances [p. 5, para. 6].

One does not have to read between the lines to understand that the framers of the code of ethics expect that some patients are likely to be whimsical in their attendance but that the psychiatrist should resort only occasionally to punishing them for misbehaving, and then only for their own good. They are silent about whether or not charging for a missed appointment would be ethical if a third-party payer is involved. At any rate, the advice to charge infrequently hardly seems to be a sound economic policy. We may also wonder if it would be a sound analytic policy.

The American Psychoanalytic Association (2001) is even more circumspect about the matter:

> All aspects of the treatment contract which are applicable should be discussed with the patient during the initial consultation process. The psychoanalyst's policy of charging for missed sessions should be

> understood in advance of such a charge. The applications of this policy to third party payment for services should be discussed and agreed upon by the patient. In the case of patients who are minors, these matters should be discussed early on with the parent(s) or guardian(s) as well as with the patient as age and capability dictate [Section III, 5].

The Standards does not address the advisability of such charging inasmuch as there is no consensus among analysts about it, but the Standards surrounds such charging with cautions.

Long before the adoption of these codes of ethics, Menninger and Holzman (1973) addressed the matter from a clinical point of view. They advocated that an analyst adopt a consistent policy, to charge either for all missed appointments or for none. Their concern was that the analyst would put himself in an unanalytic position if he were to charge only for appointments missed "without sufficient cause." They observed that, by adopting such a humane-seeming policy, the analyst would violate his basic nonjudgmental stance by setting himself up either to excuse or to punish the patient on the basis of his opinion about the quality of the patient's excuse for absenting himself. The opening this position leaves for the expression of transference and countertransference should also give concern.

A popular argument for charging for all missed sessions is based on an insufficiently thought out analogy to renting a room. That is, once one has rented a room, one pays the rent even if one does not occupy it. An implication of the analogy, however, is that the analyst has no more interest in whether or not the patient attends than the landlord cares about whether or not the renter is in residence. As long as the patient/renter pays, he may come or not as he pleases. He pays for the right to occupy the couch/room for a period of time.

You can hear the allusion to the subtitle of this section, "Who Owns Time?" for the implication is that the analyst is "selling his time." But the analyst does not own "time" and cannot sell it. He no more sells time than a grocer sells "pounds." To put it purely in the terms of a commercial transaction, the analyst sells the use of his professional skills on behalf of the patient. Should it not matter to the analyst (or patient) if the patient rejects the opportunity to use these skills? To extend the possibilities of the rental analogy, would the analyst accept a "full-fee retainer" from a patient to keep "his time" open so that he might attend at a moment's notice? To go a bit further, would he accept such payments for his entire day on the condition that he "keep his time open?" From an economic point of view, that is not too far-fetched. After all, we pay farmers not to raise grain.

Perhaps I have made the case that the arrangements between analyst and patient are not about the sale of "time" but about providing a presumably needed clinical service. If the analyst accepts the Menninger and Holzman (1973) condition that he charge for all missed appointments without exception, and also the ethically approved position that he make this position clear to the patient at the outset, he will then have to accept the implication—and it will not be lost on the patient—that he is particularly if not mainly interested in the economic value of the patient. And he will have to swallow his own sense of the unfairness of the policy when, inevitably, a faithfully attending patient is kept away for no fault of his own. He will also have a more difficult time in uncovering the possible message expressed in another patient's acting out through fickle attendance. After all, the patient has agreed to pay the analyst for the right not to attend. What further interest should the analyst have in it? Does the patient have to analyze as well as pay? Doesn't seem fair.

The alternative position proposed by Menninger and Holzman (1973)—to charge for no missed appointments—avoids the issues both of unfairness and of forcing the analyst to be a judge of the patient's behavior. Additionally, the analyst will not have announced to the patient the kind of behavior that would annoy him the most. It has the additional major advantages that it does not suggest that economically it is a matter of indifference to the analyst if the patient attends or not, and it frees both analyst and patient to inquire into the meaning of absences.

But it does seem to risk both making the analyst's income less dependable and, in effect, encouraging the patient to stay away when attending might be painful. Under this policy, the analyst might, in effect, be underwriting resistance. Experience, my own at least, does not bear out these risks. If the analyst's explanation of the reason for multiple sessions each week includes the importance of continuity and that unscheduled interruptions (that is, other than weekends) make analyzing more difficult, the engaged patient will seldom miss an appointment. If the analyst figures his income on a yearly basis, rather than weekly, the impact of unexpected absences becomes negligible. As we have already mentioned, patients suitable for analysis generally are overburdened with rules and hardly need more of them from the analyst. The analyst will be freer to notice the tendencies to ritualize attendance and promptness as virtues in their own right, which of course they are in daily life as well. The neurotic component may become clear only when the patient is anguishing about a session lateness or missing a session.

19

The Optimal Therapeutic Relationship

Research (Luborskya et al., 1985), as well as personal experience, suggests that the quality of the therapeutic relationship is perhaps the most important factor in therapeutic outcome. It is certainly true that patients credit their relationship with a particular therapist or analyst, rather than any particular thing he might have done, for the benefits they have obtained. Should it not be possible to put in systematic terms the definition of an optimal, if not ideal therapeutic relationship?

Attempting to do that, however, we run into such banalities as, "We know it when we see it," or, more precisely, "We know what it should have been when it wasn't there." Assuming that the closest model of an optimal therapeutic relationship is the relationship any one has with an ideal therapist, we should first attempt to define that paragon. Probably we would describe such an ideal as warm and sensitive, interested but objective, patient but not long-suffering, respectful but not stiff, and with values similar to our own. In short, we would like our therapist to be a good human being in the best sense of these words, and not too different from ourselves. If we put that therapist together with an ideal patient—someone also just like ourselves—would we not then have an optimal therapeutic relationship?

I expect I have aroused discomfort with this expedient solution. What is wrong with it? First of all, you might, because of native cynicism or painful experience, doubt the existence of our paragon, the ideal therapist. Perhaps equally important is the implicit assumption that there is a comparably superior patient. You may have wondered if your own experiences as a patient in psychotherapy would qualify you for the title, Superior Patient. I dare say mostly we think of ourselves as pretty tough cookies and wouldn't wish ourselves on even an optimal therapist; at least we would not want such a patient for ourselves. And how about "therapeutic?" The qualities ascribed to the ideal therapist would be just as desirable in a friend or spouse. We require additionally only that our ideal therapist be skilled and thus surely able to construct the elusive therapeutic relationship.

What Makes a Relationship Therapeutic?

Perhaps it is time to reexamine the title of this chapter. I have left unexamined the assumption that there is such a thing as a therapeutic relationship, that there is a static arrangement definable as, "that's how it is." But a therapeutic relationship is a dynamic, changing affair, sensitive to circumstance and yet resistant to external influence. We might think of it as a system that changes as the constraints of neurosis on at least one of the parties loosen.

What makes a relationship therapeutic rather than simply rewarding, constructive, or pleasurable? A therapeutic relationship is, first of all, a professional one, an instrumental relationship, one designed to serve some purpose that can be pursued only in the context of relationship. It is not intended, as is a friendship or a marrige, to be its own reward. One party in the relationship has expertise and the authority that derives both from that expertise and from being privileged by the willingness of the other party, who needs the first party's expertise, to participate in certain procedures to receive services. When the services have been rendered, or when the second party has obtained the needed benefits, or when either party decides that the benefits are unlikely to ensue, the professional relationship ends.

This straightforward definition would, of course, fit most professional relationships, whether with a doctor, a lawyer, or a plumber. And the personal qualities we hope for in the professional would be desirable in any professional relationship. Is there anything special about a professional *psychotherapeutic* relationship?

Perhaps the major difference is that the therapeutic relationship is not only the context for conducting psychotherapy, it also figures heavily in the content of the therapy. Unlike what goes on with lawyers and plumbers, much of what patient and therapist talk about, directly or metaphorically, is their relationship. As with one's lawyer, but not usually one's plumber, psychotherapy requires a degree of trust in the competence of the therapist. It also requires patience, since the desired results are not likely to occur quickly, and also willingness to bear some inconvenience and psychic pain. Unlike surgeons and dentists, psychotherapists do not provide anesthesia for the pain that is intrinsic to the process.

The therapeutic relationship is a stratified relationship, not a reciprocal one, as is a friendship or marriage. The distinction is important. In a friendship, what one party expects of the other, the other has the right to expect; not so in a therapeutic relationship. The patient usually pays a fee for the therapist's attention. And the patient has far more freedom of action than does the therapist; if displeased, the patient may simply leave. The relationship is generally defined by the patient's rights and the therapist's obligations, but it is not totally that way. The therapist has some rights and the patient some obligations, but most of the time these secondary sets are not enforceable. Often they are not really made explicit but are revealed only in the course of therapy. Distinguishing the rights and legitimate expectations of both parties from wishes expressed in the transference occupies much of the treatment. Monitoring the changing relationship is perhaps the major task of the therapist.

The term "optimal" suggests we are interested in obtaining the best possible relationship under given circumstances. I think that a better way to put the issue is, "How can we optimize the therapeutic relationship?" This revised formulation requires us to sharpen it further by addressing the key question: optimize it "for whom?"

Optimizing the Therapeutic Relationship

The question, Optimal for whom? raises the issue of diagnosis. We would not expect a single kind of therapeutic relationship to be optimal, for instance, for a patient suffering an acute schizophrenic episode and for a person depressed following the loss of a spouse.

Optimizing a relationship implies that one has discovered the sort of relationship the patient is capable of entering and remaining in long enough to accomplish the therapeutic purpose. In the broadest sense, the nature of the therapeutic relationship is dependent on the nature of the patient and on what the therapist is capable of offering. By broadest sense, I mean we must keep much more in mind than formal diagnosis. For instance, the patient's age, sex, education, cultural background, and other demographics; the patient's character or personality organization; the nature of the problems that brought the patient to treatment; the patient's strengths and vulnerabilities; the patient's recent and older experiences with helpers and authority figures; the patient's attitude toward himself, his sense of worth, his feeling of entitlement to care and to health; the meanings of illness and dependency and of asking for help.

All of these factors and more influence the emerging therapeutic relationship by shaping the patient's expectations. This does not necessarily mean that what the patient expects, the patient gets; recall that an effective therapeutic relationship includes a bearable degree of tension from frustrated expectation. The therapist should try to understand what the patient expects will happen when they get together and why the patient has these expectations. What sort of previous experiences and commitments led the patient to this pattern of expectations? By "commitments," I mean those fairly stable aspects of character and personality that frame a person's experiences.

The nature of the desired therapeutic relationship will also differ depending on the form of therapy offered. In religion-based therapies, the restoration of faith is seen as the mode of cure, and reconciliation with God is its goal. The therapist may expect to be viewed as divinely inspired. Some therapies are quite prescriptive and require that patients follow the therapist's orders and do prescribed exercises. The relationship the therapist considers optimal would differ widely among the models. Clearly, if a treatment is governed by a strict protocol, the relationship, at least viewed externally, will look different from one that develops in a treatment based on conversation without rules of procedure, one that focuses much of the time on the relationship itself. Even if the therapy follows a strict protocol, that would not prevent the patient or, for that matter, the therapist from having fantasies about the other. A patient in a relationship that officially is to remain unobserved will nevertheless develop a transference that may become manifest at inconvenient times.

We take for granted that therapy must take place within a relationship. But this idea has been tested by some who have attempted to dispense with the relationship altogether. On the assumption that it exists only to exchange information, and since the major flow of information is from therapist to patient, why couldn't audio cassettes do as well? But it would be a mistake to assume that, because the patient sits alone listening to a recorded message, there is no therapeutic relationship. Someone gave the patient the tape, and, by accepting the treatment, the patient invests that someone with the authority to advise him what to do. That someone is able to give or withhold approval and the services that the patient wants or needs. Experiments have shown that even when subjects/patients have been told that no one will listen to what they speak into a recorder, their needs and expectations create interested listeners (Schwitzgebel, 1967). The process is no different in principle from what a patient does when a therapist is present. The therapist with whom the patient deals is not necessarily the one who sits with him. Rather, the therapist the patient is dealing with is the one the patient has constructed using the actual therapist and his own expectations as raw materials.

In what follows, I consider the relationship only in psychoanalysis and the therapies derived from it. What, then, are the defining characteristics of such a therapeutic relationship? Freud (1913) recommended that psychoanalytic patients say everything that comes to mind even if it might seem silly or offensive. He promised that he would listen and comment from time to time about what he understood the patient to be saying. He recommended that the patient's attitude be not faith in the method but benevolent skepticism. Of course, that attitude also requires some faith, enough, at least, for one to be willing to go along for the time being.

As I proposed earlier (Chapter 12), the idea of the "basic rule" can be conveyed to the patient in several ways, including not mentioning a rule at all. The analyst might depend on the patient's wish that the analyst understand him and to know himself in depth. To give the patient a rule to do what he is inclined to do freely would hardly be necessary. We know that intrapsychic conflict may interfere with even the most devout wish to know oneself. By imposing a "rule," the analyst intrudes himself unnecessarily into that conflict and, in doing so, prescribes externalizing it. We can depend on the patient's discovering for himself how externalizing conflict can be used for resistance.

Perhaps, then, to define what is analytic about a relationship we need nothing more than the patient's willingness to disclose and the analyst's willingness to listen and to comment when he has something useful to say. Of course, there is more to analysis than that, but that "more" is part of analyzing—and what this book is about—but it is not part of the definition of the therapeutic relationship.

The therapeutic relationship differs from other professional relationships in other ways. A professional relationship ends when its purpose has been achieved. Of course, we still retain a sense of relatedness with our lawyer after he has written a will or with the plumber who has cleaned a drain in the sense that we remember whom to turn to when a need next arises, but we think of these people only in connection with their function. Apart from that, they are not in our minds when they are not working for us. Is it the same with a therapeutic relationship?

As each of the previous chapters has illustrated, through transference, the therapeutic relationship develops a life of its own; much of the time the attention of both parties is on their relationship. This is so much the case that, on occasion, therapist and patient alike have to be reminded that it is an instrumental relationship. I cannot emphasize strongly enough how much difficulty for the therapeutic enterprise arises from insufficient attention to the separate life of the relationship and especially its fate when the treatment nominally ends. In anticipation of a more extended discussion (Schlesinger, forthcoming), I propose that it is not true that the relationship ends when the visits stop.[1]

[1] In the best of circumstances, the therapy continues long after the visits stop. Unfortunately, it is just as common for the therapy to have ended long before the patient stops coming.

The purpose of a therapeutic relationship, of course, is to facilitate the doing of therapy. Psychoanalysis and dynamic psychotherapy cannot take place outside a relationship. Ironically that indispensable relationship can also be an obstacle to the therapy and may even make carrying out a therapy impossible. It may be only a small comfort to realize that other professions have this problem too, particularly other helping professionals. Physicians observe repeatedly that some patients overdo "compliance" and follow "doctor's orders" slavishly, even overcoming common sense. Some others do not take their medicines as directed but halve or double the dose by whim. Others do not even bother to fill their prescriptions.

Wise young physicians soon realize that technical skill alone is not sufficient to assure that they are practicing good medicine. They realize that patients collaborate with a treatment regimen to the extent that they are comfortable with the doctor, have confidence in him, and have been made partner in their treatment. Some physicians, I am afraid, write off, at least emotionally, patients who do not immediately do as they are told.

That last thought suggests one universal: namely, that what is suboptimal is the same for all therapies: the patient does not do as expected, although he may pretend to do so, or he may do something else entirely. After enduring a suboptimal situation for a while, some patients may quit. Others may continue to come while complaining that they are not getting what they came for. Still others, perhaps the largest contingent, continue to attend sessions, but do not do what they are supposed to; yet for a considerable time they give little or no hint that they are dissatisfied with the proceedings. They seem to be getting something from their relationship, although it is generally not therapy. As mentioned in our earlier discussions of resistance, the therapist ought to be concerned with what the patient *is doing* (that is, for himself) rather than merely with what he *is opposing* (that is, "resisting the treatment"). This topic will have to be pursued further under the heading of therapeutic impasse or stalemate. (Schlesinger, forthcoming)

Can we say, then, that the relationship is all there is to psychotherapy? This question, an ancient one, is still current. Some observers consider that the only effective ingredients in the various psychotherapies are the so-called nonspecific elements (Frank, 1974), such as the therapist's consistency, warmth, and wish to help. Others have referred cynically to the same factors by describing psychotherapy as a "paid friendship" and therapists as members of the "second oldest profession."

Without invoking these epithets, we can note that many therapists believe that an atmosphere of friendly interest is essential to conducting therapy successfully. Many patients in therapies that are progressing well view the therapist as a friend, even a best friend; some patients would even want the relationship to become a love relationship, even a sexual one. On the other hand, some, though fewer in number, would prefer that the relationship be "strictly business"; they are implying, if not saying, "My feelings have nothing to do with it, let's get on with the job."

Conscious preferences aside, it is certainly no secret that many a relationship that both parties intended to be therapeutic gradually transforms itself into something else. While both parties continued to speak of it as "therapy," a student of relationships might note that what actually goes on between the two more closely approximates a different model, a diluted affair, a friendship, a Platonic marriage, or even an adoption. However begun, the relationship has metamorphosed into one pursued for the sake of relatedness itself, but no longer for therapy.

It follows, therefore, that the therapist's first task with a new patient is to find out what the patient wants and needs from the relationship, as well as from whom the patient wants it (that is, the transference implications of help seeking). It is important, if paradoxical-sounding, that the therapist's first tasks include finding out who the patient is and also who he himself is, again in the transference.

To recap, we started with a proposal to dispose of defining the optimal therapeutic relationship by saying, simply, that it is what happens between good therapists and good patients. We seem now to be at the opposite pole—we see that the nature of the relationship depends on the nature of the patient and on the nature of the therapy being practiced. That is complicated enough, but would we consider the same qualities optimal at the outset of a therapeutic relationship as at the ending?

Jumping to the end of this line of questioning, I believe we can demonstrate that what is optimal in a therapeutic relationship also depends on the nature of the tasks facing the patient (and the therapist) at any time. For instance, when patient and therapist first get together and neither knows the other or what to expect, a good deal of testing of each other is realistically called for. Ideally, the therapist will feel secure enough to facilitate the patient's expression of doubt. For some time, the patient may even speak openly about his distrust of the therapist and thus signal that the vicissitudes of trusting may be a central theme of the therapy. The therapist must help the patient identify rather than suppress the anxieties that always attend the beginning of a new and risky enterprise. At the end of therapy, the tasks seem mostly to be related to the impending separation between the parties. The therapist must help the patient separate the gains achieved during therapy from dependency on the relationship and on continuing visits—the process of termination (Schlesinger, forthcoming). In this sense, beginning and ending may be thought of not just as points in chronology but, more important, as organizers of experience.

We are now in a better position to suggest a criterion for an optimal therapeutic relationship. We could say that the relationship is optimal when it best promotes the conditions required for the therapy to be effective. This criterion may sound circular, and it is. But it does contain an important idea. It emphasizes that, while the quality of the relationship may be the most important factor in the outcome, the relationship itself is not primary. The relationship exists to serve the therapy and is optimal to the extent that it facilitates the work of the therapy at the time. It is not an end in itself.

This last point emphasizes that the therapeutic relationship is an ongoing, working one. Since it continues over some time (most therapies take at least a few sessions and many go on a good deal longer than that), the relationship tends to take on a social character as well. Whether the relationship is experienced by either party as comfortable, useful, or optimal will depend in large part on the degree to which the social aspect supports the working aspect or, as is usually the case, is more or less in conflict with it, if only because it is permeated with transference.

The Therapeutic Alliance

The issue of the "therapeutic alliance" often is raised in discussions of the therapeutic relationship. The term therapeutic alliance sounds so commonsensical and so essential that you may be surprised to learn that it is especially vulnerable to misuse and when misapplied can be a source of great mischief (Brenner, 1979).

The term was coined to highlight a mildly useful distinction (of which too much has been made), between the aspects of the therapeutic relationship that are based on the realistic nature of an intentionally helpful relationship and those based on transference. Researchers (e.g., Kernberg et al., 1987; Horvath et al., 1993) have demonsrtated that the quality of fit between therapist and patient, surely an essential aspect of the therapeutic relationship, relates positively to successful outcome. But the closer one looks at the therapeutic relationship, with the hope of discriminating the reality aspects from the transference aspects, the fuzzier the distinction becomes and the more that insisting on such a distinction seems artificial and may interfere with the analyst paying sensitive attention to the shaping power of transference.

An analyst's transference and countertransference will intrude into the therapeutic relationship in all cases, not just in the treatment of patients vulnerable to severe regression that I described earlier. The intrusion, however, may not be as visible as it is in those extreme cases because patients with greater adaptive capacity and resiliency will adapt as best they can to the idiosyncrasies of the analyst, including his transference. By neither reacting to those idiosyncrasies, as with noticeable regression, nor calling attention to them, the patient, will in effect, be colluding with the analyst to distort the analytic situation by obscuring the difficulty rather than risk annoying the analyst. This painful arrangement may be a misguided effort by the patient to preserve his sense of "therapeutic alliance" against the shortcomings of the analyst.

I have found that the term therapeutic alliance is most frequently used by analysts or therapists who have come to consult me because a case is in trouble. There may have been wild acting up, or perhaps a psychotic episode by a patient for whom such regression was not anticipated, or the patient may be on the verge of quitting. Occasionally, a case is brought in because for some time nothing has been happening. The patient may have been murmuring mildly about a lack of activity but has exerted no great pressure to do anything about it. The analyst in that case usually feels uneasy and intimidated, perhaps threatened, and invariably helpless. As the story unfolds, he may demonstrate a pretty clear understanding of what is going on. But, when I ask if he has told the patient what he is telling me, the analyst looks at me as if I were out of my mind. Then, more or less patiently, he explains, "It would disturb the therapeutic alliance." I am tempted at such times to ask, "What alliance?"

Since our task is to achieve clarity rather than to win points, let me note that the term once simply referred to the minimal degree of trust and sense of common purpose that would permit patient and therapist to get together. It has come to be understood more recently as a precious state with a value of its own, something that must be nurtured and protected from too much heat, cold, or straight talk. We see here a displacement of value, actually an inversion of value. Instead of the relationship being valued because it serves the purposes of the treatment, the treatment is considered subordinate to the relationship. The analyst has put himself in a dilemma: he cannot allow himself to do what is therapeutically necessary because he believes it might harm the relationship.

Note how threatening was my implied suggestion that the analyst could have told the patient what so far he was only able to tell me. One could protest that he misused the term therapeutic alliance.

His concern for "the alliance" probably had more to do with the fear that the patient would become angry with him and, if provoked might leave him. That is exactly the point. That simple human fear—if, for the moment, we ignore both its likely source and its reality—has been elevated to the status of an analytic catastrophe. The consultant's function, of course, is to identify the problem behind the worry and help the analyst put it into perspective. It is the analyst's job to figure out, together with his own analyst, the source of the exaggerated fear of the patient's anger.

Incidentally, the consultant might point out helpfully that what the analyst fears will happen has already occurred. The patient is already angry but is withholding expressing his anger other than by closing down. Each party is afraid of what opening up matters would do to the other, and each is fearful of an ultimate disruption. The analyst would rather placate the patient than point out what the patient is doing and risk the accusation that he too is withholding. The major harm comes not alone from the placating but also from the patient's knowing, to some extent, that the analyst is more interested in being liked than he is in being helpful. Consequently the patient loses confidence in him. Often, too, that is the significance of the acting up by patients who are given to this form of expression. By refraining from dealing directly with the patient, in the misguided attempt to preserve the "therapeutic alliance," the analyst actually might be encouraging the escalation to misbehavior.

The change of focus from how to establish an optimal therapeutic relationship to optimizing the therapeutic relationship has some interesting implications. First of all, it returns us to the important therapeutic maxim, "Start where the patient is." This advice sounds banal, but it is actually profound and not always easy to follow. It is the same issue I referred to earlier as "begin at the surface." "Surface" in the previous example is the shared uneasiness between patient and analyst that they have a secret that each knows but each is fearful of letting the other know that he knows.

Countertransference, as we saw in that account, warps the therapeutic relationship just as transference does. But that way of putting it assumes once again that there is a relationship with an independent status to be warped. It would be closer to the facts to say that the relationship is an emergent one, constantly being re-created and optimized by both parties; and that the essence of analyzing lies in keeping track of where it is, and for what purpose it is being optimized, that is, where the "surface" is right now. We could also say that optimizing the therapeutic relationship is what psychotherapy and psychoanalysis are all about. We do it by clearing away the misinformation, conscious and unconscious, that disturbs the relationship.

20

Psychoanalysis and Psychoanalytic Psychotherapy

You must have noticed that occasionally I seem to have slipped and written of "the therapist" rather than "the analyst." It is time to confess that the slips were intentional and occurred when the issues under discussion applied equally to therapists doing psychotherapy or psychoanalysis. Indeed, there could have been more such instances, for there are very few occasions when it is necessary to draw a principled distinction between psychoanalysis and psychoanalytic psychotherapy, as they are practiced. I stress as practiced, to preclude argument about differences at the level of philosophy.

I have just thrown down at least two gauntlets. First, do I mean to imply that only analysts can do psychoanalytic psychotherapy? Here you may substitute "modified psychoanalysis" or any of the other terms of mild disdain that imply that the clinician is doing the best he can under less than ideal circumstances but knows that it is not the "real thing." And, second, am I proclaiming that there is no difference between psychoanalysis and psychoanalytic psychotherapy? To jump to the bottom line, the answer to both questions is no. Of course, this blunt answer must be qualified.

Both no's draw support from the same observation. Every analyst I have helped to train has remarked that he now does much better psychotherapy. On inquiry, it turns out that not only does the analyst now have a better understanding of his psychotherapy patients, but also he now understands the process of psychotherapy better. In particular, he recognizes that, from time to time, all his psychotherapy patients slip into a state in which they seem to be associating freely and that he can engage them interpretatively much as he might if they were "in psychoanalysis." Indeed, one might say that for those few minutes, or however long, those patients effectively were in psychoanalysis. It would be fair to refer to those moments in psychotherapy as "opportunistic psychoanalysis."

A little reflection might yield the wry observation that much of psychoanalysis as all of us practice it would deserve that epithet as well. If one can analyze, one analyzes when one can, regardless of what the therapy is called officially. So, does that mean that only trained analysts can do good psychoanalytic psychotherapy? No, again. But it is worth noting that many conscientious psychotherapists who, for whatever reasons, do not want to undertake psychoanalytic training nevertheless seek a personal psychoanalysis, not just for therapeutic reasons, but also to raise their level of practice.

I must discuss the topic of differences at some length because I am proposing that the principles that govern psychoanalysis also apply to the psychotherapies closely derived from it, although they may not always be applied in precisely the same way. By analogy, the principles of sterile technique in surgery are the same whether the surgeon operates on the brain or on a bunion, and few would confuse the procedures or the anatomical sites. Of course, both forms of treatment should be held to the same standards of care.

The question of how to differentiate psychoanalysis from the psychotherapies derived from it bothered analysts during generations past (see, for example, JAPA, 1954) but my impression is that the question seems less preoccupying today. Still, in conversations among analysts and in case conferences at institutes, one still hears psychotherapy used as a term of disparagement. Instead of saying of another, as is meant, "He doesn't do psychoanalysis properly," a colleague will say, "Well, he just does psychotherapy. It may be good psychotherapy, but it isn't psychoanalysis." The implication that psychoanalytic psychotherapy is a lesser or less worthy form of treatment must be rejected out of hand. Psychoanalysis done badly cannot be good psychotherapy.

Let me jump to another bottom line. I believe there are differences that are worth keeping between psychoanalysis and psychoanalytic psychotherapy, but the differences are relative, not absolute. A logical complication in making this distinction is that the treatments we are comparing are not unitary. In this respect, at least, psychoanalyses are unlike pills, every one of which has the same chemical composition and weight. From the beginning, analysts have found it necessary to adapt the procedure of psychoanalysis, as ideally conceived and presented, to the needs, circumstances, and limitations of patients. The term usually applied here, "the widening scope" (Stone, 1954), merely recognized what had become common practice, if not an officially approved one. And the term parameter (Eissler, 1953) carries the same implication. The term "modified psychoanalysis" has now come into vogue, and, while the reasons may be practical and political, those who use the term implicitly recognize that the couch no longer can be viewed as Procrustean. One might even question if the term is necessary since, to fit the patient, all analyses are modified from the ideal to some degree.

Anyone who has treated, for instance, persons with borderline, narcissistic, or impulse-ridden character disorders by making use of psychoanalytic principles knows that the principles must be applied differently in each case. Tact, dosage, and timing, and the therapist's attunement to the therapeutic relationship are much more critical than when doing psychoanalysis proper, not because the principles are more important in one form of treatment than the other, but because those patients are far less forgiving of lapses in technique than are other analytic patients.

Range of Application

The psychoanalytic psychotherapies have a much broader range of intended application than unmodified psychoanalysis. At one end of this range are treatments for conflict-based psychopathology that are problem focused. Although they may not aim specifically at personality change, the means of solving the problems may well be through modifying or softening certain character attitudes, which is the basis for their claim to being psychoanalytic. Such a treatment regimen may take relatively little time and could even fit within a liberal definition of brief therapy. Therapeutic success may or may not involve structural change.

Degree of Support Needed

At the other end of the continuum—or perhaps the other ends of continua, since I am not at all sure that all the adaptations of psychoanalysis ought to be arrayed on a single continuum (perhaps they ought to be arrayed like spokes of a wheel with "ideal psychoanalysis" at the center)—are treatments often of considerable duration. They are designed to sustain the patient, to forestall or mitigate unwanted regression. Thus they are suitable for treating persons with severe psychopathology whose personalities depend on fragile and brittle defensive structures. These adaptations of psychoanalysis may encompass the full range of treatments including many commonly termed supportive or expressive (Schlesinger, 1969).

Transference Neurosis Facilitated or Not

I believe that with all these qualifications, the major difference between psychoanalysis and psychoanalytic psychotherapy is that, when conducting any of the psychoanalytic psychotherapies, unlike when conducting psychoanalysis "proper," the analyst or therapist will (that is, should) attempt to preclude the development of a transference neurosis. Perhaps this stipulation would be better put as, the therapist should avoid encouraging more regression than the treatment requires and that the patient can stand. I realize that, with this assertion, I am striding onto unstable ground. The term transference neurosis, while part of our traditional lexicon, a clinical heritage from Freud (1914a), and advanced by Glover (1971), has periodically come under attack, its very existence or usefulness as a concept disputed (e.g., Brenner, 1982). Nevertheless, it remains one of my favorite concepts. Perhaps the reasons for my partiality will become clear in the course of this discussion.

Freud's genius lay in recognizing that what he was hearing secondhand about Breuer's patient Anna O (Breuer and Freud, 1893–1895) must be true of the mind in general and in supposing that it must be a natural tendency of the mind to function associatively and thus to be able to put into words more than the speaker consciously knows. When a "talented" patient uses the permission to speak what comes to mind, the familiar phenomena of transference and resistance, of conflict-driven expression will emerge.

When the mind functions in this way, it is closer to the mode of primary process, with the further implication that this tendency might (though not necessarily) predict a tendency toward easy regression in ego functioning and in object relationships. Whether to facilitate or discourage the tendency toward easy regression becomes discretionary for the analyst, depending on the needs of the treatment and the risk to the patient. Diagnosing the potential risk of encouraging regression and the undesired and unneeded transference neurosis takes a high order of clinical skill, and, while it is a topic central to our present interest, it demands its own platform. Let me add only that, in doubtful cases at least, skilled psychological testing can be helpful in estimating the risk associated with regression.

We should remind ourselves that regression is not a function of technique; regression is not caused by the psychoanalytic situation. The psychoanalytic situation is designed to make manifest the level of regression that is already at least potentially present. Similarly, it is the responsibility of the psychotherapist—and in this instance I am referring to an analyst functioning as therapist—to facilitate only as much expression of regression as would be useful for the therapy. In this sense, at least, we may speak of the "suppressive" as opposed to the "expressive" purpose of an essentially psychoanalytic psychotherapy.

Choice of Treatment

This point of view toward diagnosing the problem also permits the therapist to discover whether a problem-focused treatment is called for. It is worthwhile to digress here to sketch some of the forms of treatment that patients may require. For the largest number of patients seen in an outpatient setting, a problem-focused treatment is suitable.

The life situations in which most patients' problems arise are common to all of us. Of course, conflict, too, is ubiquitous in human life and the condition of having two opinions about something is not necessarily an indication for treatment. What makes a situation a problem requiring therapy is that the patient is in painful conflict, which he is unable to resolve because aspects of it are not easily available to consciousness. The patient, therefore, tends to recycle unworkable solutions to a problem he does not see clearly in a way that impairs the quality of life. The conflicts that fall within our purview are those that arise from character or neurosis, in short, from the psychopathology of the patient.

These same clinical facts and how the patient deals with them are also the material from which we derive a formal *DSM* diagnosis of the "disorder." But the organization of the facts and their relative emphases are different for the purposes of arriving at a formal diagnosis and for planning psychotherapy. If the therapist were to ask, "What would have to obtain in your life so that you would not have to be in treatment at this time?" then it would be clear he is not treating the patient for a diagnosed disorder but, rather, for a problem from which the patient may be unable to extricate himself, that is, for a degree of disability. Many persons with adjustment reactions, as well as persons with schizophrenia or borderline conditions, are able to use problem- or task-focused treatments. Perhaps the descriptive term supportive psychotherapy is more familiar than problem-focused treatment (Schlesinger, 1969; Pinsker, 1997).

Whether or not a patient can profit from a problem-focused treatment depends on several factors: (1) whether or not the patient's problems are reasonably focal in nature, and (2) whether or not the patient has the ability, or can develop it with help, to take a different (cognitive and affective) point of view toward the problem in its natural setting. The distinction is between a focal problem and a highly diffuse one. If many areas of the patient's life work pretty well (by his standards, not the therapist's), if the patient's neurosis regularly gives rise to problems in certain areas of his life but these problems are not acute and do not generally lead to severe regressions, then the likelihood is that a problem-solving treatment would be useful. The assumption is that, as a system, the personality itself might be altered by effectively solving a problem, even a seemingly peripheral one.

If, on the other hand, the patient's character structure and personality resources are too poorly organized or fragmented to support an acute conflict without severe regression, if the problem seems diffuse and "all over the place," if the patient's frustration tolerance is so low that panic attacks or severe rages are common ways either of dealing with or avoiding conflict, then a more sustaining type of treatment, rather than a problem-solving one, would be in order. These categories are, of course, not exclusive of each other, and a sustaining type of treatment, which is to say a chronic treatment, generally will have periods in it that are distinctly problem solving in nature

Where does psychoanalysis fit in this scheme? Is it a problem-solving treatment or a sustaining type of treatment? My answer may seem paradoxical: It isn't either—and it is both. Psychoanalysis proper is a process designed for the treatment of chronic neurosis, a chronic pathological condition involving a degree of developmental arrest that continually generates acute problems. After repeated efforts to solve the acute problems one by one show that a problem-solving approach is futile, it becomes necessary to consider treating the patient by a method that permits and encourages a controlled regression. The technical goal is to mobilize the enduring conflicts that gave rise to the current problems in the treatment situation itself, by way of a transference neurosis, and resolve them through largely interpretive efforts.

We could hold with equal assurance that psychoanalysis is both a sustaining and a problem-solving treatment. The purpose for the frequent visits, recumbent position, and other trappings of psychoanalysis is that they afford the patient the support of a continuing relationship. Within that relationship it is safe to risk the regressive experience needed to mobilize the chronic conflicts and to experience them again together with the pain that once had to be avoided in order to arrive at a different resolution of the conflicts.

To return to the question, What would have to happen for this person not to be a patient at this time? we can see now that it could have several kinds of answers. Through their mutual diagnostic process, therapist and patient might define one or several problems that, if solved or viewed differently, would permit the patient to resume his life with less trouble. In that event, a problem-focused treatment would be in order. Here is an example of indications for a problem-solving treatment:

A man had been troubled for many years with recurrent mild depressions but nevertheless had managed to finish professional school and had competed for and won a job that required rather more skill, experience, and maturity than he could be expected to bring to it at this stage of his life. Within a year, his fellow workers and superiors sensed his inadequacy and made it difficult for him to continue. When his subordinates rebelled, he demonstrated that, indeed he was not up to the demands of the job. He threw himself on the mercy of those subordinate and superior to him. He lost that job, became depressed, and felt unable to seek another.

Coming to treatment, he expected the therapist to tell him that it would take a good deal of time in therapy before he would be fit to try working again. Instead, the therapist worked with him just long enough for him to see that, while one of the sources of his failure was this characteristic way of solving conflicts by fleeing into helplessness, his immediate problem was how to remobilize himself, find a job within his capacities, and bring his earning power to a point where he could afford to invest himself in a more extended therapy.

Although the patient was angry at not being "accepted as a patient" he could also see that he could not afford to indulge his wish to be taken care of, which was also represented by the wish to become a patient.

After six visits the therapist and patient agreed to interrupt their meetings until the patient could get his life in order. At that time, a second evaluation might be called for to determine what the two might work on next.

Let me assume that, when the patient returns, it becomes clear there is no single problem (or few problems) to work on but rather a chronic weakness of, or an impending collapse of, important personality functions. Then a sustaining type of treatment would be called for. In such a treatment, although the immediate focus would still be on solving the problems of living the patient might bring and on addressing the conflicts that gave rise to them, there would not be the expectation that the treatment would end when the problem under discussion had been resolved. Rather, the therapist would continually gauge the integrity of the patient's personality functions in order to estimate the patient's readiness to go on alone.

During treatment, such a patient would have the opportunity to borrow, as it were, from the resources of the therapist to supplement and strengthen his own deficiencies. For example:

A woman in her late 50s had been married for almost 30 years to a difficult and alcoholic man. With the help of AA, she had sustained him through a long series of life crises, raised several children, and supported his career. She felt badly treated in the marriage but looked forward to the day when they would be able to retire, free of the responsibilities of job and children, and enjoy themselves. When her husband finally retired, he told her that he no longer wanted to be married to her. She reacted with rage, a sense of betrayal, and an acute suicidal depression.

She was hospitalized for several months, during which efforts at reconciliation failed. When considered no longer a suicide risk, she was discharged and referred for psychotherapy and after-care. Her therapist's evaluation showed that she had good strengths but low confidence in them. She had been raised to be a wife, had married early, and had never been on her own or responsible only for herself. She seemed to need permission to recognize how angry she felt.

She used the relationship with the therapist to test out her ideas for what she was going to do and connected herself with support groups for divorced and widowed women. She was able to make good use of these groups plus her friendships. She also was able to use her therapist to solve several problems, chiefly about her feeling that she was not entitled to the support of her children, that she was such a "bitch" that she had driven her husband away, and that she therefore deserved to be alone. When it became clear that she was using her therapist for much the same purposes as she used the support groups, it became possible for her to reduce her visits to biweekly with the expectation of ending them shortly.

You might ask if these really are "pure" examples of problem-solving and supportive therapies. Are they not both mixed forms? Indeed, both examples are mixed. I would be hard pressed to think of a pure case and am willing to state categorically that there are no pure cases. Neither are there distinctly categorical treatments. In any actual treatment supportive and expressive approaches are matters of emphasis whereas the medium of problem solving is characteristic of all psychotherapies.

21

Analyzing and Life Change

A Personal Note

When I was young in the field, somewhere between my first and second control cases, I had a particularly liberating experience. My supervisor, a charismatic person I would have followed anywhere at the time, proclaimed that analysts do not worry about what their patients do outside the consulting room. Our only concern is for the conduct of the analysis; the analyst should analyze and not care if the patient "gets well" or care about whatever else the patient might do with what he learns. The remark was aimed at my overdeveloped sense of responsibility, but I took it more generally. It was salve to my conscience and also probably allowed me to listen to my patient less intently and more usefully as I became less concerned about what I might be doing wrong.

My happiness was short lived, however, for, when I described my newly found sense of freedom to my second supervisor, he looked at me quizzically and asked, "Do you really mean that you don't care about what happens to your patients?" Hearing it put in that gentle way exposed the nonsense of my position but left me puzzled. The doctrine I had grasped so gratefully made no literal sense, and yet there seemed to be a profound truth nestled in the paradox—how could an analyst attend to how the patient's mind was working if his attention was captured by whether the patient is making a success or failure in his life outside? And, if we were not concerned with what brought the patient to analysis in the first place, if we had no interest in what he might do with what he learns, why bother analyzing? I learned to live with the paradox by putting it aside, and I did not really come to grips with it again until I began to supervise analyses. My students had the same problem, but I now saw it in a different way.

As an issue in logic, of course, the trouble comes from posing the matter as a dialectic, for there is no true antinomy here. The mind at ease, especially the analyst's mind, divides regularly and easily. Fluctuating, flitting, unfocused attention is the desired state of mind for both analyst and patient. There should be no problem for the analyst to shift his attention, from time to time, to whether and how the patient is making use of what he has learned or, more frequently, how he avoids making use of it. That shifting stance is an essential aspect of analyzing. My teacher's admonition had to do with my trying to correct my excessive concern with the patient's life outside. He did not feel comfortable enough to tell me what he also must have known: that my zeal for results was a sign of countertransference, at least a function of anxiety that I might not do my job well enough, that nothing would come of my analyzing. My concern, indeed, was about my feared ineffectuality. Could I really help this patient, or would I let him down much as had all the other disappointing would-be helpers and authorities in his life?

As with Samuel Johnson's condemned prisoner, anxiety is the villain that concentrates the analyst's mind. For my supervisees, as for me, anxiety had led to losing the analytic stance. They too became caught up in the story the patient was telling; they too found themselves first witnessing the events being told and then becoming drawn into the story. From being absorbed listeners to the story, they became actors in it. They had lost the sense that their main focus had to be on the *telling* of the story rather than the content, why was it being told now, and what the patient's purpose was in involving the analyst in this way.

Countertransference comes immediately to mind in connection with such observations. I am not sure, though, that countertransference is a sufficient explanation for the phenomenon, for I have observed it in seminars and case conferences as well as in supervision. Indeed, we can observe the same phenomenon when we read a novel or watch a good movie. If the novel is well written, or the film is well made, we can lose ourselves in it. Yearning for the temporary suspension of disbelief, after all, is the reason we pick up a novel or go to the movies. We can have the same experience listening to a patient tell about his life. If the patient is good at dramatic story-telling, and most are good enough, it is easy to lose ourselves in the story and forget that, primarily, we must attend primarily to the act of story-*telling*

This account oversimplifies matters by omitting consideration of an essential element in what I have termed the analytic stance. To be able to move freely back and forth between observing the patient as he tells his story and feeling himself as a witness to the events in the story, or a participant in it, the analyst must cultivate a "split" in himself, a "vertical" split into participating and observing selves. You might prefer that I use analytic terms rather then sociological language and label the sides of the "split" as "transference figure" and "therapeutic ally" or transference figure and analyst, but it would amount to the same thing. One cannot analyze and still remain firmly fixed in one's chair. Neither can one analyze if one loses oneself totally in the patient's story. One must be able to move about between these positions and yet still allow oneself to feel the shoves and tugs to take sides and the demands that one commit oneself to be a player, not merely stand on the sidelines.

Understand that I have been talking about issues that are usually discussed under the general heading of analytic neutrality, that is, technical neutrality. The usual advice with regard to neutrality is that the analyst should not take sides in the patient's conflict.

You will recall, that my first supervisor liberated me from an overdeveloped feeling of obligation to be "for the patient"; I was freed from my urge to protect him lest he become a victim of my as yet undeveloped analytic skill. I, indeed, had unwittingly set myself up to be an advocate for the patient, though not an effective one; and, to the extent that I gave myself to that role, neither was I an effective analyst. I certainly had achieved a "split," but not necessarily a therapeutic one, for my two roles or selves were in conflict too.

Technical Neutrality versus Meddling

"Technical neutrality" demands that the analyst be even-handed between the competing interests in the patient's conflict, since he recognizes that both sides of the conflict are aspects of the patient himself. The analyst is not to take one side of the patient against another. But technical neutrality does not require that the analyst refrain from becoming an advocate *for* the patient, whether as a whole or in conflict. That is a different matter.

It is a great discovery when a candidate finds that he can split in this way and enjoy the freedom to move about the psychological space that includes the consulting room, the scene of the patient's story, and the portion of the patient's history on which the current story is modeled. When we can do that, we feel that we understand the patient analytically. Once we have learned to achieve and cultivate the split, we next discover how easily that ability can be impaired.

While the presence of any strong emotion can impair that ability, mostly it is anxiety that makes it unsafe to split. An image my students have found compelling comes from the classic Western movie; when a war whoop signals that the Indians are about to attack, the settlers draw the wagons into a circle and prepare to defend themselves. Similarly, when anxiety threatens, the analyst's "split" is rewelded; the analyst pulls himself together and becomes defensive. "Pulling himself together" usually implies that the analyst cannot tolerate some aspect of the patient's transference and becomes anxious, and defensive and either withdraws or counterattacks.

Rejection of transference is an action; properly speaking, it is an enactment, an enactment of part of the patient's story, modeled on the actions of one of the actors in it. Thus, whether the analyst falls into the story or pulls himself out of it, he is acting in a frame defined by the story. As soon as he does so, he becomes part of the problem, which is to say he has allowed himself to become part of the patient's story and has identified himself, positively or negatively, with a transference figure.

He thinks of what the patient might have done better or how the patient can solve the dilemma he is facing, how to avoid the disaster he is courting. Impatiently, he thinks, if only the patient would get out of the way, I could solve that problem for him. The identification may be temporary but, for the time it lasts, the analyst has surrendered his "therapeutic leverage." It is a great achievement when a candidate grasps that his attention ought mostly to be on the patient's act of *telling* the story here-and-now rather than on the actual or fantastic events in the story that occurred in a different place and at another time.

To return to my personal development, you might wonder if I understood then that I was responding involuntarily to the patient's transference wish to be rescued and that my countertransference also fed my dilemma. You might also wonder if my own character structure gave rise to transference to the patient to adopt him as an object of rescue. And let us not leave out my well-intentioned supervisor, who, at least for a brief time, rescued me—and also set me up for another rescue by my second supervisor's act of kindly humiliation. All these forces were at play. The analytic swamp was awash with eddies and crosscurrents. Unlike the surgeon to whom Freud liked to compare us, analysts work in a necessarily dirty field. How can we stay honest, if not clean, when we are subject to such pushes and tugs, pressures and temptations?

The question is rhetorical, of course, insofar as the method of freeing ourselves is concerned, for one's personal analysis, supervision, and later self-analysis all provide initial calibration and the instruments to keep us on course. But these trusted methods do not dictate the outcome of the process. Granted that we work in a "dirty" field and that we must be aware of the multifarious forces that play on us, to what extent may we feel concern for and take a position about what the patient makes of his analytic experience in his life outside the consulting room? To what extent may we play an active role in the patient's life outside? And at what point does our well-intentioned interest slip into ill-advised meddling?

I hope I have not misled you with my willingness to consider how to stay clean in a dirty field, how to analyze and also play an active role in the patient's life. Perhaps I posed the question badly, for I do not believe it possible for the analyst both to be an actor in the patient's life and also to remain his analyst. To remain an analyst, however, is not an absolute value. The analyst, after all, is not a blank screen; his opinions, values, and attitudes toward life are apparent in all his interventions, to say nothing of the way he furnishes his consulting room. The analyst is a "real" figure in relationship with the patient, as well as a hat rack for transference, and to that extent may influence the patient in his life outside as well as within the analysis.

Beyond that sphere of unavoidable influence, circumstances may arise when an analyst must act openly in the patient's life. These circumstances mainly are emergencies ranging from a patient's threatening suicide to the analyst's belief that harm to another person or child abuse may be occurring or impending. And when the analyst does believe that he must intervene in the patient's life outside, he must be fully aware that doing so likely will preclude his remaining the patient's analyst. The analyst, like all members of society, occupies several roles; and the law, ethics, custom, and tradition dictate the hierarchy of those roles and the conditions under which one may fill each appropriately. Instances that require the analyst to interrupt analyzing to act in the patient's life fortunately are rare. But the temptation to construe circumstances as demanding that one intrude into the patient's life are far more common; it arises almost daily. Here is an example:

> The patient was a musician, a "Heldentenor" of some note who gave concerts worldwide. His major reason for wanting analysis was an inability to commit himself to any relationship. He was uncomfortably aware that he could easily take advantage of students and fellow musicians who idealized him because of his musicianship and his performance personality and would lend themselves to exploitation.
>
> The analyst also was an opera lover and valued his patient on that account as well. He thought he had been able to keep from disclosing his knowledge of music and his deep interest in the career of his patient and of his patient's colleagues. The patient, on his part, never raised the question of how invested the analyst might be in the affairs of music or for that matter how the analyst might feel about the patient's affairs with other musicians and students; but he always made it clear where and when he would be performing. The analyst was very curious about the patient's glamorous life. He wished he could be part of that scene and also deplored the patient's easy hitting on his students as unfitting a person of the patient's stature.

> One day, the patient remarked at the end of a session in which he had been describing an upcoming sell-out recital, "By the way, there will be a pair of tickets waiting at the box office if you would care to use them." The analyst was torn between acknowledging that his interest in the patient's life was excessive, and yet he could not turn down the chance to hear this artist. Although his supervisor counseled against it—and we can only presume what the analyst's analyst might have said, the analyst did attend the concert.
>
> Although it was all it should have been artistically, the analyst could not enjoy it fully. The seats were excellent and in full observation from the stage. The analyst could feel both the pull of the music and dismay at finding himself one of many admirers in the retinue of his patient. He could then appreciate that he literally was out of place, that he could not analyze and at the same time be a fan. In the subsequent session it became clear that the enactment was mutual, for the patient was fully aware of the analyst's extracurricular interest in him and that he had played on the analyst as on his colleagues and students. Making use of his chagrin, the analyst was able to bring the entire matter into the analysis. It proved possible for the two of them to deal with the collusion that had interfered with analyzing and to move on to more productive analyzing.

Things do not always turn out that well in analysis when boundaries are crossed. It is not always possible to resume an analysis when all three of the technical principles—neutrality, abstinence, and anonymity—have been ignored, as in the following example:

> The patient was a businessman with enough surplus cash to want to be a small-time venture capitalist. Unfortunately, he was impaired neurotically by a combination of indecisiveness and impulsivity, among other self-defeating character traits. The analyst was well trained and also shrewd about financial matters; he handled his own investments quite well. It was difficult for him to listen dispassionately as the patient described his haplessness at playing the market.
>
> The analyst never gave advice, of course, but his financial opinions of what the patient was planning to do somehow filtered into his interventions. They were impeccably neutral in content and invariably were directed at the patient's character traits. But more often than not they were offered at such times and in such a way that the patient felt that one path rather than another would be the "healthier" course to take. And he started to make money as his

investments paid off. Health became wealth quite literally. As anyone with the slightest awareness of Skinnerian behavioral principles might have predicted, the "analysis" drifted imperceptibly toward an almost exclusive preoccupation with the vagaries of the market.

The patient's investments did well, and he felt fine; "analysis" had done wonders for him. But though he no longer had any complaints, he did not think of ending the analysis, nor did his analyst suggest it. Only a cynic might have noted that in a time of rising market values it would have been difficult to lose money, for formerly the patient had actually managed to do just that.

But the market boom finally slowed, the great investments went sour, and margin calls increased. As the patient became more anxious, symptomatic, and pleading, the analyst became more active, anxious himself that his patient might "lose it" in several senses. His formerly subtle, not fully conscious, tweaking of his interventions became more open suggestions and directions. But he had become so fully identified with his patient's wish to succeed that he could not give the patient the conservative advice to cut his losses and instead encouraged him to stick it out.

The result was that soon the patient was all but wiped out. His original business had also suffered from the recession, and the funds he might have used to keep it alive had been invested in the market. The patient had bragged to his friends how much his analysis had helped him, and now their envy rose to the occasion and they urged the formerly grateful patient to sue the analyst. To make a long and sad story short, the patient did sue. The analyst's insurance company believed that the patient had a good case and settled the matter out of court. Subsequently, the analyst gave up his practice. Possibly there were other reasons that led him to that decision.

Insight and/versus Action

Psychoanalysis has had an uneasy relationship with the question of insight. While insight is now valued in its own right, it came fully into its own with the rise of ego psychology. Originally change, or, more particularly, cure, was thought to come about through the discharge of strangulated affect-charges associated with repressed complexes. But the goal of analyzing gradually became to disinter or reconstruct missing memories as well. It was thought that one would have to obtain insight into the causes of the neurosis to become free of it. One of the problems raised by this view was that occasionally, or frequently, the proper order seemed to be reversed. When a patient was able to act differently in his life, the insight that should have made it possible seemed to become available only then. The question remains, in the most general sense, does insight lead to action or does action lead to insight? Notice that I have substituted "action" for "change."

Jacobs (2002) posed the question:

> Is it enough to make the unconscious conflicts and fantasies conscious, increase a patient's continuous understanding of his or her patterns of thinking and behavior, and, provide insight into how our patients' minds work? Do we also concern ourselves with how this knowledge is used or not used in the patient's life? Or is it counterproductive to be so concerned? What about our patients' resistances to translating insight into action? Do we focus on this problem or do we believe that the gaining of insight is a sufficient goal in itself.

Thus far I have suggested that it is not possible to be both an analyst and an agent in the patient's life, and yet it surely must be possible for the analyst to be concerned that the patient be able to make the best use he can of the insights he gains. But the way Jacobs put the issue begs two implied questions. First, it assumes that the analysis was conducted at least competently and, second, that, if the analysis had been done competently, the patient inevitably would apply his new knowledge to his best advantage. Let us take the second implied question first. Freud (1895b) told us in a sad witticism that all analysis can hope to do is to replace neurotic misery with ordinary unhappiness. A corollary would be that, although we may free the will from neurotic compulsion, we cannot prevent the patient from making bad decisions or ordinary errors. We should not expect to be able to provide our patients with a happy life, although that outcome does eventuate sufficiently often to lead us to believe we had something to do with it, especially as our patients so often thank us for doing just that.

The first assumption, that analyses are done competently, contains the more serious issue for us to face and reopens the second question as well. My experience in over 40 years of supervising analyses and consulting about them leaves me uncertain about the safety of that assumption. Admittedly, I have seen a biased sample of analyses. After all, I was not consulted about cases that were going well. But the problems that are brought to me are similar to those I have seen in supervision of candidates and in the cases reported to seminars, and they tend to ignore two essential factors in the translation of insight into action.

The first has to do with translating insight into action *within* the analysis. By action within the analysis, I mean does the patient take an active stance toward an interpretation? Does he test it against experience? Does he weigh his emotional reaction to it? Does he challenge it perhaps? And, finally, does he take ownership of it by having worked through his objections to it? I have found that analysts usually assume that the patient has "gotten" the interpretation because he raised no strong objections to it. On the contrary, he quietly acquiesced to it.

But the analyst did not observe that the patient had not tried to test the idea for himself, and the analyst did not mark this crucial step as missing. Before we can expect a patient to apply an insight appropriately in his life outside, we should see it applied first within the analysis. And, before it can be applied, it must be tried on for fit. I say that an insight must be applied appropriately because a common way to defend oneself against the truth of an interpretation is to take it as a suggestion and then mock its intent and that of the analyst by enacting a caricature of it. The damaging consequences of heedless acting on insight show the analyst how wrong, even harmful, was his "advice" (Schlesinger, 1994b).

The second essential factor has to do with use of the term resistance. as in Jacobs's challenge, "What about our patients' resistances to translating insight into action?" Using the term resistance in this context tends to obscure the fact that the patient is in conflict and that the interpretation that led to the insight, and should have set the patient free in his life, probably addressed only one side of the conflict. "Resistance" implies that the patient is doing something "against the analysis"; it ignores that the patient may be doing something that we should construe to be for himself, that is, for the benefit of the other side of the conflict.

A competent analysis should consider that acting on the insight as the analyst would think proper might expose the patient to a danger not yet fully explored. As always, it is necessary to understand what the patient's behavior is *for*, not just what it is against (Schlesinger, 1981b).

I believe it is the business of analysts to analyze as best they can and not to expect that analysis will do a better job than would normal development had normal development been given a chance. To meddle in the patient's life is always ill advised, for it assumes, usually wrongly, that the analyst knows all the pertinent facts and knows better than the patient the conditions under which the patient must live and work. The analyst should subject to self-analysis the fantasy that he could solve the patient's problems if only the patient would get out of the way. To analyze effectively, the analyst must recognize the multifarious ways in which patients prefer to maintain the safe *status quo* rather than risk change. These "resistances" are at play in every analysis, and they show most distinctly in the way patients deal with interpretations and insight (Schlesinger, 1995a).

22

Conclusion

Interpretation and Change

I have proposed that interpreting is best viewed as a process. Of course, the ideas in an interpretation ought to be correct; and, if the construction is fractionated and built collaboratively with the patient, the ideas are more likely to be correct. But correctness is only part of what makes interpreting effective. The way an analyst puts his contributions to the process also has a great deal to do with the way the patient hears them and the effect they have.

Another important matter implicit in the concept of process is what happens at the moment when the interpretation, which has been building for some time, seems to "come together." If the analyst is not overly eager to press the point, he may hear one of a variety of responses that indicate the patient has "heard it" and something also about the patient's readiness to acknowledge hearing "it" and "its" meaning to him. Occasionally, one hears an "Aha!" of happy surprise or its equivalent. But usually one hears a note of grudging or resigned acceptance as the patient conveys something like, "Well here we are again. Maybe I better take this idea more seriously. It sounds right, but if it is right, so much will have to change. I don't know that it's worth the trouble."

I may have made the patient more dour than necessary to make the point that the process of working through overlaps with and continues the process of interpretation. Thus, when the patient "gets it," with or without an "Aha!" we have not come to the end of the road; more likely, we have arrived at a fork in the road without signposts. It is difficult, and not particularly useful, to try to figure out when an interpretive process came to an end. When an interpretation has been built stepwise, working through also can occur in step. But even when analyst and patient have come to the point where "it" can be identified and named, the emphasis merely shifts to working through the implications of an alternative way of looking at matters, as the patient's personality accommodates to this change.

Recall that a major goal of technique is to promote the activity of the patient in analyzing. As we have noted, psychoanalysis is not what analysts do but what patients do with our help. I have proposed that the point of analysis is to help the patient discover how his mind works. It is not our task to change his mind, although it is likely that, in the course of discovering how his mind works, the patient will change significantly how it works. As I hope I have made clear, what analyst and patient do is only partly responsible for the outcome of their joint project, for there are many forces at work that facilitate achieving useful change in personality and perhaps at least as many that oppose it.

To facilitate the patient's becoming active, the analyst should strive to intervene with brief comments that "go with the resistance"—which is to say, that go where the patient wants to go—rather than oppose the resistance. The analyst should particularly avoid forms of speech that conflict with this intention; one of these forms notably is questioning. As would-be writers are often advised, simple and direct is best. In these remarks, I have gone to some length to spell out the many ways in which the questioning form can undermine an analyst's conscious intention to facilitate the patient's activity. While in social discourse we value uttering important ideas—especially intentions—indirectly out of concern that a direct statement might seem crude or overbearing, to do so in analysis conflicts with our overall purpose. It testifies to our uncomfortable awareness of the power we have to influence the patient with our words. It is ironic that we use the questioning form in this way, for as questioning the patient can have the effect of arrogating to ourselves the very power we try to eschew. It is a situation reminiscent of La Rochefoucauld's (1665) wry definition of an apology, "Unsaying something in a way that leaves nothing unsaid."

In addition to misusing the questioning form, analysts concerned about the possibility of doing harm may speak obliquely, soften statements with qualifiers, use complicated grammatical forms such as the subjunctive, or speak in the passive voice.

I hope it is clear that there is no objection to both wanting to propose an idea to a patient, particularly one the patient would rather disown, and wanting to avoid offending or hurting. These are separate intentions and deserve separate expression. Trouble arises when the analyst expresses one intention in the content of a statement and the other in the form.

The moment a patient is faced with opposing views, that is conflicting ideas, both of which are his, something has to give. Freud's (1894) first theory of neurosis placed this dilemma at the core. The patient may feel called on to choose one idea over the other, although he may not realize he is doing so. And the analyst is there to help him catch a glimpse of how his mind functions as it wrestles with this "new" experience, one that the neurosis, as it were, was designed to preclude.

Another way of addressing this issue is that the analyst observes and attempts to understand how this patient goes about changing his spots as he helps him to appreciate that, at this very moment, by facing up to his conflict, he already is changing one of his spots. The significant point is that the patient chooses, and the analyst hears him choose and helps him to see that he is choosing. What the patient chooses at that moment is less important than that he has made a choice. Saying no to an idea is a choice, provided it is neither reflexive nor compelled; and determining the nature of the patient's response is the business of the analysis. By way of illustration:

> The patient had been sulking for several days about being ignored by the very people who should care about him but who, because of his diffidence, just overlook him, as if he were part of the furniture. The major figures in his life—wife, boss, children, and parents—were all denounced in turn, and the analyst was warned not to, "stick your nose in, the way you usually do. You're not pure, but I'm not talking about you now." The analyst took this counsel to heart and kept silent. After a while, the patient began to slow down. He had been decrying how ungrateful his children were. He had mentioned, in passing and with a bit of a sniff, that the oldest one had just won a national scholarly prize.
>
> After a brief pause, the patient's mood changed. He ceased his tirade and began to play with his thoughts about an upcoming family vacation. The analyst relaxed, sensing how tense he had been during the patient's angry lament. He knew he must have been implicated, yet he felt constrained to stay out of it. He felt tempted to leave well enough alone and let peace settle. But his analytic conscience got the better of him; he realized that something important had happened and ought to be looked into. Staying "on the surface," he said to the patient, "A few minutes ago you were feeling miserable and vindictive, but now I sense a greater friendliness."
>
> Seemingly embarrassed, the patient replied, "I started to feel silly. All that carrying on. What was it all about?" The analyst waited. The patient was silent and moved about uneasily. Finally, he asked, "What was I talking about just before my mood brightened?"
>
> The analyst remained silent for about half a minute and then reminded the patient, "It was just after you mentioned that Jerry had won a prize."
>
> The patient sniffed and started to cry. "I remember now. I felt a flash of anger and envy. You remember, I didn't win that Boys Club

> contest. It was stolen from me, and I instantly thought, you jerk, how can you think that way, envious of your own son? I won't think that way."
>
> The analyst waited a bit while the patient cried quietly, and then he added, "You shocked yourself when you realized what was feeding your anger."

The analyst assumed the patient was doing the best he could, and he did not ask him to account for the way he felt or to justify the change in the way he felt, although the patient did feel he had to do so. The analyst's purpose was to see if the patient had noticed the change in mood and whether he was curious about it or might want to dismiss or devalue the change. Instead, and to the surprise of both analyst and patient, when the analyst called attention to a minor emotional shift, a new line of analysis was opened.

We may also consider the question of what makes analysis work in the larger context of how psychological or emotional change occurs in general. Consider this phenomenon:

> A new patient came to see the clinician. He had felt desperately anxious when he called for the appointment, so much so that the doctor took some trouble to accommodate him with an earlier appointment than would have been convenient. Within a few minutes, the patient obviously felt better and in the next few appointments, he reported fewer moments of feeling anxious. The clinician had not begun any form of specific treatment. Indeed he had not yet arrived at much understanding of the patient. Nonetheless, the patient began to talk about other matters in a way that clearly was not urgent. At the moment, he seemed to be in no further need of treatment.

This example is a commonplace. What is there to understand about it? That is just the point. We have no easy way to understand patients who "get better" without specific treatment. We may be so annoyed and dismayed by such patients, who first demand our attention and then leave us puzzled, that we fail to give the phenomenon the weight it deserves. Indeed, we have several dismissive pejoratives at hand for these events. We call them "transference cures" or "flights into health" to avoid "real treatment." Or perhaps we tell the patient, Portnoy-like, "Now that the emergency is over, the treatment can begin."

Is it not remarkable that we denounce patients who have the nerve to feel better without our permission? And it is dismaying how easily we discount a phenomenon that points to the heart of a most important question, namely, how do we explain personality change that occurs in psychoanalysis, or in psychotherapy, or indeed without any professional attention whatever (Schlesinger, 1988; Appelbaum, 1994)? If a patient begins to feel better in response (or so we would like to think) to an intervention we considered particularly clever, we would have no trouble explaining his improvement, *post hoc ergo propter hoc*. Such salutary changes in the patient's sense of comfort, optimism, hopefulness, sense of community, relatedness, empathy, and other good things occur regularly during psychoanalysis. And, in truth, they often, although not always, occur when the patient discovers a new way of looking at things. But it is not always obvious what the patient might be responding to when, at least for the moment, he seems better.

The point of these musings is that it is essential that we not discount as trivial or worthless improvements we do not, for the moment, understand. For if we do discount them, it is more than likely we will never understand them, and neither will our patients.

Early in my training years, when youthful optimism and therapeutic zeal worried my teachers, I was taught, either explicitly or by example, to temper my enthusiasm and not to expect too much from my efforts. Instead, we were to strive for a dignified acceptance of the dictum that the only kind of change acceptable to analysts was that achieved with arduous effort on everybody's part, and over a long period of time. We were, after all, in dogged pursuit of "analytic change," "structural change." Simple, everyday change was unworthy and would not do. We were allowed to absorb the remarkable idea that in psychoanalysis nothing good happens in finite time; and anything good that seems to have occurred is suspect as unanalytic. Fortunately, neither idea is true (Schlesinger, 1995a).

I do not mean to imply that I have found a way to do brief psychoanalysis or to relieve a chronic neurotic problem over a weekend, although you may recall that Freud had done just that (see Breuer and Freud, 1893–1895). After a while, he discovered that the several apparent successes that led him to think of psychoanalysis as a specific and brief treatment for neurosis were highly unusual cases (and besides, usually there was no follow-up). But there is an infallible way to make analyses go on longer than they have to. One need only disparage the minor changes that occur frequently during analysis and feel no need either to explain them, or to make use of them, or to place them in a theoretical context. The issue, I believe, is not so much how to achieve structural change as to recognize when change is occurring and knowing how to help the patient to "structuralize" the changes that do occur (Schlesinger, 1995a).

I have been discussing some of the pragmatics of change in psychoanalysis without alluding to the theories that have been advanced to account for change (Schlesinger, 1988). In closing, I would like to remind you that many factors in the analytic situation (and elsewhere) seem to be at play, and they combine variously at different times. The findings of research suggest that the major factor is the relationship with the therapist (Luborsky et al., 1980, 1985). The time is long past when one could say with confidence, but without data, that only insight can lead to structural change. There are also, of course, conservative forces that oppose change. At the very least, however, I hope you will agree that I have strengthened the case for the analyst's paying attention to the effect he is having on the patient following interventions, as well as at other times.

To end as I began, the point of my concern for understanding the role of technique in psychoanalysis is merely to assure that analysts will be able to take responsibility for the only thing they properly can—to allow their patients the best chance at analyzing.

References

American Psychiatric Association (2000), *Diagnostic and Statistical Manual of Mental Disorders*, 4th ed. Washington, DC: American Psychiatric Association.

——— (2001), *Principles of Medical Ethics with Annotations Especially Applicable to Psychiatry*. Washington, DC: American Psychiatric Association.

American Psychoanalytic Association (2001), *The Principles and Standards of Ethics for Psychoanalysts*. New York: American Psychoanalytic Association.

Appelbaum, A. H. (1994), Psychotherapeutic routes to structural change. *Bull. Menninger Clin.*, 58:37–54.

Azim, H (1998), "Dosage" and "accuracy" of transference interpretations in short-term psychoanalytic psychotherapy. Presented to American Psychoanalytic Association, May.

Bibring, E. (1954), Psychoanalysis and the dynamic psychotherapies. *J. Amer. Psychoanal. Assn.*, 2:745–770.

Bowlby, J. (1973), *Attachment and Loss, Volume II: Separation*. New York: Basic Books.

Brazelton, T. B. (1973), *The Neonatal Behavioral Assessment Scale*. London: Spastics International Publications Monograph 50.

Brenner, C. (1981), Defense and defense mechanisms. *Psychoanal. Quart.*, 50:557–559.

Breuer, J. & Freud, S. (1893–1895), Studies on hysteria. *Standard Edition*, 2. London: Hogarth Press, 1955.

Canetti, E. (1962), *Crowds and Power*. New York: Continuum.

Deutsch, F. (1955), *The Clinical Interview*. New York: International Universities Press.

Dorpat, T. (1996), *Gaslighting, the Double Whammy, Interrogation, and Other Methods of Covert Control in Psychotherapy and Analysis*. Northvale, NJ: Aronson.

Eissler, K. R. (1953), The effect of the structure of the ego on psychoanalytic technique. *J. Amer. Psychoanal. Assn.*, 1:104–143.

Erikson, E. H. (1954), The dream specimen of psychoanalysis. *J. Amer. Psychoanal. Assn.*, 2:5–56.

——— (1959). *Identity and the Life Cycle. Psychological Issues Monograph* 1. New York: International Universities Press.

Feigl, H. & Brodbeck, M., eds. (1953), *Readings in the Philosophy of Science*. New York: Appleton-Century-Crofts.

Fenichel, O. (1941), *Problems of Psychoanalytic Technique*. Albany, NY: Psychoanalytic Quarterly.

Fierman, L., ed. (1965), *Effective Psychotherapy: The Contribution of Hellmuth Kaiser*. New York: Free Press.

Ferenczi, S. (1919), On the technique of psycho-analysis. In: *Further Contributions to the Theory and Technique of Psycho-Analysis*. London: Hogarth Press, 1950, pp. 177–188.

Fliess, R. (1953), *The Revival of Interest in the Dream*. New York: International Universities Press.

Frank, J. D. (1974), *Persuasion and Healing*, rev. New York: Schocken Books.

Freud, A. (1936), *The Ego and the Mechanisms of Defense*. London: Hogarth Press.

Freud, S. (1894), The neuro-psychoses of defense. *Standard Edition*, 3:45–68. London: Hogarth Press, 1962.

——— (1900), The interpretation of dreams. *Standard Edition*, 4. London: Hogarth Press, 1953.

——— (1901), The psychopathology of everyday life. *Standard Edition*, 6:1–290. London: Hogarth Press, 1960.

——— (1905), Jokes and their relation to the unconscious. *Standard Edition*, 8: 9–236. London: Hogarth Press, 1960.

——— (1912a), Recommendations to physicians practicing psycho-analysis. *Standard Edition*, 12:109–120. London: Hogarth Press, 1958.

——— (1912b), The dynamics of transference. *Standard Edition*, 12:97–108. London: Hogarth Press, 1958.

——— (1913), On beginning the treatment. *Standard Edition*, 12:121–144. London: Hogarth Press, 1958.

——— (1914a), Remembering, repeating and working-through. *Standard Edition*, 12:145–156. London: Hogarth Press, 1958.

——— (1914b), On the history of the psychoanalytic movement. *Standard Edition*, 14:3–66. London: Hogarth Press, 1957.

——— (1915a), Observations on transference love. *Standard Edition*, 12:157–171. London: Hogarth Press, 1958.

——— (1915b), The unconscious. *Standard Edition*, 14:159–216. London: Hogarth Press, 1957.

——— (1919), Lines of advance in psycho-analytic therapy. *Standard Edition*, 17:157–168. London: Hogarth Press, 1955.

——— (1923a), Two encyclopedia articles, (A) Psychoanalysis. *Standard Edition*, 18:235–254. London: Hogarth Press, 1954.

——— (1923b), The ego and the id. *Standard Edition*, 19:3–66. London: Hogarth Press, 1961.

——— (1924), An autobiographical study. *Standard Edition*, 20:3–74. London: Hogarth Press, 1959.

——— (1926), Inhibitions, symptoms and anxiety. *Standard Edition*, 20:77–174. London: Hogarth Press, 1959.

Frijling-Schreuder, E. C. M. (1966), The adaptive use of regression. *Internat. J. Psycho-Anal.*, 47:364–369.

Gilbert, W. S. & Sullivan, A. S. (1885), The Mikado, or the Town of Titipu. In: *The Complete Plays of Gilbert and Sullivan*. New York: Norton, 1976.

Gill, M. (1982), *Analysis of the Transference, 1: Theory and Technique Psychological Issues Monogr. 53.* New York: International Universities Press.

Glover, E. (1971). *The Technique of Psychoanalysis.* New York: International Universities Press.

Greenson, R. (1967), *The Technique and Practice of Psychoanalysis.* New York: International Universities Press.

Grünbaum, A. (1990), "Meaning" connections and causal connections in the human sciences: The poverty of hermeneutic philosophy. *J. Amer. Psychoanal. Assn.*, 38:559–577

Herzog, P. (1991), *Conscious and Unconscious; Freud's Dynamic Distinction Reconsidered. Psychological Issues Monogr. 58.* Madison, CT: International Universities Press.

Hoffman, I. Z. (1983), The patient as interpreter of the analyst's experience. *Contemp. Psychoanal.*, 19:389–422.

Horvath, A., Gaston, L. & Luborsky, L. (1993), The therapeutic alliance and its measures. In: *Handbook of Dynamic Psychotherapy Research and Practice*, ed. N. Miller, L. Luborsky, J. Barber & J. Docherty. New York: Basic Books.

Isakower, O. (1957), Preliminary thoughts on the analyzing instrument. Presented to Faculty of the New York Psychoanalytic Institute.

Jacobs, T. (2002), Charge to the panel on psychoanalysis and life change. Presented to the American Psychoanalytic Association, Philadelphia, May 12.

Jaffe, J. (1966), Formal language patterns as defensive operations. In: *The Collected Award Papers.* Port Chester, NY: Gralnick Foundation.

James, W. (1892), *Principles of Psychology.* New York: Henry Holt.

Kafka, F. (1925), *The Trial.* New York: Knopf, 1992.

Kernberg, O. (1987), An ego psychology-object relations theory approach to the transference. *Psychoanal. Quart.*, 56:197–221.

——— Selzer, M. A., Koenigsberg, H. W., Carr, A. C. & Appelbaum, A. H. (1989), *Psychodynamic Psychotherapy of Borderline Patients.* New York: Basic Books.

La Rochefoucauld, F. de (1665), *Maxims.* Boston: Branden Press, 1982.

Lewin, B. (1958), *Dreams and the Uses of Regression.* New York: International Universities Press.

Loewenstein, R. (1958), Remarks on some variations in psycho-analytic technique. *Internat. J. Psycho-Anal.*, 39:202–210.

Lorand, S. & Console, W. (1958), Therapeutic results in psycho-analytic treatment without fee. *Internat. J. Psycho-Anal.*, 39:59–64.

Luborsky, L., Mintz, J., Auerbach, A., Christoph, P., Bachrach, H., Todd, T., Johnson, M., Cohen, M. & O'Brien, C. P. (1980), Predicting the outcome of psychotherapy—Findings of the Pennsylvannia psychotherapy project. *Arch. Gen. Psychiat.*, 37:471–481.

——— McLellan, T., Woody, G., O'Brien, C. & Auerbach, A. (1985), Therapist success and its determinants. *Arch. Gen. Psychiat.*, 42:602–611.

MacKinnon, R. & Michels, R. (1971), *The Psychiatric Interview in Clinical Practice.* Philadelphia, PA: Saunders.

Menninger, K. A. (1938), *Man Against Himself.* New York: Harcourt Brace.

——— & Holzman, P. S. (1973), *Theory of Psychoanalytic Technique, 2nd ed.* New York: Basic Books.

Olinick, S. (1954), Some considerations of the use of questioning as a psychoanalytic technique. *J. Amer. Psychoanal. Assn.*, 2:57–66.
——— (1957), Questioning, truth, pain and negation. *J. Amer. Psychoanal. Assn.*, 5:302–324.
Peterfreund, E. with J. T. Schwartz (1971), *Information. Systems and Psychoanalysis: An Evolutionary Biological Approach to Psychoanalytic Theory. Psychological Issues Monogr.* 25/26. New York: International Universities Press.
Pinsker, H. (1997), *A Primer of Supportive Psychotherapy.* Hillsdale, NJ: The Analytic Press.
Poland, W. (1975), Tact as a psychoanalytic function. *Internat. J. Psycho-Anal.*, 56: 155–162.
Racker, H. (1968), *Transference and Countertransference.* New York: International Universities Press.
Ramzy, I. (1974), How the mind of the analyst works: An essay on psychoanalytic inference. *Internat. J. Psycho-Anal.*, 55:543–550.
Rapaport, D. (1957), A theoretical analysis of the superego concept. In: *The Collected Papers of David Rapaport*, ed. M. M. Gill. New York: Basic Books, 1967, pp. 685–709.
Reich, A. (1951), On countertransference. *Internat. J. Psycho-Anal.*, 32:25–31.
Reik, T. (1949), *Listening with the Third Ear.* New York: Farrar, Straus.
——— (1959), *The Compulsion to Confess.* New York: Farrar, Straus & Cudahy.
Rothstein, A. (1998), *Psychoanalytic Technique and the Creation of Analytic Patients*, 2nd ed. Madison, CT: International Universities Press.
Santayana, G. (1905–1906), *Reason and Common Sense*, New York: Dover, 1980.
Schafer, R. (1976), *A New Language for Psychoanalysis.* New Haven, CT: Yale University Press.
——— (1982), *The Analytic Attitude.* New York: Basic Books.
Schlesinger, H. J. (1969), Diagnosis and prescription for psychotherapy. *Bull. Menninger Clin.*, 33:269–278,
——— (1978), A contribution to a theory of promising: I. Developmental and regressive aspects of the making of promises. In: *The Human Mind Revisited: Essays in Honor of Karl Menninger*, ed. S. Smith. New York: International Universities Press, pp. 21–50.
——— (1981a), The process of empathic response. *Psychoanal. Inq.*, 1:393–416.
——— (1981b), Resistance as process. In: *Resistance in Psychodynamic and Behavioral Therapies*, ed. P. Wachtel. New York: Plenum, pp. 25–44; 245–250.
——— (1988), A historical overview of conceptions of the mode of therapeutic action of psychoanalytic psychotherapy. In: *How Does Treatment Help? On the Modes of Therapeutic Action of Psychoanalytic Psychotherapy*, ed. A. Rothstein. Madison, CT: International Universities Press, pp. 7–27.
——— (1989), The therapeutic impasse, Unpublished ms.
——— (1990), On "interminable analysis." Association for Psychoanalytic Medicine, New York.
——— (1992), What does psychoanalysis have to contribute to the understanding of character? *The Psychoanalytic Study of the Child*, 47:225–234. New Haven, CT: Yale University Press.

——— (1993a), In defense of denial. Unpublished ms.

——— (1993b), Work and play in the analytic situation: The pleasures of analyzing. Rado Memorial Lecture, Association for Psychoanalytic Medicine, New York.

——— (1994a), How the analyst listens: The pre-stages of interpretation. *Internat. J. Psycho-Anal.*, 75:31–37.

——— (1994b), The role of the intellect in the process of defense. *Bull. Menninger Clin.*, 58:15–36.

——— (1995a), The process of interpretation and the moment of change. *J. Amer. Psychoanal. Assn.*, 43:662–685.

——— (1995b), Facts is facts, or is they? *Internat. J. Psycho-Anal.*, 76:1167–1177.

——— (1996), The fear of being left half-cured. *Bull. Menninger Clin.*, 60:428–448.

——— & Appelbaum, A. H. (2000), When words are not enough. *Psychoanal. Inq.*, 20:124–143.

Schwaber, E. (1979), On the "self" within the matrix of analytic theory: Some clinical reflections and reconsiderations. *Internat. J. Psycho-Anal.*, 60:457–479.

Schwitzgebel, R. (1967), Short-term operant conditioning of adolescent offenders on socially relevant variables. *J. Abnorm. Psychol.*, 72:134–142.

Shapiro, D. (1965), *Neurotic Styles*. New York: Basic Books.

——— (1999), *Psychotherapy of Neurotic Character*. New York: Basic Books.

Solms, M. (1997), What is consciousness? *J. Amer. Psychoanal. Assn.*, 45:681–703.

Spence, D. (1982), *Narrative Truth and Historical Truth*. New York: Norton.

——— (1984), Perils and pitfalls of free floating attention. *Contemp. Psychoanal.*, 20:37–59.

Stepansky, P. (1999), *Freud, Surgery, and the Surgeons*. Hillsdale, NJ: The Analytic Press.

Sterba, R. (1934), The fate of the ego in analytic therapy. *Internat. J. Psycho-Anal.*, 15:117–126.

Stolorow, R. (1991), The intersubjective context of intrapsychic experience: A decade of psychoanalytic inquiry. *Psychoanal. Inq.*, 11:171–184.

Stone, L. (1954), The widening scope of indications for psychoanalysis. *J. Amer. Psychoanal. Assn.*, 2:567–594.

Strachey, J. (1934), On the nature of the therapeutic action of psychoanalysis. *Internat. J. Psycho-Anal.*, 15:127–158.

Thurber, J. & White, E. B. (1929), *Is Sex Necessary? or Why You Feel the Way You Do*. New York: Harper, 1950.

Vaughan, S. C. Spitzer, R., Davies, J. M. & Roose, S. (1997), The definition and assessment of analytic process: Can analysts agree? *Internat. J. Psycho-Anal.*, 78:959–973.

Virchow, R. (1866), *Cellular Pathology as Based on Physiological and Pathological Histology*, trans. F. Chance. Birmingham, AL: Classics of Medicine Library, 1978.

Yorke, C. & Wiseberg, S. (1976), A developmental view of anxiety: Some clinical and theoretical considerations. *The Psychoanalytic Study of the Child*, 31:107–135. New Haven, CT: Yale University Press.

Index